*A future well
much intended.*
*Steve
Nowicki 12/7/16*

CHOICE OR CHANCE

Understanding Your Locus of Control
AND WHY IT MATTERS

STEPHEN NOWICKI

 Prometheus Books

59 John Glenn Drive
Amherst, New York 14228

Cover images © Media Bakery
Cover design by Liz Scinta

Inquiries should be addressed to
Prometheus Books
59 John Glenn Drive
Amherst, New York 14228
VOICE: 716–691–0133
FAX: 716–691–0137
WWW.PROMETHEUSBOOKS.COM

20 19 18 17 16   5 4 3 2 1

Library of Congress Cataloging-in-Publication Data Pending

Printed in the United States of America

CHOICE OR CHANCE

CONTENTS

PREFACE

I have wanted to write a book about Locus of Control for a very long time. The idea first crossed my mind when I published my initial article on the topic in 1971.[1] Way back then, I saw how the Locus of Control scale uniquely captures how we attempt to understand the world and our place in it. If we see ourselves as governed by fate, luck, chance, or powerful others, we are externally controlled, or "External." If we see ourselves and our own actions as the cause of the circumstances of our lives, we are internally controlled, or "Internal."

Many researchers joined me in the study of Locus of Control. New information continued to accumulate, and I was so busy trying to keep abreast of the literature that there was never enough time to stop and write my book. Before I knew it, decades had passed. Then I heard the sad news that Julian Rotter, the man who originated the concept, had passed away at the age of ninety-six. I decided it was finally time to face up to the challenge of distilling findings from well over twenty thousand published papers and research presentations.

This book, *Choice or Chance*, is the result of my efforts. It is not, however, a detailed scientific review. Rather, after nearly five decades of publishing Locus of Control research, using the concept in my psychotherapy and clinical work, teaching it to my undergraduate and graduate students, and applying it in my business and educational consulting, I offer my best judgment of what is important for others to know about this subject.

I have tried not to overwhelm you with footnotes, statistical analyses, and academic jargon. When I have spoken to people in educational, business, athletic, or medical settings, I have found that, while they don't mind hearing some science, they are mainly interested in learning what Locus of Control can tell them about their own lives and those of their loved ones.

The organization of the book is based largely on what they have told me they want to know.

The Locus of Control ride has been exciting, and the story continues, but we are entering what I consider to be a crucial time. As you will read about, we are becoming increasingly External as a country. We have been on a thirty-year slide toward greater Externality, and that has implications for all we value in life. As you read *Choice or Chance*, I think you will be impressed by what is associated with being Internal and what it means if we are becoming more External. I hope that making you aware of the importance of Locus of Control and what it has allowed us to find out about ourselves will contribute to efforts to reverse what I and many others view as the potential blight of our current collective outlook.

ACKNOWLEDGMENTS

When you have been involved in something as important as the study of Locus of Control for as long as I have, you understand how vital your relationships with colleagues, students, family members, and friends are.

Of course, we all owe so much to Julian Rotter, a true pioneer in the study of human behavior. His unique insights brought the concept of social learning in general and Locus of Control in particular to the forefront of psychology.

Marshall Duke has been my colleague, confidant, confessor, and best friend on this journey. I cannot imagine the trip without him by my side.

Bonnie Strickland introduced me to Julian Rotter and his work and was responsible for my learning so many things about what it means to be not just a professor but a professor who values teaching and students above all else. The gifts of her friendship and guidance have helped keep me on the right academic path through the years.

Academic colleagues like Jean Golding, Don Gordon, Klaus Scheewind, Albert Osborn, John Carton, and Tom Johnson, have joined me in Locus of Control research at various times and given me the energy and insights I needed to continue my work.

And then there are my students. The thought of them fills me with emotion as I consider how much they have contributed to my enjoyment of the academic life. Undergraduates and graduates alike have committed themselves to the study of Locus of Control with me and by doing that have contributed in many nuanced ways to my own education, both scientific and personal. There are too many honors theses, convention papers, publications, master's theses, and dissertations to list here, but I have mentioned many of them in the text.

Before I had my academic family, there was my biological one. My mother and father were my initial teachers of the benefits and liabilities of either an Internal or External way of perceiving what happened to me.

Finally, there is my own family, the one I chose to have and grow old with: my wife, Kaaren, who always provides me with what I need and keeps me in line; my son, Andy, who has helped me to see life in so many different ways; my daughter-in-law, Jenny, whose humor and caring are always appreciated; and my grandchildren, Hannah Ruth and Soren, who every day give me reason to be optimistic about life. Thank you all for making this book possible and my life so satisfying and rich.

But of course the book never would have been seen the light of day if it were not for the unflagging encouragement and help of Bridget Matzie Wagner, my literary agent, in developing the proposal; Jackie May Parkinson, who made my words sound so much better; and the people of Prometheus Books, Steven L. Mitchell and Jade Zora Scibilia, who actually said yes to making it all happen. Thank you.

INTRODUCTION

This book is a collection of helpful information for you to know about Locus of Control. To whet your appetite, here is a sneak preview.

What is Locus of Control? Locus of Control is a concept that reflects the impact our behavior will have on what happens to us. It can be assessed by self-report questionnaires that measure our expectancies regarding the effects of our behavior. As mentioned in the Preface, if we perceive that luck, fate, chance, or powerful others determine outcomes, we are External. If we perceive that our circumstances are the result of our own actions and choices, we are Internal.

How can I measure my Locus of Control? Questionnaires and instructions are included in the text. You can use these to calculate your own Locus of Control.

Is Locus of Control inherited? Locus of Control is not inherited; it is learned.

What is the best Locus of Control to have? This is a tricky question. There is no "best" Locus of Control orientation, although Internality (seeing a connection between what we do and what happens to us) is often preferred to Externality (seeing little or no connection between what we do and what happens to us). The particular situations we face determine the appropriateness of perceptions of Locus of Control.

Does our personal Locus of Control change over our lifetime? Yes, our Locus of Control will likely change, becoming more Internal as we get older until the latter stages of adulthood, when it levels off.

Can we choose to change our Locus of Control? If so, how? Yes, we can decide to adjust our Locus of Control. Since it is learned, learning principles can be applied to change it.

What do we know about Locus of Control and achievement in school, business and athletics, relationships, and mental and physical

health? Locus of Control has a consistent effect on achievement: academically, athletically, professionally, and socially. In most instances, Internals do better than Externals in setting and meeting life's goals.

Are there Locus of Control differences between females and males? Women and men apply their Internality and Externality differently. For example, we know Internality is associated with greater academic achievement for both females and males until around age twelve, when, for no obvious reason, it becomes more difficult to predict female academic achievement from Locus of Control (see chapter 4).

From research on physical fitness, we know that Internals work out more frequently and intensely than Externals, but it turns out that Internal females and males stick to their fitness routines for different reasons—reasons that may surprise you.

Do Internals and Externals learn differently? They do. If you want Internals to learn, give them the freedom to choose what they study and how to study it. In contrast, if you want Externals to learn, provide them with a firm structure and a leader who will tell them how to study the material. This information can be used to help all learners, from children in school to adults in advanced education settings.

How is Locus of Control related to health issues? The answer to this question can literally have life-or-death consequences. Internals are more likely to comply with medical instructions if they are given relevant information and the time to evaluate its worth. Externals, on the other hand, are more prone to comply if they are given clear instructions by someone of high status and authority, followed by consistent, "nagging" reminders.

THE TAKE-HOME MESSAGE

Internals often do better than Externals in many arenas of life. They fend off failure, illness, and loss and achieve more in most performance areas, such as academics, sports, and business. However, this does not mean it is always better to be Internal than External. What also needs to be considered is how your personal Locus of Control fits with the situation in which you find yourself. Externality is best when you are flying from Atlanta to Paris; there is nothing you can do to make the flight safe and smooth, so you must simply trust that the pilot is a professional and knows what he or she is doing. Similarly, in the midst of a recession there is only so much you can do to find a job. Recognizing the limits of your power is healthy and sensible in such circumstances. Every day, you face a succession of situations in which your personal Locus of Control may be more or less appropriate. Your task is to make yourself aware of that possibility.

I invite you to read, learn and enjoy. I hope you will have as much fun reading this book as I did writing it. I am always open to comments, questions, and admonitions at my e-mail address, snowick@emory.edu.

PART 1

BEGINNING THE STORY OF LOCUS OF CONTROL

INTRODUCTION TO PART 1

"What really frightens and dismays us is not external events themselves, but the way in which we think about them. It is not things that disturb us, but our interpretation of their significance."

—**Epictetus**

In the initial three chapters, you will find out why Locus of Control is so important, how it came into being as a scientific concept, and what we know about its origins and development in our own lives.

In the first chapter, I argue that Locus of Control should be front and center in our collective consciousness. I want readers to understand that this concept is a true treasury of insight into the human mind. LOC has occupied center stage in psychology for a half century because it has proven to be intimately connected with most everything we value in life. Standing up to critical evaluation for fifty years is no mean feat in the harsh climate of psychological research. We psychologists pride ourselves on our critical acuity. We reward those who spot flaws in theoretical and empirical offerings. Of the many thousands of concepts that have risen up in psychology, only a handful can survive the concentrated and thoroughgoing scrutiny of our scholarly community. Locus of Control is one of those few.

Following the first chapter, I take you on a personal journey: how I became involved first with the idea of Locus of Control and then with the many ways it can be applied to our lives. In chapters 2 and 3, I describe how Locus of Control came to be a tangible, measurable, and useful psychological concept accessible to the public, instead of an abstruse conceptual notion largely held captive within the ivory towers of academia.

Along the way, I introduce the men and women who played major roles in the unfolding of the Locus of Control story. This will help illustrate where this concept comes from and why it remains worthy of our continued attention. The story's characters range from a Jewish war veteran from Brooklyn who came through the ultracompetitive elite midwestern university system and became one of the foremost psychologists of the twentieth century to a woman raised in rural Alabama who overcame unbelievable obstacles to become president of the American Psychological Association. I also describe how I, a working-class kid raised in the inner city of Milwaukee, joined the Locus of Control story early on.

I close this first part of the book with an overview of what we know about how our own Locus of Control orientations develop and change over our lifetimes. It will be no surprise that parents are intimately involved in the development of their children's LOC, but what might be surprising is that the children themselves play a significant part in this process via their temperament, personality, and energy level. As children grow older, their relationships with their parents expand, and parents' impact is increasingly shared with other significant adults.

CHAPTER 1

LOCUS OF CONTROL: WHAT IT IS AND WHY IT IS IMPORTANT

"You only live once, but if you do it right, once is enough."
—Mae West

You've met people who just seem to get life "right." They are a joy to be with and are utterly dependable. If you need someone to write an article for the community paper, pick the children up from school, get a report done at the office, or call you back at a specific time, they're the ones you choose. You can relax around them because they know what to say and how to act. You like and respect them because they follow through on what they say they are going to do, and if you have a problem, they are the ones who will come up with solutions. They approach life confidently, as though they have something to do with how it is going to turn out.

What they excel at is excelling. They make excellent teachers, bosses, athletes, friends, coworkers, and parents. They seem to squeeze every bit of potential out of their ability, be it in school, in the workplace or in social situations. We look with wonder at how exquisitely they manage to balance life's challenges. How do they do it? Do they know something the rest of us don't?

Were such people merely born ready to do the right thing? Or have they gone through a special learning process open to only a select few? Maybe they take supplements of some sort—vitamins made from exotic animal parts. Maybe they have gone through some secret neurological enhancement operation that allows them to use that "unused" 90 percent of the human brain we hear about. What is clear is that they believe they have control over their lives; that, for them, life presents a continual succession of choices that will determine failure or success; and that, more often than not, they make the correct selections.

They are the *Internals.*

And then there is another type of person, whom you also recognize. They are the ones who have trouble getting life right. They start many things but often fail to follow through. When they fail, they give a million ready-made excuses for why their failures weren't their fault. They vow to do better the next time, but when the next time comes, they don't. Rather than initiating things, they seem more comfortable reacting to whatever pressures are operating on them. You wish you could depend on them, but too often they are not where they said they would be or doing what they are supposed to be doing. Others see their potential, but they don't. Their relationships are shaky and unsatisfying, and their lives are largely unfulfilled and unhappy. When something bad happens to them, they react with behavior paralysis. They are convinced that fate has handed them a bad deal or that they have been unlucky.

They are the *Externals.*

DEFINING LOCUS OF CONTROL

Before picking up this book, you may not have heard of Locus of Control, but it is an extraordinarily important concept in modern psychological circles. In fact, over the past fifty years, more studies have been published on this concept than most any other in the history of personality psychology. A search of the database PsycINFO using the keyword "Locus of Control" found 17,812 articles published on this topic as of summer 2015, with 6,600 appearing after 1996 and 1,426 between 2010 and 2015.[1] Locus of Control is a resilient concept that has shown incredible sustainability within the scientific community.

LOC has its origins in the influential social learning theory of Julian Rotter, one of the true giants of American psychology. Quite simply, LOC reflects how we have learned to perceive what happens to us. The more we have learned to expect connections between our actions and outcomes, the more Internal we are; the less we expect such links, the more External we are. If we are more Internal, we tend to view ourselves as able to influence the course of our lives; if we are more External, we tend to view our lives as governed by forces beyond our control.

Though most people fall somewhere between these two extremes, an Internal or External orientation has far-reaching effects. For example:

- The more External mothers are, the more likely their children will have behavioral problems in school, as well as greater feelings of depression and anxiety.[2]
- Externals live somewhere between 2.5 and 7 years less than Internals.[3]
- The more External CEOs are, the less financial success and the more bankruptcies their companies are likely to have when economic times are difficult.[4]
- Internality is one of the best predictors of managerial success across an amazing variety of organizations.[5]
- Externality at age ten predicts higher blood pressure and/or greater obesity by age thirty-five.[6]
- Internals facing Parkinson's, diabetes, kidney disease, heart disease, joint injury, or the prospect of major surgery cope better and have better treatment outcomes than Externals in the same circumstances.[7]
- Externals are more likely to be diagnosed as depressed, anxious, dyslexic, attention-deficit hyperactive disordered, schizophrenic, or bipolar than Internals.[8]
- Wendy Kopp, CEO of the well-respected organization Teach for America, looks for applicants who are "internally controlled."[9]
- A massive study conducted under the auspices of the United Nations of nearly one million people in eighty-four countries found the major predictor of "happiness" was having an Internal Locus of Control.[10]

WHY INTERNALS DO SO WELL

What is the secret of Internals' success? You might think they are smarter, but, in fact, Internals and Externals don't differ in IQ. Instead, the crucial difference seems to be the way Internals perceive, and then take on, their everyday tasks. It turns out Internals are motivated by, perhaps even driven by, the simple but powerful assumption that what they *do* is important in determining what happens to them. This assumption, in turn, produces a constellation of benefits, which have collectively been called the *Big Five*.[11]

The Big Five

The Internals' strong belief that their behaviors and outcomes are connected motivates them to deal with life's problems and challenges in dissimilar ways to Externals. Each aspect of the Big Five functions as a piston driving them forward to find the best solutions to their problems.

Internals are more likely than Externals to:

1. *Take responsibility* for what they have done. This means they are more likely to look back over their behavior to see what they did right and what they did wrong, a process that increases the likelihood of learning from both their successes and their failures.
2. *Be persistent* in their efforts to solve problems and meet challenges. It follows that because they believe personal actions are associated with personal outcomes, Internals are more likely to persist to increase their perceived chances of success.
3. *Delay gratification*. Because Internals believe they are more able to control what happens to them, they are more likely to trust that rewards for their effective behaviors will be given later. Externals, who depend on luck or fate to determine how they are rewarded, tend to give up if a reward is not presented quickly. This leads Externals to be more impulsive and less reflective than Internals.
4. *Gather information*. What is more useful for solving problems than having the best possible information? Internals are like human

information vacuum cleaners; they constantly suck up information wherever they go. They know what they learn may come in handy in the future, even if not immediately.

5. *Resist coercion.* "Show me," Missouri's state motto, could only have been written by an Internal. Internals only change their minds about a topic, belief, or attitude when they are presented with material that persuades them to change. Pressure from "powerful others" is met with resistance unless dependable facts and figures make the pressure understandable. Internals are anathema to tyranny of any sort.

I was reminded of the truth of this fifth aspect of Internality when I was invited to give a talk at the Hungarian Scientific Congress in Budapest when Hungary was under the control of a Communist dictatorship.

I traveled by train from Munich, where I was spending my sabbatical leave, to Budapest, where the event was being held. On the ride there, I could not help but notice the contrast between the freedom, affluence, and openness of the flourishing democracy in West Germany with the grey, tattered, and depressing atmosphere that pervaded the Communist state of Hungary. When I arrived in Budapest, I was assigned a "host" by the Communist party. I was told he would help make my visit "more pleasant," but, in reality, he was there to make sure I didn't talk too long with Hungarian colleagues or go off the approved routes prescribed for me. I felt unnerved to be followed by an ever-watchful "guide" everywhere I went.

The more I got a taste of what it was like to live in a totalitarian state, the more confused I was as to why I was asked there to talk about LOC. The power of Internality seemed like the kind of "Western," "capitalistic" idea that would not appeal to the Hungarian system of the time. I eventually shared my confusion with my academic colleague from Budapest University. "Why," I asked, "would the Communist party be interested in how to help people to become Internal? Internals are always questioning and evaluating. It seems to me that more Internals would be a giant pain in the neck to this government!"

My colleague looked around to be sure our "guide" was not within earshot and whispered, "Dr. Nowicki, they are not interested in how to help people become more Internal; you are here because they want to learn how to make them more External. If they can do that, the people will be much easier for them to manage."

I have never forgotten this experience because it reminds me that scientific information can be used for good or ill purposes.

BUT WHERE HAS OUR INTERNALITY GONE?

By now, I hope you are convinced that being appropriately Internal is a goal worth pursuing. In the United States, the Great American Dream promises our country will give the opportunity for success to everyone who is willing to work hard. Because the concept of Internality fits this notion so well, we in the United States should be at the forefront of fostering its development and growth.

But we are not.

We in the United States are failing to produce the conditions necessary for the growth of Internal Locus of Control. In fact, our failure to do so is stunning. Consider an epic study completed in 2004 by Jean Twenge, Liqing Zhang, and Charles Im from San Diego State and Case Western Reserve Universities.[12] They collected thousands of LOC scores from thirty years of studies of children and adults. When they took the average score of each year and plotted it over time, it showed that over the past thirty years, children and adults in the United States had become significantly less Internal and significantly more External.

For someone who had been studying the attributes of Internals and Externals for decades, these findings were devastating and hard to believe. I thought there must be groups of people who would buck this trend toward Externality, especially those with superior intellectual ability. I decided to evaluate this possibility at my own school, Emory University. During my time there, I had watched the school become one of the premier institutions of its kind in the country, if not the world. On average, only one out of five students who applied was accepted, and the average SAT scores of incoming students had risen by hundreds of points over the decades.

Truly, I thought, Emory freshmen, who were among the brightest and best students in the nation, would be immune to the national movement toward Externality found by Twenge, Zhang, and Im.

Fortunately, I had the means to test this hypothesis. My faculty colleagues Dan Adame and Tom Johnson had collected LOC scores from freshmen each year for ten years.[13] All I had to do was analyze these scores and find out whether Emory students had resisted whatever forces were causing the rest of the country to spiral downward toward Externality.

Sadly, I found they had not. On the contrary, the scores of Emory students showed a similar steep rise in Externality over the past decade to the rise found in the general population.

Clearly, then, being academically astute and attending a prestigious college did not protect or insulate bright, advantaged young adults from whatever was producing increased Externality in our country.

The loss of Internality and the growth of Externality is a frightening trend because it strikes at the very core of who we are as a country and a people. Our democratic system not only requires but demands its citizens assume their opinions and the efforts they put forth to support those opinions matter. For a democracy to work well, or work at all, it needs a continuous stream of active, informed, competent, Internal citizenry.

What are the implications of us becoming more External?

POSSIBLE SYMPTOMS OF OUR INCREASING EXTERNALITY

Fewer people voting. Is greater Externality affecting our voting behavior? Are changes in the frequency of voting paralleling the changes in our Locus of Control?

Unhappily, the answer is yes. According to the Information Please website using data secured from the Federal Election Commission, over the thirty years covered by Twenge and her associates, the number of people voting in national elections began at nearly 62 percent (1968) and fell consistently below 60 percent, reaching an all-time low in 1996, when only 49 percent of eligible voters voted. President Obama's election in

2008 reversed this trend, but the 57 percent of voters who voted was still below the turnout of the late 1960s. Disappointingly, the percentage of voters in the following presidential election fell again to 53 percent.[14]

Poorer physical health. Fewer of us exercising our right to vote is but one indication of our fading Internality. We are also becoming less physically healthy. One clear example can be found in the increasing incidence of obesity in our country. Obesity has been identified as a major contributor to a cascade of other physical maladies, including heart disease, diabetes, and cancer. I do not think it is an accident that three decades of increasing Externality have seen a corresponding rise in obesity. In fact, the Centers for Disease Control and Prevention have declared obesity a national epidemic. Indeed, obesity rates have *doubled* for adults over the past thirty-five years. The average American weighs twenty-four pounds more today than he or she did in 1960. And the news is even worse for children, whose rate of obesity has actually *tripled* over the same time period. The statistics are still more abysmal for minorities like African Americans and Latinos.[15]

Poorer mental health. The negative trends associated with Externality also can be found when we look at mental health. One of the most often replicated findings in the field of mental health is a strong association between Externality and depression. This is easy to understand. The core of this disorder is a feeling of helplessness in the face of suffering. We all know the dark, heavy feeling of depression; everyone feels that way sometimes, even if only for brief periods. But for those diagnosed with clinical depression, that feeling is a chronic and omnipresent state of mind, sucking all the joy out of their lives.

One of the potential unpleasant legacies of increasing Externality may be a conspicuous increase in unhappiness. Indeed, more Americans than ever before in the history of mental health are being diagnosed with major depressive disorders. And depression is occurring at increasingly younger ages. In fact, today's young adults are much more likely to be diagnosed with a major depressive disorder than their peers were thirty years ago. Some studies have suggested they are even as much as ten times more likely to receive this diagnosis. This finding is all the more alarming because it is estimated that around 80 percent of suicide attempts originate in people suffering from depression. Not surprisingly, then, as depression has increased, so has the incidence of suicide.[16] While part of this increase may be due to greater knowledge about the disorder of depression itself and increased sensitivity to its occurrence, it is unlikely these factors account for all the rise in frequency. It is more likely there are other personal, social, and cultural contributors as well. Since External LOC has consistently been found to be associated with depression, it qualifies as one of the possible contributors to its occurrence.[17]

BUT, ON THE OTHER HAND, INTERNALITY MAY NOT *ALWAYS* BE GOOD

Up to this point, while I have been touting the advantages of being Internal, it is important to point out that it is not always better than being External. There are times when being too Internal can have negative consequences. Some idea of these consequences was proposed by Kurt April and his associates. They used surveys to examine the interaction between Locus of Control and well-being and suggested extreme Internality could affect individuals negatively in a number of possible ways:

1. Stressing them because they take too much responsibility for what is happening.
2. Increasing their anxiety because of their inability to cast responsibility or blame on other people or factors.
3. Increasing their feelings of guilt and self-criticism when their goals are not achieved.
4. Causing them to fear losing their sense of control.
5. Breeding feelings of insecurity because they do not trust others and their capabilities.
6. Increasing their loneliness because they lack compassion for others.[18]

Personal LOC versus Situational

As I explained earlier, none of us is totally Internal or External; rather, we fall between the two extremes. The situations we face can straddle these categories as well. We sometimes find ourselves in circumstances in which our behavior has little or no effect on what happens to us. Think of being strapped into a seat on a roller coaster or airplane. Or what about a visit to the dentist? How Internal can we be while sitting in a dentist's chair with a mouthful of instruments? We can mumble or nod, but we can't do much to change the situation or its outcome. It is in the hands of a powerful other. Our best bet, now that we are there, is to take deep breaths and let the doctor get on with the work. In other words, being External in this situation is the appropriate choice.

Mindlessly approaching all circumstances as though we can control all aspects of them ignores the very real possibility that such control may not be attainable. We can avoid counterproductive expenditures of energy by learning to distinguish those instances in which our effort will and will not have positive effect.

Misapplied Internality can lead to problems. Gamblers can make the mistake of being too Internal when they believe they can control the outcome of all their wagers. Internally controlled job hunters may blame themselves for not finding work during times of economic recession, when, in reality, there are no jobs to be found no matter how persistent the search. Then there are athletes like Lance Armstrong, whose Internality propelled him to outstanding athletic accomplishments, but who blundered terribly when he tried to extend his control by taking banned drugs and dictating the behavior of his teammates and others around him.

Perhaps a helpful example of the advantages and disadvantages of Internality can be found in the career of golf superstar Tiger Woods.

The Good and Bad about Internality

One way to show how Internality worked to the benefit of the "early" Tiger Woods is to compare him to Sergio Garcia, another successful (if less known) golfer. Both Woods and Garcia entered professional golfing with glittering credentials at about the same time. Both could hit a golf ball a mile, and both had a magic touch around the green. Their promise seemed unbounded. Yet they have wound up on very different career trajectories. Tiger Woods is now regarded as perhaps one of the greatest golfers of all time. He has won fourteen major championships, while Sergio Garcia has yet to win one. Sports experts have tried to explain the wide discrepancy in the achievements of these two seemingly equally gifted athletes. One fundamental difference is clear: they have opposite Loci of Control.

In 2008, Tiger Woods was playing on a left knee that had two stress fractures, and, although doctors recommended immediate surgery, he decided to play one more tournament. It was not just any tournament—it was the US Open, the most demanding of all the majors. Woods stayed in contention throughout the game and was close to the lead when the final round began. Anyone watching him play the final eighteen holes on one good leg could not help but be impressed by his grit, persistence, and courage. In the end, he won the Open in a playoff against Rocco Mediate. In the post-tournament interview, his Internal perspective was clear. When asked how he felt, he said, "Rocco played so very well that I knew I was in for a real fight. I just tried to take care of my own game. I knew if I paid attention to my own shots and just grinded it out, I might have a chance." His knee was operated on the very next week.[19]

Contrast that with Sergio Garcia's performance during one of the four majors: the British Open in 2007. He, too, played well enough to get into a playoff, but he lost to Padraig Harrington. According to Jim Litke of the Associated Press, Garcia "couldn't stop whining about all the forces that conspired against him." He led by three strokes going into the final round and would have won if he had shot par, yet he did not take ownership of his poor performance. According to Garcia, "It seems to me like every time I get in this kind of position, I have no room for error. I can't miss one shot and I rarely get many good breaks."[20]

What are the chances of Garcia changing his basic External perspective and developing a more Internal approach to his game? Not great. When asked if he was open to changing his attitude and the way he played golf, he said, "I can change a little bit, but not too much because then I wouldn't be myself." It is this kind of thinking that keeps Externals stuck in self-defeating behavior and prevents them from reaching their true potential.

Contrast Garcia's stubborn reluctance to change with Woods's dogged determination to do whatever he needed to do to win. After winning seven major titles, including the Masters, by double digits, Woods decided his swing needed to be upgraded if he was going to remain competitive in the future. He didn't opt for this strategy because he was playing poorly but because he believed he needed to make his game even better. He spent nearly a year working with a well-known golf teacher to perfect a new swing. During that time, Woods did not win a single tournament (recall that Internals show a propensity to delay gratification), but once his new swing was perfected, he returned to the tour with a vengeance, winning seven more majors and thirty-seven tournaments.

Unfortunately for Woods, he has faltered in recent years, and his behavior represents the kinds of problems being too Internal can generate. His later career has been one of escalating failures on the golf course and in his personal life. In 2009, his family was shattered when his wife discovered his affair with Jamie Grubbs, a call girl. Since then, his professional golf performance has had more downs than ups, with the result that instead of being idolized, Tiger Woods now has become an object of pity and derision for some. Writing for *FOX Sports* in the summer of 2015, Robert Lusetich led his article about Woods's disastrous play with the headline, "Stop the Spin Cycle, Tiger: Just Admit You Are Completely Lost, and Get a Head Guru."[21]

What has created this negative backlash is Woods's reluctance to accept the reality that outside forces such as his declining physical ability are affecting his capacity to control outcomes. Instead, he continues to believe he can be just as good as he was before if he tries hard enough. His inappropriate Internality prevents him from observing and accepting what is obvious to others: he's just not that good anymore. As Greg Norman, one of golf's greatest players, concluded: "You can see the physical side of it about where his weaknesses are and what he's doing wrong but I think it's more deep-seated. I think it's deep inside his head and maybe deeper than that."[22]

Robert Lusetich pointed to Woods's comments about his game that do not reflect the reality of his performance. After shooting ten bogeys (a stroke above par) at the US Open and finishing better than only seven other golfers, one of them an amateur, Woods came up with the following reasons for his failures: "I hit the ball solid. It's just that it wasn't getting through the wind. I don't know what was causing that, and it's something that we're going to have to take a look at; look at my numbers, see if the spin rates are on or not."

He is talking as though he can still solve the problem of the ball not going as far or as accurately as it used to by changing his own swing behavior, instead of accepting the fact that the ball is not going as far now because his physical skills have deteriorated. In essence, Woods is denying reality to stay Internal, and this is having a deleterious effect on his interactions with others.

Take Robert Lusetich again: "Spin rates . . . It is mind blowing to contemplate both the absurdity of this sentiment and just how much Woods seemingly takes his audience for idiots. Failure masked by insulting intelligence is becoming a Woods trademark. He now routinely trots out obfuscating jargon that means nothing—glutes deactivating, shifting his baseline, stuck between patterns—to mask an unpalatable truth: He is totally lost as a golfer." Tiger Woods and Sergio Garcia illustrate how Internality and Externally can affect the approach and reaction to performance. I hope once you're familiar with the characteristics of Locus of Control, you'll not only be able to spot Internal and External behavior easily, but you'll also identify aspects of both in yourself so you can work toward developing an appropriate balance.

WHY I WROTE THIS BOOK

I would like to explain my reasons for writing a book about Locus of Control. The American slide toward Externality concerns me greatly; I want to alert readers to that danger. While I'm aware that having too much Internal LOC can create its own set of problems by making us feel inappropriately distressed and frustrated when we fail, I am also sure that healthy Internality lies at the core of our ability to be our best selves. An appropriate level of Internality that is consistent with what the situation demands is one of the most powerful problem-solving tools we can possess to deal successfully with our personal, social, and community challenges.

I also have a very personal reason for writing this book. Its source can be traced to a conversation I had with my granddaughter, Hannah Ruth, nearly a decade ago, a conversation I've never forgotten.

When she was about three years old, Hannah Ruth visited me in Atlanta. One morning, we went for a walk to a nearby pond, as was our wont in those days, carrying bags filled with week-old bread to feed to the ducks and geese. After satisfying the hungry birds, we rested together on a park bench.

Hannah Ruth was usually quite a talker, but on this day, she just sat quietly with her head resting on my arm. After a time, she looked up at me and asked in a soft voice, "Papa, will you watch over me?"

Although startled at her serious tone, I recovered quickly and said, "Of course, Hannah Ruth, I'll watch over you." She settled back into her own thoughts but soon raised her head again, looked me straight in the eye, and asked even more intensely, "Papa, will you *always* watch over me?"

Now, how does one answer a question like that? It struck me then, as I think it would strike any parent and grandparent, how difficult, if not impossible, this question is to answer. How can we *always* watch over our beloved ones—not only to protect them but to assure them of the best chance for a healthy, happy, and fulfilling life?

Hannah Ruth's challenging question was especially relevant for me. I've discovered that being a grandfather is a uniquely wonderful experience. Hannah Ruth filled a place in my heart that I never knew existed until she came along. But one bittersweet aspect of being a grandparent is that I know I will *not* be there to help her or my younger grandson, Soren, for most of their adult lives. So the big question is this: what could I give them, and all the other grandchildren in the world, to help them watch over themselves when I am not there?

My answer to Hannah Ruth's question is this book.

I want those people responsible for guiding her and all children into adulthood to know all they can about Locus of Control. I want to give parents the knowledge necessary to raise appropriately Internal children who also have the skills necessary to identify when they should be appropriately External. This set of abilities will give them the best chance of solving whatever problems they face. Now that would be a worthy gift to last Hannah Ruth and Soren a lifetime.

MOVING FORWARD BY LOOKING BACK

If I've been at all successful in this first chapter, you should have some appreciation for the importance of Locus of Control and my reasons for writing this book. In the next chapter, our journey continues with a trip back to the 1960s and 1970s, when the concept of LOC was born. It was a time of great chaos but also groundbreaking scientific breakthroughs by people like Julian Rotter, who helped us to rethink the fundamental ways we learn and live.

CHAPTER 2

A LITTLE HISTORY OF LOCUS OF CONTROL

"If you don't know history, then you don't know anything. You are a leaf that doesn't know it is part of a tree."
—**Michael Crichton**

ROTTER'S REMARKABLE DISCOVERY

When I look back at how the concept of LOC was born, I'm sure it was helped along by the political turmoil and social upheavals of the 1960s. Peace, love, anger, and war mixed liberally to create a sometimes lethal cocktail of ill-supervised rock concerts, assassinations of political leaders, and massive riots. It was a time when many felt powerless and disconnected from their government, their employers, and one another; conditions that seem uncomfortably familiar today.

In the middle of it all, in 1965, my wife, Kaaren, and I travelled to West Lafayette, Indiana, where I began a doctoral program in clinical psychology at Purdue University. In spite of all the turmoil, it was a very exciting time. I and many others of my age were optimistic about the future and believed if we just tried hard enough, we could make the world a better place. As evidence of that belief, many of my peers were departing for the Peace Corps in response to John Kennedy's call: "Ask not what your country can do for you, but what you can do for your country." While I did not leave the country, I, too, had worked for the Peace Corps while studying for my master's degree at Marquette University in Milwaukee in the early 1960s. Looking back at the thousands of college-age adults who were going off to "save" the world, I am now convinced they were examples of Internality in action. They expected their efforts to bring positive change, a core assumption of Internality that lives on in what remains of the Peace Corps and other, more domestic programs like Teach for America.

Teach for America is a program that asks college graduates to spend one or two years of their lives teaching high school students in low-income, high-risk urban and rural areas of the United States. The "corps" has gained in prestige and importance over the past twenty-five years and today counts more than forty-two thousand members from diverse backgrounds who have had a profound impact on the students they instruct.[1]

And what does Teach for America have to do with Locus of Control? Well, when CEO Wendy Kopp was asked what she looked for in the teachers she recruited, she said, "The No. 1 most predictive trait is perseverance, or what we would call internal locus of control. People who in the context of a challenge . . . have the instinct to figure out what they can control, and to own it, rather than to blame everyone else in the system."[2]

So in at least this one major American institution, the belief in Internality is alive and well. Within this organization, they are especially looking for individuals who expect a positive effect from their efforts and sacrifices.

Back to the 1960s

Of course, at the same time thousands of college-age students were gladly choosing to face the challenge of the Peace Corps, many others were being drafted into the armed forces to fight a war they did not support, halfway around the world in Vietnam— a classic example of induced Externality.

To add to the increasingly chaotic nature of the times, America saw some of its greatest leaders—John Kennedy, Robert Kennedy, and Martin Luther King Jr.—die at the hands of murderers. In response to these assassinations, mob violence and riots broke out in cities across the United States. At times, it felt as though our society was coming apart at the seams. Many people felt helpless and at a loss for how to fix things. Internality and Externality were like separate streams crashing into one another. While the Peace Corps volunteers were applying their Internality to solve problems around the world, many of the rest of us were feeling more and more External, as it seemed that powerful others were determining our fates.

Such was the world in which Julian Rotter and his colleagues at Ohio State University found themselves when they began the process that eventually would lead to the development of social learning theory, in which Locus of Control would be a major concept. Rotter, like most of us at that time, wondered where all this behavioral madness was coming from. Why did some people erupt in self-defeating violence while others chose to sacrifice themselves for the good of others? Rotter was driven by the need to understand why these contradictory events were occurring with the hope that through that awareness he could gain the kind of knowledge that could foster positive change. The opposite possibility—that human behavior was just a crazy, unpredictable, and uncontrollable mess that could not be explained—was simply not acceptable to him. It is easy to understand, in light of prevalent societal attitudes that included both individuals who believed they could affect change and others who believed control was beyond them, why Rotter would later come up with the idea of Locus of Control.

Rotter believed through interactions with others, we come to envision and value certain goals and to anticipate reaching them. Here, "anticipate" is another way of saying we learn to predict our chances of obtaining rewards or punishments if we behave in a certain fashion. We are driven to meet certain needs, such as recognition and status, physical comfort, and love and affection, and, consequently, to learn the actions that increase our chances of meeting our needs. In contrast to psychoanalytic views of battling entities like the id, ego, and superego within us that often ignored outside influences, Rotter emphasized the unity of our personality, our basic humanity, and the importance of our social experiences.[3]

Through a combination of novel experiments, dogged persistence, and some well-placed flashes of genius, Rotter and his colleagues generated a socially based learning theory that was used to generate findings that would help us understand where self-defeating behavior comes from and how to change it.

I BECOME PART OF THE LOC STORY

In 1969, I had just begun my career as a professor of psychology at Emory University. I was twenty-seven, a brand-new professor, looking to make my mark. It was a time when the mainstream explanation of human behavior was Freudian theory, which I found difficult—if not impossible—to evaluate on a logical, scientific level. I was fortunate at this early phase of my career that Bonnie Strickland was already a member of the psychology faculty.

Born and raised in the Deep South by a single mother, Bonnie and her brother were the only two of fifty or so cousins who went on to college (her brother became a dentist) and got professional degrees. She played every sport available to her as a girl. Although she went to school in Birmingham, many of her summers were spent visiting her grandparents' home in rural Florida with no running water. Her chores included, as she told me, "slopping the hogs and feeding the chickens." She always told me she felt more at home there than she ever did in Birmingham.

Bonnie loved school and found it to be a steadying influence in her life. It was the springboard to higher education and, eventually, graduate work with Julian Rotter. Bonnie has had an immense impact on psychology through her energetic pursuit of women's issues and the study of Locus of Control, leading eventually to her election to the presidency of the American Psychological Association.

When I first met Bonnie, I was relatively new to the academic world of psychology and valued her guidance. We became research collaborators and, with time, close, lifelong friends.

I came to Emory right after I defended my dissertation on how attitude similarity creates interpersonal attraction. I was no longer interested in that topic and was on the lookout for a new research area, especially one with a well-thought-out theory that could guide my work. Bonnie was enthusiastic about her work with Rotter and his social learning theory. She described Rotter as a brilliant, kind, and empathetic man who was devoted to making the world a better place. But she also told me he was a stern taskmaster who expected nothing but the best from his students and himself.

Rotter was born in 1916, the middle child of a Jewish immigrant family in Brooklyn.[4] His father was a successful businessman who lost most of what he had worked for during the Great Depression of the 1930s. The economic devastation of the Depression left a lasting impression on Rotter (as on millions of others) and sensitized him to the impact of the environment on behavior. It also made him aware of the prevalence of social injustices in American society, which, in turn, motivated him to strive to understand the sources of such outcomes and to develop ways to promote justice and fairness.

The more I read about Rotter's theory and the research it was generating, the more excited I became. Rotter had been conducting experiments, first at his lab at Ohio State University and later at the University of Connecticut, where he spent the majority of his academic career. I especially liked his emphasis on *expectancies*. Rather than trying to make sense of how we behaved by looking back at what we had already done, Rotter wanted us to pay more attention to what people thought and believed *before* they acted. While the emphasis on expectancies makes perfect sense to us today, that was not true when Rotter first introduced his theory. Largely through Rotter's efforts, the concept of expectancies has moved front and center in American psychology. Although Rotter did not fully realize its importance early on, it soon became apparent that a particular general expectancy called *locus of control of reinforcement* was especially relevant and meaningful. To explain why, I need to introduce the notion that "perception is reality."

PERCEPTION IS REALITY

In the 1960s, learning theorists believed to get people to behave a certain way, you simply rewarded or punished them. Say you wanted a child, Zoe, to pick up her toys. A sure way to get her to do that was to give her a reward, like candy, when she completed the task. In the jargon of the trade, you were "reinforcing" her behavior to increase the likelihood that it would repeat in the future.

Rotter made a wonderfully perceptive observation about the reinforcement process that helped to further define LOC and change the way we think about rewards and punishments. He pointed out that to evaluate the true impact of reinforcement, we need to know if Zoe actually *perceived* the connection between her behavior (picking up toys) and the reinforcement (candy). If Zoe realized the reward was connected to her behavior, she would learn to anticipate that if she behaved similarly again, a reward would follow. But what if Zoe did not perceive the connection between the treat and her actions and instead concluded that the reward happened because of luck or the whim of a parent or babysitter? Then the reward could lose much of its punch. If it lost its connection to her "cleaning up" behavior, it could also lose some of its ability to motivate her to pick up her toys in the future. In other words, Zoe would fail to see the obvious connection between what she did and what happened to her, and this alone could affect how she would behave in that similar situation later. Learning to see the connection between what we do and its consequences is called *contingent reinforcement* and is a crucial process for becoming aware of how much actual Internal control we have and how often and to what extent we can expect our behavior to produce particular outcomes.

AN EXAMPLE OF WHAT A LACK OF AWARENESS OF CONTINGENCIES CAN CAUSE: *CALVIN AND HOBBES*

Because of the different ways they have learned to anticipate what to expect in the future, Internals and Externals can experience the same events but remain unaware of whether the outcomes were contingent on their actions. Externals have learned to see life as largely characterized by chance, while Internals view it more or less as typified by skill and effort. This dichotomy is demonstrated well in the comic strip *Calvin and Hobbes*. Calvin is a young boy, and Hobbes, a stuffed animal, is his imaginary playmate. The pair's daily activities often play out as parables of Internality and Externality. Calvin (usually an External) bitterly complains about his accidents or difficulties being caused by ill luck, while Hobbes (most often an Internal) patiently but indirectly keeps suggesting to Calvin that it is his behavior and not luck that is causing his problems.

In one of my favorite strips, Calvin and Hobbes are shown riding in a coaster wagon that is careening down a hill at breakneck speed. As they arc flying through the air and about to crash, Calvin angrily exclaims how unfortunate he is to have this bad thing happen to him. "Yes," Hobbes replies, "just like it did yesterday and the day before that, and the day before that on this very same hill, in this very same wagon."

Because Calvin is not aware of the connection between his actions and what is happening to him, he does not learn to avoid the inevitable outcome his actions are repeatedly causing. It reminds me of the old saying that insanity is defined by doing the same thing over and over again but expecting a different outcome. Every time I read *Calvin and Hobbes*, I secretly hope maybe this time Calvin will stop and consider what Hobbes is saying and change what he does. So far, no success.

ROTTER'S MEASURE OF LOCUS OF CONTROL

In 1966, after many years of preparation, Rotter published the scale for assessing Locus of Control in adults. Consistent with the meticulous approach Rotter took in all his research endeavors, the twenty-three-item scale with six "fillers" was accompanied by a massive amount of information gleaned from testing thousands of different participants from all walks of life and on all sorts of issues.[5]

The publication of Rotter's scale triggered research that has caused it to become one of the most often used and cited instruments in the history of personality psychology. A recent check of Google Scholar showed Rotter's article has had more than half a million hits. When the scale was published, scientists from the United States and all over the world were pleased to finally have a valid way to measure the impact people expected their behavior to have. The scale generated studies that showed, without a doubt, that scores on Rotter's test predicted important outcomes in people's lives. As a testament to its usefulness, the test continues to be used in studies today by researchers across the world, some fifty years after its introduction.

Rotter's scale is most appropriate for testing college-educated adults, but its reading level is too difficult to be of use for testing children. That is where Bonnie Strickland and I entered the Locus of Control picture. In 1970, we began a program of research that culminated in the 1973 publication of the Children's Nowicki-Strickland Internal External control scale (CNSIE), a downward extension of Rotter's measure. It has been used by researchers in more than a thousand studies in the United States and thirty-eight other countries. Soon after its publication, I collaborated with Marshall Duke, another Emory colleague, in constructing several more LOC scales.

Marshall was hired the year after my arrival, quickly became part of our Locus of Control team, and then became my best friend. Originally from New Jersey, he attended Rutgers University as an undergraduate and Indiana University as a graduate student. His clinical internship was served with the army at Fort Ord in California before he arrived on the scene at Emory. He went on to claim honors in psychology, both as an award-winning teacher and an acclaimed researcher in resilience in children. He continues his work at Emory as the Charles Howard Candler Professor of Psychology.

What Marshall brought with him was a background in learning theory that helped shape our research program for years to come. He was especially astute in translating theory into practice and was invaluable in bringing LOC into our clinical work. As a result of our collaboration, we were given the American Psychological Society's award for applying scientific work to clinical settings. But all that came later.

Soon after Marshall arrived, he and I published additional LOC scales: one with an easier reading level for adults (Adult Nowicki-Strickland Internal External control scale, ANSIE) and one appropriate for preschool children (Preschool and Primary Nowicki-Strickland Internal External control scale, PPNSIE).[6] Over a three-year span, Bonnie Strickland, Marshall Duke, and I had put together useful and dependable ways to measure general LOC in children as young as four and in adults as old as ninety.

What we have found using these scales is far beyond what we could have imagined. They have taken us into areas of study ranging from obesity and high blood pressure to academic achievement, athletic performance, and the effectiveness of CEOs.

IDENTIFYING YOUR OWN LOCUS OF CONTROL

What follows is a scale that has been administered to nearly a million people. Taking it will help you understand the kinds of questions that are asked to determine Internality and Externality, and it will tell you where you fall along the LOC continuum and how you tend to approach life.

The Opinion Survey

If you wish to give the test to children under the age of twelve, we would want you to read the items aloud. The following are the usual instructions given to test takers:

We want you to answer the following questions based on the way you feel. There are no right or wrong answers. Don't take too much time answering any one question, but do try to answer them all and try to pick one response for all. Do not leave any item blank.

One of your concerns taking the test may be, "What should I do when I feel as though I could answer both yes and no to a question?" It's not unusual for this to happen. If it does, the way we would like you to handle this is to think about whether your answer is more one way than the other. For example, if you'd assign a weight of 51 percent to the yes and a weight of 49 to the no, then make your answer yes.

LOC Questionnaire

YES NO

_____ _____ 1. Do you believe that most problems will solve themselves if you don't fool with them?

_____ _____ 2. Do you believe that you can stop yourself from catching a cold?

_____ _____ 3. Are some people just born lucky?

_____ _____ 4. Most of the time, did you feel that getting good grades means a great deal to you?

_____ _____ 5. Are you often blamed for things that just aren't your fault?

_____ _____ 6. Do you believe that if somebody studies hard enough, he or she can pass any subject?

_____ _____ 7. Do you feel that most of the time it doesn't pay to try hard because things never turn out right anyway?

_____ _____ 8. Do you feel that if things start out well in the morning that it's going to be a great day, no matter what you do?

_____ _____ 9. Do you feel that most of the time parents listen to what their children have to say?

_____ _____ 10. Do you believe that wishing can make good things happen?

_____ _____ 11. When you get rejected, does it usually seem it's for no good reason at all?

_____ _____ 12. Most of the time do you find it hard to change a friend's opinion?

_____ _____ 13. Do you think that cheering, more than luck, helps a team to win?

_____ _____ 14. Did you feel that it is nearly impossible to change your parents' mind about anything?

_____ _____ 15. Do you believe that parents should allow children to make most of their own decisions?

_____ _____ 16. Do you feel that when you do something wrong there's very little you can do to make it right?

_____ _____ 17. Do you believe that most people are just born good at sports?

___ ___ 18. Are most of the other people your age and sex stronger than you are?

___ ___ 19. Do you feel that one of the best ways to handle most problems is just not to think about them?

___ ___ 20. Do you feel that you have a lot of choice in deciding who your friends are?

___ ___ 21. If you find a four-leaf clover, do you believe that it might bring good luck?

___ ___ 22. Did you often feel that whether or not you did your homework had much to do with what kind of grades you got?

___ ___ 23. Do you feel that when a person your age decides to be angry with you, there's little you can do to stop him or her?

___ ___ 24. Have you ever had a good-luck charm?

___ ___ 25. Do you believe that whether or not people like you depends on how you act?

___ ___ 26. Did your parents usually help you if you asked them to?

___ ___ 27. Have you ever felt that when people were angry with you, it was usually for no reason at all?

___ ___ 28. Most of the time, do you feel that you can change what might happen tomorrow by what you do today?

___ ___ 29. Do you believe that when bad things are going to happen, they just are going to happen, no matter what you do to try to stop them?

___ ___ 30. Do you think that people can get their own way if they just keep trying?

___ ___ 31. Most of the time, did you find it useless to try to get your own way at home?

___ ___ 32. Do you feel that when good things happen, they happen because of hard work?

___ ___ 33. Do you feel that when somebody your age wants to be your enemy, there's little you can do to change matters?

___ ___ 34. Do you feel that it's easy to get friends to do what you want them to do?

____ ____ 35. Did you usually feel that you had little to say about what you got to eat at home?

____ ____ 36. Do you feel that when someone doesn't like you, there's little you can do about it?

____ ____ 37. Did you usually feel that it was almost useless to try in school because most other students were just plain smarter than you were?

____ ____ 38. Are you the kind of person who believes that planning ahead makes things turn out better?

____ ____ 39. Most of the time, did you feel that you had little to say about what your family decided to do?

____ ____ 40. Do you think it's better to be smart than to be lucky?

Scoring Key (Items are keyed in the External direction)

1. Yes
2. No
3. Yes
4. No
5. Yes
6. No
7. Yes
8. Yes
9. No
10. Yes
11. Yes
12. Yes
13. No
14. Yes
15. No
16. Yes
17. Yes
18. Yes
19. Yes

20. No
21. Yes
22. No
23. Yes
24. Yes
25. No
26. No
27. Yes
28. No
29. Yes
30. No
31. Yes
32. No
33. Yes
34. No
35. Yes
36. Yes
37. Yes
38. No
39. Yes
40. No

Each time your response agrees with the keyed responses, you receive one point toward Externality. Your score is the total number of times your answer agrees with the keyed item.

What Does Your Score Mean?

The test is scored in the External direction. This means that the higher your score, the more External you are, while the lower your score, the more Internal you are. Keep in mind that the following descriptions are general and do not mean everyone scoring in a particular zone will behave the same. The zones have been corrected for the increase in Externality over the past three decades.

Low Scorers (0 to 8). Scores from zero to eight usually mean you would be classified as Internal. As such, you probably see what happens to you as the result of your effort and skill rather than luck, fate, chance, or powerful others. You most likely believe you have had something to do with the good and bad things that have occurred in your life. You probably tend to take the initiative in most instances, from job-related activities to relationships. In addition, you often are described by others as vigilant in getting things done, aware of what's going on around you, and willing to spend energy in working for specific goals. You would probably find it uncomfortable to sit back and let others take care of you, since your test answers stressed that you like to have your life in your own hands.

Although being Internal is most often a positive way to approach life, you have to be aware of those instances when it is not. Overreaching your Internality can lead you to think of yourself as a failure even when an outcome wasn't your fault or responsibility. So when you are feeling bad about what you've done, check to be sure it truly was your fault rather than a situation in which there wasn't any control to be had.

Average Scorers (9 to 16). You've answered questions in both Internal and External directions, which suggests you may be a bit hesitant to act as though you can determine what happens next but also not so quick to depend on luck, fate, and chance to decide your future outcomes. Though your general Locus of Control is usually the best predictor of how you behave, you might believe you have more impact on one set of outcomes, like work, than another, like relationships. You may find it helpful to review the questions and group them into those you answered in the Internal direction and those you answered in the External direction to see if they fall into a common content area.

High Scorers (17 to 40). If you scored seventeen or above, chances are you are External in your view of the way life operates. You are likely to be a follower rather than a leader and to have problems persisting at tasks. In approaching a problem situation, you are likely to make the mistake of believing there isn't anything you can do to help solve the problem when, in reality, there is. When you fail, you are protected against feelings of disappointment because you do not see yourself as responsible.

There are different reasons for an individual to score in the External control direction. For example, psychologists have found that many people in minority and disadvantaged groups tend to score this way. One recent suggestion is that people in these groups perceive their life situations realistically: minorities and members of lower socioeconomic classes really do have more restrictions on their successes, fewer job options, lower pay, and less opportunity for advancement, no matter what they do or don't do. An Internal belief in such situations may be unrealistic and inappropriate. Thus, your own high External control score could be a realistic perception of your current life circumstances.[7]

On the other hand, your score may represent a strong belief in luck or superstition and a concurrent feeling of helplessness in controlling your life. Research studies have shown a relation between unrealistic External control beliefs and problems like anxiety, depression, low self-concept, and poor physical health.[8] If this is the case, it might be helpful for you to reflect on whether you may actually have more control over your outcomes than you have expressed on the test. You may be then more likely to engage in behaviors that might bring about more positive results.

MEASURING DIFFERENT ASPECTS OF LOCUS OF CONTROL

The test you just took measures a generalized LOC similar to what is measured by Rotter's scale. That is, it reflects how you typically perceive the connection between how you behave and what happens to you across most situations; it does not favor or focus on any specific content area or attempt to separate Externality into luck, fate, chance, or powerful others. Almost from the moment Rotter introduced his generalized expectancy scale, other researchers began to construct tests that measured LOC for specific content areas such as academic achievement, physical health, parenting, and work. Still others sought to separate Externality into luck, fate, chance, and powerful others. Combining these two goals has resulted in an explosion of more specific scales. While it is difficult to say exactly how many of these measures exist, I have counted more than one hundred.

While the idea of having more specific LOC scales is a sound one, it turns out many scales aren't very good. They may lack *reliability* (yielding the same score from one testing to the next) and *validity* (measuring what the scale says it does). Some haven't been given widely enough to diverse groups of people to test their generalizability. Some have only been used in a study or two. Most telling of all the criticisms is that although these scales are more specific, many lack what is called *incremental validity*, meaning they do not provide evidence they improve on the already-established tests. There is little use for a more specific LOC test if it does not predict better than the general measure.

In this book, I only report findings gathered from reliable and valid tests. Eliminating results from tests lacking scientific support still leaves us with thousands of studies and an amazing amount of valuable information. Here are some basic facts about Locus of Control.

LOC and Age

For any test of Locus of Control to be useful, it has to be reliable. That is, it has to produce a score that remains relatively stable across time. If we score a twelve at ten o'clock Monday morning, we should get a similar score if we take the test again later in the week. The score should not swing wildly from day to day.

However, being stable does not mean the score is static. Rather, our individual LOC, like our weight, commonly changes with age. If someone asks what we weighed when we were children, we wouldn't give one answer because weight changes from year to year. In that sense, our weight is not absolutely consistent because we are constantly gaining weight, but it is stable because we usually weigh the same in comparison with our peers, who are also changing and gaining weight each year.

Similarly, our LOC scores tend to become more Internal as we grow older. The trajectory toward Internality is powered by our improving physical and mental abilities, which help us gain increasingly greater control over our environment. As we become older, not only can we run faster and throw farther, but we can think more complexly and reason more acutely.

Due to our increasing skills, our parents and teachers give us more opportunities to engage additional aspects of our environment independently. As we interact more independently with others, we are given new opportunities to learn who we are and what we can do, and we learn through experiences that allow us to observe the positive and negative consequences of our behavior. Typically, we grow to be more Internal as we get older, but, through greater parental support and richer learning experiences, some of us learn to be Internal more quickly than others.

As a scientist who has spent his life measuring what Locus of Control is and is not, I've found out that understanding the stable but changing nature of the trait can be confusing. Often, people ask me which test score separates Internals from Externals; they tend to become annoyed when I tell them it all depends on age. Because our LOC scores change throughout our lives, our state of Internality and Externality is always in flux. For example, a score of fifteen on a test taken at age eight would put children in the Internal group, but the same score at age twelve would place them in the External group, since children tend to become more Internal as they advance toward adulthood.

Perhaps this is a good place to remind you that we use the terms "Internal" and "External" as a convenience. There are not separate Internal and External groups of people. Rather, our scores fall somewhere along a continuum between totally Internal and totally External.

Based on four decades of Locus of Control information, we know that, on average, we become increasingly more internally controlled throughout childhood. This trend toward Internality continues, although at a slowing rate, into late adulthood, when we stop becoming more Internal and begin to become more External.

LOC and Gender

We know LOC changes with age, but does it differ between males and females? The simple answer is no. But (and there always seems to be a "but" when trying to fully explain what LOC is all about), although male and female test scores don't differ in absolute terms, the same score can predict different outcomes for each group.

Let me show you what I mean by using academic achievement (which will be covered more thoroughly in chapter 4). My Locus of Control test, the Nowicki-Strickland Internal External control scale (NSIE), has been used in many studies to examine the association between LOC orientation and academic achievement. Two general findings are pertinent to our discussion of LOC and gender. One: from third grade through high school (and in adulthood as well), boys and girls do not differ in their average LOC scores. Two, and perhaps relevant to our conversation about gender: Internality in boys is a predictor of their academic achievement from third grade through high school and into college, but Internality in girls only predicts academic achievement up to about eighth grade. By high school, LOC scores no longer predict girls' academic achievement as well as they do boys', even though the scores are similar. Why should this be? Is there some other factor that enters in around the age of twelve that might affect the ability of LOC to predict female academic achievement? One intriguing possibility is the type of relationship between daughters and their fathers.

LOC and Fathers and Daughters

One advantage of studying Locus of Control for as long as I have is that I get to read literally thousands of studies about it. Every so often, I run across something so distinctive that it stays with me over the years and bells go off when I find it again. That's what happened in regard to daughters and fathers.

The story begins in the fall of 1971, when I was beginning my second year at Emory. A wonderfully bright, hardworking, and perceptive senior college student, Wendy Segal, had asked me to be her undergraduate research advisor. At this stage of our research, we knew next to nothing about the interplay between parent and child LOC and how it related to children's academic achievement and social activities.

Wendy decided to use high school seniors as her research participants. The students completed LOC scales: one for themselves and one each for how they thought their mothers and fathers would score on it. Students also described how each parent interacted with them. Finally, we received permission to acquire the students' grades and social activities from their school records.

Though boys and girls had similar LOC scores, these scores predicted different outcomes: Internality predicted a higher academic grade point average for boys but not girls. Likewise, Internality predicted a greater number of social activities for girls but not boys. These facts were interesting on their own because they were one of our first hints that though actual LOC scores did not differ by gender, they were predictive of different outcomes for boys and girls.

We also found students' perceptions of how their parents interacted with them differed by gender: perceived maternal nurturance was associated with boys' Internality, and perceived paternal nurturance was associated with girls' Internality. What this seemed to suggest was that the perceived nurturance of the opposite-sex parents was more important for children's LOC than that of the same-sex parents.

But perhaps the most thought-provoking result for me, and the one that stayed with me over the years, was that although the girls' LOC did not predict their academic performance, how they perceived their *fathers'* LOC did. Something unique was going on between how adolescent girls saw their fathers' Locus of Control and how the girls performed academically.[9]

Fast-forward to a study completed by my German friend and colleague Klaus Schneewind.[10] Dr. Schneewind is an internationally acclaimed expert in family relationships who has published more than a dozen books and dozens of research studies. Early in his career, he was kind enough to sponsor me on my first sabbatical leave, at Trier University in Germany. At that time, he was working on a project to investigate the effect of parent-child relationships on the personal adjustment and academic performance of children. He included my LOC scales in the assessment of both parents and children. The children were ten years old when the study began.

Some eighteen years after the initial study, Dr. Schneewind was able to locate a significant number of the original participants and obtain their permission to be tested again. And here is where the father-daughter story gets really good. Of many outcomes, the one that stood out for me echoed the special relationship of fathers and daughters I had noticed twenty years previously. The best predictor of daughters' Locus of Control at age twenty-six was not their own LOC at age ten but their fathers' LOC. As with the high school seniors in 1971, fathers' Internality seemed to have more to do with their daughters' LOC and behavior than the daughters' own Internality did.[11]

Indeed, these two findings suggest the father-daughter relationship during the daughters' childhood, and possibly beyond, is a major determiner of the daughter's adult LOC and achievement. While this is still a possibility that needs additional research to confirm, the findings resonated with the personal experiences of the female students in a course I am teaching called the Psychology of Leadership at Emory's Goizueta Business School. Every semester in which I have offered this study for discussion, female students have volunteered examples of how their fathers played a part in their pursuit of achievement success in high school and college. I was impressed by how fathers stood out so boldly and clearly in the minds of these young women as a source of support and a person to emulate.

LOC AND BIRTH ORDER

While Locus of Control scores may be similar for males and females, they do differ by birth order. Alfred Adler, a prominent psychiatrist of the early twentieth century, was among the first to suggest that birth order would produce different kinds of personality.[12] He assumed because of the way families operated, firstborn children would be responsible, serious, motivated, goal-directed, rule-conscious, organized, and driven to be successful in whatever they pursued. Why? Adler suggested it was because parents put a great deal of pressure on themselves and their firstborn children to get things right.

In contrast, middle-born children, according to Adler, tend to develop a more diverse range of personalities because they mix the experience of being the youngest for a time with the loss of the limelight when a younger sibling is born. Because of their more diverse incidents, Adler felt that middle-born children were likely to be more natural mediators and to develop more social skills and peer relationships outside the family.

The youngest child, the "baby," was predicted to be outgoing and a likely entertainer who enjoyed having a good time. Because youngest children have many people paying attention to them, they are in danger of being pampered too much. Adler believed pampering can lead young children to become selfish and grow into irresponsible adults.

If any of the Adlerian suppositions about birth order are true, firstborns should be more Internal than later-borns. However, though research findings have been mixed, a closer look shows that researchers often fail to take into account the gender of the children, the age separation among the siblings, and the size of the family.[13]

I have access to data that control for all these factors and are longitudinal to boot—that is, following the same participants over time. The Avon Longitudinal Study of Parents and Children (ALSPAC) has been following about twenty-five thousand children who were born over an eighteen-month span between 1991 and 1992 in Bristol, England. My Locus of Control tests were given to the children when they were eight years of age.

We found that the larger the family, the more externally controlled were the members, but, regardless of number of family members, those born earlier tended to be more Internal than those born later, regardless of gender.[14]

ROTTER'S REACTION TO THE SUCCESS OF HIS CONCEPT

As reflected in the brief introduction of basic findings above, there was instant interest in Locus of Control from the moment of its introduction. In fact, the number of studies that followed the publication of Rotter's scale in 1966 threatened to overwhelm him. Although Rotter was always quick to point out that Locus of Control was only one aspect of his overall social learning theory of human behavior, his cautions fell on deaf ears. On the twenty-fifth anniversary of the publication of his scale, Rotter lamented what had happened to the concept: "It was like I was walking in the woods and I put a match to my pipe and then I threw the match over my shoulder. I took a few steps and when I turned around the woods all around me were on fire."[15] In the twenty-five years following Rotter's declaration, it appears the fire is still raging.

WHAT COMES NEXT?

Now that you have some idea of the historical context out of which the concept of Locus of Control sprang, the many available ways to measure it, and some basic information about your own LOC, it is time to get more personal. How do you and I get the LOC we have? Let's find out next.

CHAPTER 3

HOW WE GET OUR LOCUS OF CONTROL

"If you can't control your peanut butter, you can't expect to control your life."
—**Bill Watterson,** *The Authoritative Calvin and Hobbes*

Louisa lies in her crib, but she is not still. Her eyes dart about, and her arms and legs move in excitement. Why? Because she is gazing at a mobile hung over her crib that has five multicolored angels jiggling from it. Why are they jiggling? Because there is a thin ribbon tied to Louisa's foot that, in turn, is tied to a pulley connected to the mobile. When Louisa moves her foot, she sets the mobile in motion. The more she moves her foot, the more the mobile jiggles and bounces. The more the mobile jiggles and bounces, the more Louisa moves her foot. You get the picture. Louisa is interacting with her environment, and, although she has little control over her surroundings at her early age, she's learned that she can at least manipulate the mobile. The smile on her face and the excited kicks from her feet indicate that she is truly enjoying exercising some measure of dominion over her surroundings. Even as an infant, she is happy to be Internal!

We all seem to have an innate need to control what's happening around us. We feel comforted and secure when we are able to find ways to manipulate our environment in a manner that pleases us. Thus, we can understand why Louisa delights in having control over the wonderful creatures floating above her; after all, we, too, seek to control the circumstances of our lives. However, our efforts are often unsuccessful. Much as we like to call the shots, there are times when we're left to the whims of luck, fate, chance, or powerful others. We can only hope these unpredictable external regulators will be kind to us. Yet, even as we tremble a bit under their capricious rule, we wonder: would it not be better if we could chart our own course and steer clear of challenges?

Such an aspiration is, in fact, one of the things that motivate us to grow in knowledge during childhood. Even if you have spent your earlier years as an External, it is quite possible to move toward greater Internality. As previously discussed, most people do tend to become more Internal with age.

If you took the Locus of Control test in the previous chapter, you have some idea of where you fall along the continuum and what your score suggests about how you behave. But do you know what led you to obtain your present personal LOC? Did you inherit it from your parents or learn it from your life experiences, or was it determined by some combination of these sources? What forces helped you become more Internal, and which ones contributed to your Externality? Was the process the result of the unfolding of messages from your genes, similar to what happened as you matured sexually? Are there significant behavioral experiences that played a part? How important were your parents, other adults, and your peers in determining how much of what you experienced would be seen through an Internal or External lens?

To answer these crucial questions, we must look back to the beginning of our lives, when we were forced from the comfort of our mothers' wombs and brought kicking and screaming into our new world. As newborn babies, we couldn't possibly have been more External. We even had trouble distinguishing between ourselves and the objects and people around us. But that slowly changed, and, eventually, we began to develop separate concepts of "me" and "them." Although we had an innate need to seek and gain control over our world, the truth was we couldn't control much of anything in the beginning.

But soon, our developing brains began to note that certain events followed one another. When we were uncomfortable or hungry and cried, someone responded and did things to fulfill our needs. Later, we learned that a smile was important; it was difficult to know exactly when or how that happened, but we began to exchange smiles with those people who were consistently in our perception, and, for some reason, this felt good.

As our coordination improved and we had more control of our arms and legs, we found that we could reach for and grab things. Some of the things we took hold of made noises when we shook them, and—marvels of marvels!—if we stopped shaking them, they fell silent. Apparently, we enjoyed this power to control this something, because we exercised it over and over again. As with Louisa in the above vignette, there was pleasure in controlling outcomes. We wanted to control more and more of what went on around us. It was fun when we pushed our cereal bowl off the table and found that someone picked it up and put it back for us, so we decided to do it over and over again. This control thing could really be a good time!

As time passed, we grew stronger, more coordinated, and better able to think and reason. We became more aware of the ways our behavior affected us and the world around us. With speech came a new powerful way to test the limits of our control. Some of us found a well-placed tantrum or, perhaps, uttering the word "sorry" (accompanied by a very sad face and tone of voice) could postpone or even avoid punishment. Our Locus of Control was developing and changing from general Externality to a greater degree of Internality via the learning process called contingent reinforcement. As you may remember from the earlier account of Zoe, contingent reinforcement is when a reward or punishment occurs immediately following a behavior or interaction, thus helping establish an "expectancy link" that future similar behaviors will produce similar predictable consequences.

AN EXAMPLE OF CONTINGENT REINFORCEMENT

When my grandson, Soren, was about eighteen months old, his mother, father, older sister, grandmother, and I all sat around the dining room table finishing a happily chaotic family meal. Soren was not a very talkative child at this point, in part because his sister, Hannah Ruth (a proficient talker), often spoke for him. Interested in helping him talk independently, we asked him to name everyone at the table. We reminded Hannah Ruth to let her brother speak. Soren looked hesitantly at his mother and said, "Mommy," then at his father, saying, "Daddy," and, with steadily increasing confidence, he looked across the table at his sister and said, "Hannah," and then at his grandmother and said, "Nanna." Finally, he turned his head slowly toward me, hesitated for just a moment, smiled mischievously, and said, "You a monkey." The table erupted in laughter, and Soren looked around at everyone, pleased with the effect he'd had on his audience. His words had power. They'd had a dramatic impact on the behavior of his family. He had received contingent reinforcement for his joke. From that point on, he talked much more frequently and expected his words to be heard and reacted to. This is a favorite family story—and an excellent example of how contingent reinforcement works.

If we take the time to notice, we can see contingent reinforcement taking place all around us. A child washes her face, and her mom exults, "Good!" A youngster finishes sweeping the walk, and his dad plays catch with him as promised. A teenager fails to complete her homework and has her video game privileges taken away for the night. A woman makes a presentation at a business conference and gets a text message from her boss congratulating her on "a job well done."

Such practices make us aware that our behavior has consequences, and, through that awareness, we learn to expect which of our actions will consistently produce the same positive (or negative) outcomes in the future. It is a basic way we learn to be more internally controlled. Although this learning process is not rocket science, many parents (and teachers) fail to use the process of rewarding contingently as much as they could. Instead, they promise to reward (or punish), but they miss seeing the relevant behavior or don't reward (or punish) it promptly, so when they get around to finally delivering the reinforcement, it is not tied to the appropriate behavior. Still worse, some parents shower children with constant rewards (or punishments) that have nothing to do with what they have or haven't done. This is a sure way to teach children to expect their actions to have little or nothing to do with what happens to them—in other words, to make them more External and thus, in the long run, less happy and well adjusted.

HOW BEING TOO "GOOD" A PARENT CAN BE BAD

Xavier and Caroline thought they would never be able to conceive and have their own child. They tried for years and years and had just about given up when Caroline became pregnant. "Joy" was hardly a strong enough word to describe their reaction to the news. The pregnancy proved to be difficult, and the birth involved some complications, but Caroline and Xavier greeted a six-pound, seven-ounce baby girl they named Josephine (after the maternal grandmother). From the minute they brought Josephine home, they fawned over her and responded to her every perceived need. As Josephine became a toddler, she moved about the house grabbing everything at her height; Aunt Evelyn's expensive vase went "boom," as did a number of important first editions. But Josephine never heard the word "no." On playdates at other children's homes, Josephine was allowed by her mother to "rumble" through toy boxes, cupboards, and bookcases and take whatever she wished to throw, jump on, or put in the toilet. Although other mothers often directed their children's play and reprimanded them when they misbehaved, Josephine's mother did not. Whatever Josephine wanted was what she should have; she was the "miracle" child, and everything she did was OK. Soon, Josephine and her mother were not being invited to as many playdates as they had been before. Parents were not willing to put up with a child who did not follow the rules and created conflicts with other children.

No matter what Josephine did, she was rewarded. As a result, she did not receive the kind of information required to learn what to expect from her behavior in the real world. There was no need for her to learn to discriminate between what she should and shouldn't do when she was at home. As a result of this kind of parenting, Josephine was being taught to be External by an overabundance of tolerance. Whatever she did was reinforced positively by her indulgent parents. One can only imagine what happened when Josephine began preschool, away from her parents, and had to face situations where some of her learned behaviors would bring great consternation and disapproval.

HOW PARENTS AFFECT THE DEVELOPMENT OF INTERNALITY

If we simply inherited our Locus of Control scores from our parents, there would be no need for this chapter. My advice would be brief and to the point: if you want to have an Internal child, just be sure to have two Internal parents!

Alas, I'm afraid it's not that simple. While some temperamental characteristics related to the concept may be inherited, studies reveal our own individual LOC is not inherited but learned.

Let me give you the best evidence I know of regarding the heritability of Locus of Control: comparing fraternal twins (i.e., those born at the same time but from different eggs) with identical ones (i.e., those born from the same egg with identical DNA). If the trait is inherited, it will be shown more convincingly in the identical than the fraternal twin pairs. In this case, if one identical twin is Internal, then the other will be also. This is less likely to happen in the fraternal twins because they are less genetically similar.

Researchers Susan Bullers and Carol Prescott analyzed findings from hundreds of twin pairs and concluded that "results suggest that perceived control is determined in large part by *non-inherited psychosocial factors*" (emphasis mine).[1] The factors they mentioned were education, income, earnings, marital quality, age, and single-parent status.

The lack of heritability evidence is consistent with the lack of association we have found between parents' and children's Locus of Control scores. It is clear that something else is contributing to our LOC. The rest of this chapter is an exploration of what that something else might be.

PARENTS' LOCUS OF CONTROL

Just because we don't inherit our LOC directly from our parents doesn't mean they don't play an important role in determining it. We learn our LOC from the way parents (or other caregivers) discipline and interact with us. We learn it from the life experiences they provide for us and the ways in which they model Internality and Externality at home, at school, and at play.

We can't help but be affected by adult models during childhood, and there are few models as important as our parents. This is as true about Locus of Control as it is about any other important set of behaviors. Our task of learning from parental models in this area can be a complex one, especially when our parents don't share the same LOC as one another.

A PERSONAL EXAMPLE

When I consider my own childhood and my parents, I'm immediately struck with how different parental Locus of Control models can be. My parents had diametrically opposed LOC orientations. My father was an Internal's Internal—a strong, silent man, proud of his "old country" Polish heritage. He believed a person was responsible for his or her failures, just as he believed a person was well within his or her rights to take credit for successes. Fishing with my father provided numerous reinforcements of this mind-set for me. On one particular trip, I remember casting and retrieving a lure hundreds of times without any success. Then, unexpectedly, as I was retrieving what felt like my thousandth cast, my lure was hit by a large fish near the boat. After a loud splash, the fish was gone. It took about a millisecond for it all to happen. And it took about the same amount of time for my father to begin explaining what I had done wrong to lose the fish. I tried to explain to him that it all had happened much too quickly for me to do anything, but my complaints fell on deaf ears. I want to be clear that my father wasn't angry with me; rather, he wanted to take that opportunity to teach me about what he saw as the "control" I had in that situation. I can remember him calmly describing how, among other actions, I should have held the rod tip closer to the water when I was casting. His response was consistent with his belief there was always something you could do to turn failure into success.

And then there was my mother, a superstitious Sicilian. She never felt an emotion she didn't immediately express intensely. My mother was as much an External as my father was an Internal. For her, life was all about luck and fate. If you wanted to catch fish, you put lucky stones in your pocket. When I was nine years old, I lost a ten-dollar bill on an ill-fated shopping trip to the corner store. In those days, ten dollars was a great deal of money, especially for a family living on the edge of poverty. My sizable extended family immediately stepped forward to help me look for the missing money, but not my mother. Instead, she stayed home and sat quietly by the statue of Saint Anthony, the patron saint of lost items. When we found the missing money, we all celebrated the success of our efforts to track it down, but what I remember most vividly is the knowing look on my mother's face. For her, the real reason for our success was the kindness of Saint Anthony. Nothing I or anyone else could have said would have convinced her otherwise.

Like many, I was presented with a choice of contradictory Locus of Control models to emulate during my childhood. How could I deal with such a disparate pair of choices? I had a number of options.

1. I could combine the two models and split the difference so my eventual LOC would be somewhere in the middle of my two parents'.
2. I could attempt to reflect both of my parents' LOC at different times, with the result that I would swing from Internality to Externality, depending on the situation.
3. I could adopt my father's Internality and the way he modeled it because I would grow to someday be a man.
4. Finally, I could copy my mother's Externality because I spent most of my time with her.

WHAT IS THE IMPACT OF PARENTAL LOCUS OF CONTROL ON CHILDREN?

A few researchers have looked at the association of parents' LOC with their children's behavior. What they have found is intriguing, especially with respect to Internality. According to Duane Ollendick's study, when both parents were External, their fourth-grade children were likely to be more anxious and lower achieving in school.[2] But when one parent (either father or mother) was Internal, the negative associations with anxiety and achievement disappeared. He concluded there were "benefits of children having at least one internally controlled parent."

However, bad news about the effects of parental Externality was uncovered by Rachel Freed and Martha Tompson of Boston University.[3] Maternal Externality, as measured by a parental Locus of Control scale, appears to co-occur with behavior problems in elementary school–age children.

Freed and Tompson took their study a step further by retesting the mothers and children a year later. Unfortunately, not only had children's "acting out" problems increased in the year that had elapsed, but the mothers' LOC had become even more External. The researchers concluded this result reflected a "bi-directionality," otherwise known as a vicious circle between parental Externality and children's difficulties—that is, each influenced changes in the other in an ongoing spiral of negativity.

For some reason, researchers seem more interested in the influence of mothers' Locus of Control than fathers'. In the studies mentioned above, mothers are often studied alone. But there are exceptions. Erin Tone, one of my finest graduate students and now a professor at Georgia State University in Atlanta, teamed up with me and Liverpool University's Stephanie Goodfellow to look at fathers more closely.[4] We took advantage of available information from an ongoing large-scale longitudinal study taking place on the Isle of Man (located off the west coast of England). In this study, fathers' LOC was assessed before their children's birth. Children's adjustment outcomes were then obtained when the children were seven. In examining these data, we found fathers' (but not mothers') prenatal Externality was related to their sons' negative adjustment, especially hyperactivity, as measured by teacher ratings.

SUMMARY OF PARENTAL LOCUS
OF CONTROL AND CHILDREN'S BEHAVIOR

Parental Locus of Control is important to children's adjustment. Parental Externality, especially in both parents, is associated with feelings of anxiety and depression. On the other hand, parental Internality seems to have a positive effect on children's lives, both in and out of school. What is missing is research on children's adjustment to Internality or Externality in single-parent families. With no competing model, it is likely that whatever the LOC is of a single parent, its effect would be magnified.

In light of the information from the studies above, I realize I was fortunate to have at least one Internal parent. My father's Internality contributed to creating a more positive learning environment for me while perhaps also allowing my own Internality to develop. But it was also true that I absolutely loved school, where I found additional Internal models to emulate.

HOW DO PARENTS FACILITATE THE DEVELOPMENT
OF INTERNALITY IN THEIR CHILDREN?

We know there is a relationship between parental Locus of Control and children's behavior, but what we don't know is what other parental characteristics, attitudes, and behaviors play a central and meaningful role. Fortunately, Julian Rotter and his colleagues June Chance and Jerry Phares have provided some help here.[5] They suggested the Locus of Control of our parents (and other important adults) is significant, but only as a starting point for learning our own. What is more important is how our parents interacted with and disciplined us. Regardless of parents' LOC, to teach children to be Internal, parents (and other adults) must consistently and contingently reinforce their behavior; allow them autonomy and independence; and nurture them with warmth, support, and acceptance.

I know the following will sound simplistic. But, at the risk of showing my age, I'm struck with how Rotter's description for facilitating the development of Internality bears an uncanny resemblance to how American families were depicted in 1950s television shows. From *Leave It to Beaver* to *Father Knows Best*, parents were shown giving their children consistent contingent feedback about their everyday behavior. When problems occurred, as they inevitably did, they usually were resolved by the end of the show by the children (and, at times, their parents), who became aware of the connections that existed between their actions and the outcomes they received.

I remember one episode in which Beaver, an eight-year-old and not a very good athlete, scores the winning touchdown and receives much attention. It goes to his head, and he soon alienates all his friends but feels confused about how that happened. The show ends up with Beaver talking with his father, who helps Beaver understand the connections between the way he acted and the way his friends reacted. More important, they also discuss how to repair the ruptured bonds of friendship. A final talk with Beaver's brother, Wally, before bedtime reviews what happened, with Wally telling how the same thing had happened to him.

As mundane as they may sound, each of Rotter's assumptions has turned out to be supported by research.

ARE PARENTS OF INTERNALS MORE CONSISTENT AND CONTINGENT IN REINFORCING THEIR CHILDREN'S BEHAVIOR?

Research shows that mothers and fathers of Internal children are better at being consistent and rewarding contingently.

John Carton—one of my doctoral students, who now occupies a distinguished chair as a professor of psychology at Oglethorpe University in Atlanta—set out in his doctoral dissertation to see how parents of Internals and Externals behaved with their children while the children completed tasks.[6]

Here's what John did. He brought mothers and their eight-year-old sons into his laboratory. He had the children complete a series of four puzzles on their own and kept their mothers, who were seated at the opposite end of the table, busy filling out a number of forms. Children were given five minutes to complete an easy puzzle, and, when they were finished, John gave them a slightly more difficult second puzzle to solve. All children completed the first and second puzzle successfully. When they were finished with the first two puzzles, he gave them a third, very difficult, puzzle to complete. At the end of the time allotted for the third puzzle, John gave them a fourth and final puzzle, which was easily solved. (This was done so children would leave the study with a success experience.) He also let them pick out a prize from the "present" box. Each session was videotaped in its entirety.

John and his research team then set to work viewing and analyzing what they had captured on videotape. What transpired between mothers and sons revealed something quite important for our understanding of the determinants of Locus of Control, especially when children are facing challenging situations. The behavior of mothers of Internal and External children was virtually indistinguishable during the first two puzzles; all of them kept to their assigned tasks while their children worked on putting the puzzle pieces together.

Changes first began to occur when children were faced with solving the nearly impossible third puzzle. Most notable was a change in mothers' affect. As they watched their children struggle with the puzzle, mothers of Externals showed exasperation and then anger, communicated via their facial expressions and voices. Angry words soon followed: "Why aren't you trying harder?" or "Do I have to show you where the piece goes?" Along with angry words, mothers of Externals were more prone to intrude into what the children were doing, sometimes going so far as to take the task over from their sons.

The unpleasant and tense quality of the mother/External sons' interactions contrasted strongly with the warm, relaxed, and supportive exchanges between mothers and their Internal sons. Mothers of Internals calmly stuck to their assigned tasks even when their sons were obviously struggling to solve the puzzle, They also offered reassuring comments at times of greatest difficulty, like, "Just do the best you can," or, "That is a really tough puzzle, isn't it? Just keep at it; you'll get it."

Carton was quick to emphasize that comments from mothers of Internals came at the "right" time to reward their children's persistence. Their statements were never given as orders. This same phenomenon has been observed by other researchers who observed parent-child interactions. For example, Theodore Chandler, a professor at Kent State, put parents and children together on two tasks: building block designs and building a rocket. He noted that parents of Internals offered comments that were "suggestions and explanations in contrast to orders or directions and . . . positive, not negative."[7]

Finally, showing the connection between contingency and another parental characteristic, warmth, Reed Yates and his colleagues found that parents who were perceived by their children as providing contingent rewards were more Internal and were also seen as warmer and more loving.[8] In contrast, parents perceived as not delivering contingent rewards were seen as External and more rejecting, neglecting, and critical.

DO PARENTS OF INTERNALS ALLOW THEIR CHILDREN MORE AUTONOMY AND INDEPENDENCE AND CONTROL THEM LESS?

Rotter suggested too much parental control and dominance could stifle children's ability to learn the full effects of their behavior by preventing them from gaining enough experience. Two important developmental goals for children are to acquire knowledge of how the world operates and to acquire the skills necessary to obtain what they need. By inhibiting children's freedom to explore their physical and interpersonal environments, parents are depriving them of the opportunities they need to continuously learn the extent of their control.

Although it may sound positive that External children have parents who are described as "protective," this protection comes at a high cost in terms of restricting the range of behavioral opportunities and reducing the learning opportunities that come from experiencing the natural consequences of actions, both of which are crucial components for developing Internality.

This kind of protectiveness sounds very similar to the actions of what are now called "helicopter parents," who are overinvolved with their children's lives and often end up doing tasks the children should be doing themselves. Helicopter parents have become so ubiquitous in our society that the term was accepted into the *American Heritage Dictionary* in 2011. Many college professors and high school teachers have experiences with helicopter parents. Let me give you an example of one of my own interactions with such a parent.

A CALL FROM AN OVERINVOLVED PARENT

It was 9:15 on a Wednesday evening. My wife, Kaaren, and I were at home watching one of our favorite mystery shows when our phone rang. I asked Kaaren not to answer it because I thought it probably was a robocall, but she answered the phone anyway. I heard her quietly asking what the call was in reference to, then silence. Kaaren walked into the living room with her hand over the phone and whispered, "It's a parent. He wants to talk to you about his daughter's class." I inwardly groaned and took the phone.

Putting aside my annoyance, I gamely greeted the caller. However, all attempts to muster goodwill evaporated when the man began his tirade. For the next ten minutes, I only heard about how very bright his daughter was, followed by how hardworking she was and how she had never gotten any grade other than an A in any subject in high school or college. He asked how it was possible for her to be flirting with a B in my class when that class wasn't even in her major. Next, he reminded me how difficult it was for anyone to be admitted to the finest medical schools unless they had outstanding grades.

Did I realize how upset his daughter was at the grade she had gotten on her midterm? I was forced to answer that I did not. Then, it was finally my turn to speak. I explained I had offered to meet with any student who wanted to discuss the test and how they did on it. I hoped that would placate the man, but, instead, it seemed to upset him even more. Hadn't I noticed his daughter had been upset? Again, I had to admit I hadn't, but I told him

I was sorry to hear that and would be glad to meet with her. Was there any way the test could be retaken or thrown out? he wondered. I said I couldn't do that, but there was an opportunity for his daughter to do an extra-credit paper, and, with a high score on the final, there was a good chance she could raise her grade.

Even though I knew from past experiences that my next comment would not work, I couldn't help but tell the man how much I wished I was having this conversation with his daughter. If we met, we could talk about her study habits, and I could help her find more effective ways to prepare for exams.

The man told me he didn't need any help about how to raise his daughter and that he was upset with my "tone." He then said he was a significant contributor to the college and that the dean was a close friend, and he proceeded to inform me he was against tenure just because of situations like this one. I told him I was sorry he was upset and that I hoped his daughter would come to see me. At which point, he hung up.

I wish I could say this was a unique and infrequent interaction with a student's parent, but it wasn't. My colleagues have had any number of similar experiences with parents. One I just heard today went like this: a student came up to one my colleagues at Emory and said, "My mother wants to know if you will change the examination time for me."

To me, the unfortunate aspect of the phone call was that the daughter was losing an opportunity, as she probably had in the past, to become aware of her own Internality by experiencing the consequences of her behavior and learning to find a way forward. I'm not sure I would want any physician of mine to be so ready to have someone else take over their responsibility for performing.

But overprotective parents don't suddenly appear when their kids go to college. They've been around all the time. Even toddlers know what it's like to have their every move observed and controlled by their parents. Research shows overprotective parents take away the opportunity of their children to learn to be Internal.

Frank Wichern, one of my doctoral students, carried out a study that gives credence to the above statement.[9] He had a group of mothers complete an "independence allowing" questionnaire. As expected, mothers of Externals reported that their children were allowed to partake in activities significantly later than reported by mothers of Internals. I completed a similar study to Frank's with twelve-year-olds and found pretty much the same thing, but I dug a little deeper into the data and found a gender difference. Mothers of female Externals, for example, tended to allow school-based activities (such as learning the letters of the alphabet) later than mothers of female Internals. Rather than delaying school-based activities, External males were delayed in learning personal grooming skills, such as brushing teeth and tying shoes.

By restricting what children can do, parents are also reducing the number of learning opportunities for them. As Karrie Shogren and her colleagues put it, "LOC orientations are believed to develop over time, as children and young people have opportunities and experiences that enable them to learn about the contingent relationship between their actions and the outcomes they experience."[10]

Shogren and her colleagues were particularly interested in studying Internality in intellectually disabled children. More than a thousand intellectually disabled and learning disabled children, along with a control group of non-special-needs children, completed Locus of Control tests over time. Of these three groups, only the intellectually disabled children failed to show the expected increase in Internality as they got older. The authors concluded the LOC of students with intellectual disabilities did not become more Internal because these children were given fewer opportunities to act on their environment.

Scientists have offered this same argument for the failure of children with other disabilities, such as an autism spectrum disorder or cerebral palsy, to acquire an appropriate Internal Locus of Control and to learn to have a greater awareness of who they are.[11] These authors, like Shogren and her colleagues, suggest practitioners and families should develop and provide programs in which individuals with disabilities are given more opportunities to become aware of the connections between their behavior and its consequences.

OVERPROTECTION TURNS INTO ENABLING

According to parenting expert Deborah Gilboa, if you have helicopter parents, you will have your sport teams carefully chosen for you and your coaches watched and criticized.[12] Gilboa asserts that experiences of "unhappiness, struggle, not excelling, working hard with no guaranteed results, are great teachers for kids," who benefit by being exposed to these challenges. "Worry," she says, "can drive parents to take control in the belief that they can keep their child from ever being hurt or disappointed."

From the above description, we would expect helicopter parents would have children who would be more External. Shirley Lynch and her colleagues evaluated that possibility and found it to be true. Their study describes parents who prevent the school system from enforcing consequences for inappropriate behavior as "enabling parents." These parents "reinforce irresponsible and dependent behavior . . . by taking over a task, like pet care, that the child had taken responsibility for doing."[13] Enabling parenting discourages independence.

To more closely study the impact of enabling parents, Lynch constructed a test to measure to what degree parents were involved with "direct" and "indirect" enabling and nonenabling of their children.

You would be doing *direct enabling* if you agreed with the following statement: "When my teenage child calls to tell me s/he forgot his/her lunch money again, I take it to her/him."

If you agree with this statement, you would be assessed as an *indirect enabler*: "If my child wants to give a grandmother a gift but doesn't have the money, I give him/her the money."

If you agree with this item, you would get a point for *direct nonenabling*: "My child has been sent to the office for calling the teacher a name. I tell him/her such behavior will not be tolerated."

And finally, if you disagree with this item, you would get a point for *indirect nonenabling*: "My child dyes his/her hair against my advice and it is a disaster. I allow him/her to stay home from school."

(In case you wonder about your own "enabling" tendencies, I have included where the scale is published in the notes.)

To test whether enabling parents would have External children, scales were given to parents of honors students and parents of students at risk for dropping out of high school. With both sets of parents, the researchers found that the higher the scores on the enabling scale, the greater the Externality of the adolescents, regardless of gender. It appears the desire of helicopter-type parents to "help" their children short-circuits the development of their Internality, leaving these children less able to handle their difficulties than their peers.

ARE PARENTS OF INTERNALS WARMER AND MORE SUPPORTIVE, ACCEPTING, AND NURTURING?

That Internal parents are more nurturing is an intriguing supposition, and it is one that has received ample support. For children to feel sufficiently comfortable to fully explore all aspects of their environment, they need to feel safe and supported enough to make mistakes and learn from them. Herbert Lefcourt, who has contributed much to the study of Locus of Control, put the matter this way: "For a child to develop into a reality testing adult, one who is aware of his capabilities and limitations, he needs to be reared in a home in which he is relatively sheltered from aversive stimulation that could intimidate him and thus decrease his sense of freedom to explore his milieu. In becoming less exploratory the child would have too constricted a range of experience from which to discover his particular talents."[14]

John Carton and I found a number of studies that supported the connection between parental warmth and children's Internality. Internal children from third grade through senior year in high school reported that their parents were warmer, more emotionally supportive, and more accepting than their External peers did.

Not only did both Internal children and their parents describe parents as more nurturing and supportive, they were also perceived this way by researchers who observed parent-child interactions. John Carton and Erin Carton found parents of Internals used both words and nonverbal cues to communicate sympathy and support. I will have more to say about the importance of nonverbal communication in chapter 7.

In a study similar to John Carton's study discussed in the previous chapter but with different methodology, Carton and Carton looked at the interplay between mothers and their second-grade children during a puzzle-solving task.[15] The puzzle was a difficult one for second graders, and it prompted interaction between mothers and children. Mothers were given questionnaires to answer while sitting at the table with the children and were told they could help if they wished. The puzzle sessions were videotaped and later scored.

I think you will find their results interesting. The more internally controlled the child was, the more smiles and "positive touches" (e.g., hugs, pats, and rubs) they received and the longer the mother gazed at them. Internally controlled children also smiled more often and stayed more on task than externally controlled children. The nonverbal communication between externally controlled children and their mothers was quite different: here, there were fewer smiles and friendly touches, along with fewer incidents of eye contact between mother and child.

OTHER METHODS FOR ASSESSING WARMTH AND SUPPORT IN PARENTS OF INTERNALS

Family climate. Researchers have used some ingenious methods to obtain different "readings" of environments associated with Internality and Externality. One approach looked at the "family climate" or the "ecological" situation in which children live and learn at home.

My German colleague Klaus Schneewind and I wanted to see how the family climates of Internals and Externals in Germany compared to those in the United States.[16] We asked twelve- and eighteen-year-old children to complete "family climate" and LOC scales and found convergence between the two cultures on factors associated with Internal and External control. We summarized our findings this way: "Internals perceived their families as being organized, but with little conflict; in such a family a person can express him- or herself without fear of being controlled by others. Moreover, internals perceive their family as an active one that values independence and cultural as well as recreational activities." Internal children in the United States also report greater family cohesiveness than their External counterparts, according to a recent study by Erin Tully and her colleagues.[17] In the study, older elementary school–age children's Internality was found to be related to greater perceived family cohesiveness. It seems the overall feeling of belonging and sharing in a cohesive family setting contributes to a warm and supportive environment conducive to learning the connections between behavior and its consequences.

Parental discipline. Another way to look at what is going on between parents and children is to examine how parents discipline their children. Past research shows parents of Internals are more likely to use *authoritative* methods (that is, methods characterized by high acceptance and involvement as well as gradual granting of autonomy), in contrast to parents of Externals, who are more prone to use *authoritarian* techniques (which are typified by low acceptance and involvement, high coercive control, and low granting of autonomy).[18]

Working with my then Emory colleague Don Gordon, I decided to find out specifically what parents felt and did when considering how to discipline their children. We constructed the Intensity of Parental Punishment Scale (IPPS).[19] The scale presents a number of characteristic child-misbehavior situations. We asked parents to read the situation and give two responses: (1) what they *feel* like doing in terms of discipline, and (2) what they actually *do* in these situations.

The parents had to choose from a list of disciplinary actions, ranging from mild punishment to more severe forms of verbal and physical discipline.

Compared to parents of Internals, parents of Externals punished more often, punished physically much more often, and punished more severely. And there was an additional bit of information about parents of Externals that was somewhat worrisome: In contrast to parents of Internals, they also reported a wider divergence between how they felt like disciplining their child and how they actually wound up disciplining him or her. Although they already punished more often and more severely, they felt as though they would have liked to punish even more often and more severely. This finding tends to lend credence to the notion that External children are likely to grow up in a less supportive and nurturing atmosphere.

TAKE-HOME MESSAGE FOR PARENTS
WHO WANT TO RAISE INTERNAL CHILDREN

Here's what can definitively be said about raising internally controlled children. If parents want to give their kids the best chance of becoming Internal, they must create a warm and friendly environment within which their children will feel safe, nurtured, and supported. In such a positive space, parents then need to encourage children to explore their surroundings to gain information about their ability to control facets of their environment. The environment ought to be challenging enough to make failure a real possibility but not so difficult as to cause the children to feel frightened or discouraged enough to stop trying.

Our children need to fail at times, after all, so they can understand their behavior can have negative as well as positive consequences. But failure in a supportive environment gives them an opportunity to learn what they did wrong without producing high levels of anxiety and fear. When our children fail, we or other caretakers like teachers, coaches, and adult leaders can then pick them back up, dust them off, and send them back out to explore again. This is how children can learn to become Internal.

For example, when he was just a toddler, my grandson Soren loved to build towers with his blocks. He often became upset when his towers reached a particular height and fell down. I sympathized when they crashed and urged him to keep trying (by the way, when my towers fell, he seemed to think it was funny). But Soren did see I could build my towers higher than his. He began to notice how I put a number of blocks at the bottom to form a more secure base, and he tried that, too. Soon, we both were building our high towers together, and Soren looked very proud of himself for succeeding after failing so many times in the past.

Child-psychology specialists have long known about the importance of creating safe and secure learning situations for children. Much of our present-day knowledge about what characterizes a "secure" relationship comes from the groundbreaking research initiated by British psychiatrist John Bowlby and Canadian developmental psychologist Mary Ainsworth. Though Bowlby took the early lead in championing the idea we are born with an innate need to "attach" to adults and was a mentor to Ainsworth, the two soon became partners in studying the effects of the early attachment relationship.

Ainsworth was largely responsible for creating the "strange situation," a laboratory technique used to gauge the type of attachment relationship between children and their "mothering" parent.[20] Mothers and their children (usually between one and two years of age) attended a number of sessions to determine if they had a *secure*, an *anxious*, or an *avoidant-attachment* relationship. The crux of the assessment is in observing how children behave when they are left with a stranger, either with or without the mother being present. Children are categorized as "securely attached" when they are observed to use the parent as a secure base. They are uncomfortable (sometimes crying) when she is absent but are comfortable and at ease when she returns. In an unfamiliar situation, secure children will venture out from the parent to explore their environment but use the parent for comfort and support when something goes wrong in that exploration.

BEHAVIOR OF A CHILD WHO IS SECURELY ATTACHED

Sixteen-month-old Sheila and her mother attend an orientation for children and parents at a day care. It is their first time there, and the mom holds her daughter as she walks around the room looking at the colorful pictures on the wall. Sheila's eyes are open wide. "Want to get down and have a look around?" her mom asks as she places Sheila on the floor near some blocks. Sheila resists being put down and lets out a howl of concern. It is clear she is overwhelmed and needs physical contact with her mother to feel comfortable.

Mom responds by picking her up again, saying, "OK, honey, let's walk around a little more while we both get used to this nice new school." After a few minutes, Mom notices Sheila is leaning away from her, looking intently at some toy animals in a bucket on the floor. "Want to try again, honey? Let's take a look at what's in here!" She places Sheila on the floor again, and this time, Sheila does not resist.

Before long, Sheila is completely absorbed in picking through the bucket to see what else is in there. Mom sits down nearby. Soon, Sheila moves to a nearby table and tries out a bouncy paddle. Her first attempt to hit the little rubber ball fails, and the second ricochets off her forehead. Surprised by this attack, she runs to her mother near tears. Mom hugs Sheila, shows her how the ball flies all around when hit, and tells her to be careful. In a few seconds, Sheila is off reconnoitering another place in the room. A teacher comes over to talk to Mom. Every so often, Sheila looks over at her mother and holds up a little plastic animal she has found, as if to share her discovery. Mom responds with an enthusiastic, "Wow!" Eventually, Mom tells Sheila she has to leave the room and talk to the teacher in her office.

In response, Sheila begins to whimper and tries to follow her. An assistant teacher approaches Sheila and directs her interest back to the animals, diverting her attention with a toy horse. When Mom returns a few minutes later, Sheila greets her excitedly, takes the stuffed horse, and runs over to be picked up.

It is obvious this mother and daughter are securely attached. Even though Sheila is frightened (appropriately so) by the new surroundings, her mother's soothing and measured response to her discomfort helps ease her into this new place. Sheila's mother doesn't rush her but, rather, follows her child's lead. The mother is taking this opportunity to allow Sheila to learn about Internality by showing the connection between what her daughter does and what can happen as a result. Because Sheila is secure, she also feels free to explore her new environment and find out what she can and cannot control within it.

The lesson for parents is that they should take every chance to respond contingently to their children's efforts to deal successfully with their new surroundings by providing support and/or reinforcement. Likewise, when their children inevitably fail in their attempts to control things, parents should treat these disappointments as teaching moments to help children understand why they failed, to normalize what happened, and to encourage them to keep trying. This process will repeat throughout all the days of childhood because it is the major way children become aware of the full extent of their choices and the impact of their behavioral decisions. The level to which parents create these secure circumstances in their children's lives plays a huge role in determining the course of their children's Locus of Control, not only for childhood but for adulthood as well.

IMPLICATIONS FOR INTERVENTIONS
TO CHANGE LOC ORIENTATION

What we have learned about how Internal LOC expectancies are acquired during childhood could be of immense benefit in designing ways to foster the development of Internality, not only in the home but in school and elsewhere throughout childhood and later in life. Although much of the research has focused on young children, there is every reason to believe the conditions we've described for the development of Internality would have application at any age and in most any situation. Creating a warm, secure, and nurturing situation can help athletes, auto workers, managers, and others become aware of the connections between their efforts and the consequences of those efforts.

For now, though, let us to move to part 2 and see how Locus of Control plays an instrumental part in achievement, whether it be academic, professional, athletic, or otherwise.

PART 2

WHEN LOCUS OF CONTROL IS IMPORTANT IN OUR LIVES

INTRODUCTION TO PART 2: REMEMBERING JULY 7

"Sometimes you will never know the value of a moment until it becomes a memory."

—Dr. Seuss

It was an unusually hot day for July in London. Marshall Duke and I had just left our apartment in the Notting Hill area of the city, realizing we might be late catching our train on the Circle Line. This was the train that usually took us to University College London. We were looking forward to spending the final day of our summer-abroad program with our students. We were teaching a course on developmental psychology that required our students be placed in elementary schools in Scotland and Ireland for three weeks. While in the classrooms, they had collected research data that we worked to analyze during our three weeks together in London. The academic aspects of this experience were valuable, but what students had come to realize was that the interpersonal aspect was perhaps even more cherished. Our college students had fallen in love with the children who had been their research subjects. They loved their accents and their enthusiasm for all things American. Gifts had been exchanged and promises made to keep in touch, and many tears and hugs were part of the goodbyes.

It had been a wonderful session. Marshall and I had been doing these study-abroad trips for twenty-five years, but we concluded that this was one of the best groups we had ever taught. Our students had impressed us as bright, hardworking, and fun, and we were sad to see our time with them coming to an end. We had learned over the years that the final day of the study-abroad experience always elicited many feelings. To mark the end of our time together, we were going to celebrate with an after-class picnic at one of the nearby parks.

Our usual class time began at nine in the morning, but since this was the last day of the program, we had decided to give our students an extra hour of sleep by starting class at ten. Little did we realize this seemingly trivial gesture might have saved their lives.

Because of our slow start, Marshall and I just missed our train for the Circle Line at the Notting Hill Tube station. We were miffed with ourselves because we had stressed to our students that promptness was an important and expected behavior, yet here we were, setting a poor example by being tardy ourselves. We waited anxiously. Finally, the next train came into the station and we hopped on, wondering if we might still salvage our reputations by managing to be on time after all. The train was so crowded we had to stand. Our traveling companions for the fifteen-minute or so ride to our destination were the usual diverse mix of London commuters of all ages and ethnicities. The car was filled but strangely quiet. Some were on their phones or computers, some were reading books or papers, and some were just sitting. It was a great contrast to the subway in New York, where noise is everywhere. On this particular day, I remember wondering what it might have been like in the Underground during the London Blitz. I thought about the many nights when the stations had been full of people spending the night to escape the bombs.

About five minutes into the trip, we suddenly ground to a halt. A muted groan rose from the collective lips of everyone in our car. While not an unusual event, this delay had certainly come at an inconvenient time for us. We were already late, and we were going to be even later.

Marshall, his type A proclivities swinging into high gear, whipped out his cell phone to call our graduate assistants, but he couldn't get through. In fact, none of the other passengers who were trying to call out could get a connection either. None of us thought much about the lack of connection because this was a common occurrence depending on how deep you were underground. We settled into a sort of comfortable, mostly silent wait. This being England, few people talked; those who did grumbled idly about the unreliability of the Tube system. Marshall observed how different things would be if they'd been delayed on the New York subway. New Yorkers, he said, would be swearing and demanding to know "what the hell was going on." In London, however, a more genteel air of quiet irritation prevailed.

Time passed slowly. Fifteen minutes, thirty minutes. People fidgeted and tried their cell phones again and again without success. An hour passed. It was getting hot and sticky in the car. I was just annoyed at the delay, but as time passed, Marshall became more worried. His trips to Israel had sensitized him to moments like this, when most anything could happen. He leaned over and told me he was afraid of what was delaying us.

After about an hour and a half of waiting, a woman finally got through to someone on her phone. She calmly asked whomever she was talking to if that person knew what was wrong. She said "uh," "ah," and "hmmm," followed by a heartfelt "Thank you ever so much," and ended the call, her face grown pale. To no one in particular, she said in a cracking voice, "There are bombs. They've bombed the trains!" Suddenly, there were many voices asking "where," "what," and "when" questions and whether we were in danger. I can't remember feeling anything but unreal. Marshall, on the other hand, said, "It's terrorists." He was both angry and frightened.

And yet, no one moved or cried or panicked. We all sat or, in our case, stood in silence waiting—for what, I don't know. Marshall whispered to me that this would be a much more chaotic scene if this were happening in New York, but it was apparent to both of us that Londoners were choosing to be calm in a disquieting situation.

In a moment, the conductor informed us over the loudspeaker that we would all be "detraining" through the front of the car. Then, as though we were on a sinking ship, the order was given that women and children would "decar" first, followed by the elderly and then everyone else. Underground workers appeared and directed the women and children off the train. After they had left in an orderly and quiet manner, there was an order for the infirm and elderly to leave. The conductors looked at Marshall and me as though to say, "OK, you old geezers, your turn." With our vanity stung, we said, "No thanks, we will wait to leave with the other adults."

We, too, left in quiet order, walking with the others for about a half mile down a dark, narrow tunnel to a landing that led to a ladder. There, we climbed up and out onto a noisy, bright, hot, and busy street, where sirens screamed and a seemingly endless parade of speeding ambulances rushed past us. We still did not know what had happened.

We asked the personnel some questions about what was going on. We soon found out two things that disturbed us greatly. First, the train we had just missed on the Circle line was the target of terrorist bombs, and there were multiple deaths. Second, there was a separate bombing at University College, where our program was centered. A bomb had been placed in a bus that was parked directly on the street where our students walked on their way to class. As we gathered more information, we found out the bombing at the university had taken place at nine o'clock: the usual time our students would have been walking to class had we not given them an extra hour to sleep! We didn't want to think of what could have happened if we would have held class at the usual time. It was too frightening even to contemplate.

I am going to stop this story here to make a point about personal and situational Locus of Control. Up to this time in my day, my Internality had nothing to do with what was happening to me. Because of luck, fate, and/ or chance, Marshall and I had traveled safely on a train car that was not the target of bombs because we were running late, and our students were out of harm's way and had not walked past the bus when its bomb exploded because we gave an extra hour's sleep. We had been very "lucky."

However, once we found ourselves on the chaotic London street, we could reclaim our Internality because we now had important choices to make. We could just sit there and wait for something to happen, or we could take the initiative. We quickly decided to exercise our Internality with the expectation what we chose to do could help us and others cope with the aftermath of this tragedy. We agreed our first responsibility was to our students, so we opted to walk the four miles to the college rather than risk the traffic jams that would be part of traveling by public transportation or taxi. Concluding the satellite phone systems were overloaded, we thought if we were persistent with our attempts to call our wives and our graduate assistants, we might get through. We were correct; though it took a while, we eventually managed to connect with our spouses, who were frantic. They had been handling calls from family in the United States who had heard about the bombing. In the few seconds we had to talk with our wives, we told them we were safe and were rewarded with grateful sobs.

When we arrived at the university, police lines prevented us from crossing over to reach our students. But our graduate assistant, Ginger Wickline, was waiting at the police line with permission from the university for us to cross. She calmly, but emphatically, told the police, "These are our professors. Our students need them to cope with what has happened. Please let them pass." And they did. What a terrific place for Ginger to show her Internality.

We spent the rest of the morning with our students. We found ways for them to connect with family in the United States, and we immediately began helping them make plans to leave London if they wished. Some parents decided they would fly over to meet their sons or daughters and bring them home. We expected to be helpful in this new and troubling situation, and we were. I think our Internality had much to do with how well we dealt with this crisis. We did not let luck, fate, chance, or powerful others determine what would happen to us once we had regained our belief that our own actions would have much to do with reducing anxiety, making the right travel decisions, and letting the students know they could depend on us.

HOW LOCUS OF CONTROL CAN BE APPLIED TO OUR LIVES

What helps us cope with our problems is knowing how much control we actually have available to solve them. All too often, we feel responsible for things that are truly out of our control. Such inappropriate Internality causes us to waste valuable time, energy, and resources trying to solve problems that may be unsolvable. Staying calm and waiting to find out what had occurred was the correct choice for Marshall and me on the train. If we want to effectively cope with general stress or specific problems, we need to employ the Balance Rule—that is, equating how much control we would like to have with how much control is available.

For example, even though we know Internality is associated with better physical health, it cannot prevent all accidents, diseases, and disorders. We must exhibit appropriate Externality by accepting this fact.

Perhaps Internality can be of most benefit in how we respond to being sick, traumatized, or otherwise in negative circumstances. Internality may be a major weapon in our attempts to cope effectively with what happens to us, especially when what happens to us is apparently "bad." The truth is Internals and Externals don't usually behave differently when faced with unambiguous, structured, and easy situations. They diverge in what they do when the going gets tough—that is, when the situations are ambiguous, novel, or unstructured. Keep this in mind as we explore next how Locus of Control is involved with our achievement in academic, business, and athletic settings.

CHAPTER 4

LOCUS OF CONTROL IN ACTION: ACHIEVEMENT IN SCHOOL

"I'm a great believer in luck and I find the harder I work the more I have of it."

—Thomas Jefferson

THE IMPORTANCE OF ACADEMIC ACHIEVEMENT IN THE UNITED STATES

Besides knowing your children are happy and well adjusted, is there anything better for parents to hear than that their youngsters are doing well academically? We Americans value academic achievement. How much? Consider this. Our children between the ages of five and eighteen spend most of their waking hours either in school or at home working on assignments given to them in school. A survey by the online publication *FiveThirtyEight,* conducted by Mona Chalabi, revealed American schoolchildren spend more time in school than do most other children in the world. In fact, children from only three other surveyed countries—Chili, Australia, and Mexico—are in the classroom longer than American primary and elementary school students. When you add the extra time American students spend on required homework assignments, they are involved in schoolwork an astounding 1,500 hours a year, or about 42 days longer than the students in half the countries of western Europe.[1]

Of course, what's really crucial is not just the time spent in the classroom but the kind of learning that actually takes place there. We Americans want the best for our children, and we show it by supporting our schools with our wallets; over the past decade, we have increased our financial contribution to education by 14 percent. We now spend an average of $12,608 annually to educate each student, a cost that totals more than $632 billion a year.[2] Academic achievement is serious business, and the rewards for those who succeed are substantial; they earn more money, accrue more prestige, and possess greater access to a number of personal and social opportunities. Over a lifetime of working, those with a bachelor of arts degree will earn 2.5 times as much as their same-age peers with a high school degree. The longer we stay in school, the more money we will earn during our lifetime.

PREDICTING ACADEMIC ACHIEVEMENT

The truth, however, is that not everyone who stays in school achieves to the same degree. The potential payoff for identifying factors that predict who will and will not succeed academically is enormous. That is why IQ testing has become a billion-dollar business: IQ scores predict academic achievement better than any other single factor.[3]

The development of IQ tests has a long and checkered history stretching back to Alfred Binet, who constructed the first viable individual intelligence test at the beginning of the twentieth century.[4] Binet, a French psychologist, was commissioned by his government to devise a test that would identify children who needed educational assistance. Eventually, his test was translated into English and adapted for an American population by Lewis Terman at Stanford University, where it became the Stanford-Binet Intelligence Scale. This test set the standard for IQ testing for most of the first half of the twentieth century.[5]

When World War I broke out, American military forces were faced with a Herculean task of quickly but reliably assessing IQ in millions of men.[6] To accomplish this task, group tests of IQ were developed and used successfully to identify potential leaders and to place other men efficiently. After the war, these tests remained popular and were used to assess immigrants who were attempting to escape their war-torn countries for the United States. This also was a time when the eugenics movement was in full force, and with it came a strong belief in the inheritance of intelligence and racial superiority. In essence, the tests were often used inappropriately to keep out "undesirable" elements of the immigrant population. For one thing, they were administered in English, with the result that people from countries where English was a primary language or taught in school scored higher than immigrants from non-English-speaking countries. This did not bother the eugenics believers because they felt it supported their view that English-speaking people were inherently more intelligent than others.

Today, we have a more balanced view of intelligence and what IQ tests are measuring. We realize although they can significantly predict academic achievement, they are far from perfect, and we accept that non-IQ factors are also important in predicting academic success. These factors hold for any standardized IQ tests, whether they be given to elementary, high school, or college students. College admission officials acknowledge this: in addition to standardized testing scores such at the Scholastic Aptitude Test (SAT) or the American College Test (ACT), which are stand-ins for IQ measures, they ask for a variety of other information upon which to base their academic prediction. Prospective students must provide letters of recommendation, lists of extracurricular activities, and personal essays. Admission officials assume that hidden somewhere within the nonacademic material lies potentially useful information that will predict the students' academic success. I believe school officials most often are searching for evidence of the students' motivation, realizing no matter how high their IQ scores, students are not going to achieve unless motivated to do so. And what determines whether they will put forth the effort to achieve? The answer to that question brings us back again to Locus of Control.

PREDICTION OF ACADEMIC ACHIEVEMENT: LOCUS OF CONTROL

Locus of Control was catapulted into public awareness largely by results published in *Equality of Educational Opportunity*, known as the Coleman Report, a groundbreaking study of race and public education.[7] Published in

1966, the same year as Julian Rotter's LOC article, it analyzed the responses of more than half a million elementary and high school students on a wide range of educational topics and concerns. It was the first broad-based study that attempted to evaluate the state of education in the lives of both African American and European American students in the United States. Its more than seven hundred pages of text provided both facts and opinions about where American public education was and where it needed to go in regard to the impact of segregated and integrated classrooms on school achievement. Of specific interest for us in regard to Locus of Control, one relevant—and controversial—conclusion of the report was that non-IQ factors were important in determining how much students achieved, especially African American students.

Buried somewhere in the dense text and multitude of tables that filled the Coleman Report was a finding so impressive it provided an impetus for the many studies that would follow, studies that firmly established the importance of LOC in predicting academic achievement. Even more amazing, the finding was obtained using only a few LOC items (because of the number of tests given, all tests were shortened to fit in with time restrictions). In fact, because this study took place before the concept of LOC became so popular, researchers more or less sneaked these items in to see if they might be related to achievement. What the few items predicted stunned investigators. Of all the nonacademic items included in the study, they provided the best non-academic predictor of academic achievement for African Americans and the second-best one for European American students!

Locus of Control had forced its way into the narrative of what determines academic achievement, and it has remained solidly in place to the present day. Over the decades since the Coleman Report, study after study has confirmed that Internality is associated with better academic achievement. Periodically, investigators will read all that has been done concerning Locus of Control and academic achievement and write a review article pointing out what generally has been found. This seems to happen about every ten years: one review was completed in the 1970s and one in the '80s, and in the '90s, I collaborated with Ari Kalechstein, one of my doctoral students, on yet another such study.[8] Though all the reviews conclude that Internality predicts better achievement for children, adolescents, and adults than Externality does, predicting the academic achievement of females past the age of twelve has sometimes been problematic.

PREDICTING THE ACADEMIC ACHIEVEMENT OF FEMALES: A MORE COMPLEX PROPOSITION

In the 1970s, Herb Lefcourt noted findings were much more consistent for males than females in the area of performance. He suggested perhaps "fear of success"—that is, the fear academic success might produce social failure—played some part. Some twenty years later, after reviewing 208 studies of academic achievement in males and females, Maureen Findley and Harris Cooper concluded the association with LOC was stronger for males than for females. However, they offered few reasons for why this should be.[9]

When I began my career at Emory, the majority of students in our clinical psychology doctoral program were male. After a decade or two, the majority of our department students were women, and for a five-year period, my lab was made up of undergraduate and graduate women and me. This reflected a change that has occurred in clinical doctoral programs across the country since the late 1980s. The women in my lab wanted to find out why Locus of Control didn't predict academic achievement as well for them as it did for males.

In one study, Julia Roundtree, one of my undergraduate students, found Internality was associated with better academic achievement (and more votes for class president) for high school males but not females.[10] Instead, female Internality was related to being involved in a great number of extracurricular activities. Julia suggested this occurred because "our culture rewards males more than females for academic performance and females more than males for involvement in extracurricular activities."

Two of the undergraduate women in my lab, Celeste Pappas and Charlotte Walker, thought they knew what was going on.[11] They figured true Internal women would be likely to present themselves as Externals to be congruent with what is expected of women in our culture. Why?

Because expressing their Internality would create a social dilemma for them, especially in competitive achievement relationships with men. Publicly accepting responsibility for their academic success, especially if it is greater than their male friends', might threaten the men and reduce the women's chances for social acceptance.

So how could the students in my lab find out if their reasoning was accurate? How could they find and identify those Internal women who were hiding among their peers? If they could identify them, it should follow that these concealed Internals would show the predicted association between Internality and academic achievement.

The students chose a creative and unique way to uncover the Internal females who were trying to operate under the radar by claiming an External LOC. They gave high school and college students an LOC scale as well as a test that measured something called *social desirability*.

Social desirability is a fascinating concept. It is predicated on the assumption there are people who want to present themselves as darn near perfect, regardless of their true nature. Social desirability measures the tendency to put ourselves in the best possible light when answering questions about our personality, regardless of the truth of the answers. Here are some representative questions.

"I read every editorial in the newspaper every day."

"I never hesitate to go out of my way to help someone in trouble."

"When I don't know something, I never hesitate admitting it."

The higher your social desirability score, the greater is your tendency to compulsively project an impeccable image.

My students predicted the true Internal females would answer Internally on the LOC measure but low on the social desirability scale. Not overly invested in the social impact of their LOC orientation, these would be the females who showed the theoretically predicted association between Internality and academic achievement.

My students were correct. What they called "true" Internals (i.e., those Internals with low need for social desirability) had higher academic achievement than any other grouping, male or female (Internal, high social desirability; External, low social desirability; External, high social desirability).

With these results, we now had two ways to predict the academic achievement of women by using LOC scales. Remember the first way I described in chapter 1? We found when we asked females to complete these scales in the way they thought their fathers would complete them, the fathers' perceived Internality predicted the daughters' achievement. Now, we have a second way to predict women's academic achievement: find Internal females who score low on a social desirability scale, and they will be the Internals who show academic achievement. Predicting academic achievement based on Locus of Control remains a tricky business, but we are making progress.

A final issue in predicting women's achievement: do they compete differently with men than with women?

Mary Pat Duncan Crouch, another woman from my research lab, experimented with ways to answer this question.[12] Mary Pat, now a vice president of a nonprofit firm in Atlanta, was a college senior at Emory when she completed an honors research project that looked at the question of women's academic achievement.

She assumed Internal women would be more sensitive to the gender of their competitors because Internals believe acquiring information may help them achieve more. Therefore, they would be more likely than External women to compete intensely with men. To examine this possibility, men and women completed LOC scales as well as a "digit-symbol" task. In this task, they had a minute and a half to copy one of ten different symbols into randomly numbered empty boxes. Participants received one point for each correctly placed symbol.

About two weeks after the first phase of the experiment, participants were asked back for a second trial. This time, they were placed in pairs with either a man or woman opposite them and given instructions that set up either competition or cooperation. In the competitive situation, they were led to believe they had been called back because they had the same score as the person with whom they were now matched, so the experimenter needed to retest them to break the tie. They were urged to do their best and promised that the highest score would receive a monetary reward.

In the cooperative situation, they were led to believe their score would be added to their partner's, with the promise that the pair with the highest combined score would receive a monetary award that would be shared by both.

What Mary Pat found was most interesting. Internal women increased their performance significantly when they were competing against a male but not when they were cooperating with a female. (The other two conditions—competing against a female and cooperating with a male—fell between these extremes.)The difference in performance was obvious; in competition against women, Internal women increased their performance by five additional points, but against men, they more than doubled their score.

If what happened in this study transfers to achievement in other venues such as athletics and business, having Internal women compete against men or cooperate with women would produce the best performance. None of these factors influenced the achievement outcomes for men; they achieved at the same level regardless of whether they were competing or cooperating with men or women.

IS LOCUS OF CONTROL THE CHICKEN OR THE EGG?

Here's an important question you may have been wondering about. Does our academic success help us to take responsibility for our academic performance and lead us to be Internal? Or is it the other way around—does Internality provide the motivation and skill we need to do what we need to do to perform better academically? In other words, is Locus of Control the chicken or the egg?

The answer to this question has relevance for a variety of reasons. If LOC comes first, then we must make stronger efforts to design parent interventions and school-based programs to help children develop greater Internality. If, on the other hand, Locus of Control is the result of academic success or failure, then our energies can be better spent finding ways to increase academic performance that would, in turn, help students to become more Internal.

The chicken/egg question was a concern from the very earliest days of LOC research. Deborah Stipek was one young researcher who joined the hunt for its answer.[13] Stipek used first graders in her dissertation research because they were just beginning their formal schooling and had little or no experience being graded for their academic work. Locus of Control differences are most likely to show themselves in just this kind of new, ambiguous, stressful situation within which the children have had little or no prior experience.

What Stipek did was simple, yet powerful. She and her assistants administered IQ and achievement tests as well as an LOC measure to students at the beginning of the school year and at the end. Using complex statistical procedures that controlled for students' IQ and social class, Stipek found that Internality preceded and influenced students' academic achievement in her first-grade students. Locus of Control was the cause of academic achievement, not its product.

More evidence for LOC being the cause, not effect, of academic achievement comes from what is called the British Cohort Study. In this study, Eirini Flouri at University of London measured Locus of Control when children were ten years old and then gathered information from 1,737 men and 2,033 women twenty-six years later when they were thirty-six.[14] Dr. Flouri was most interested in whether Internality at ten years of age would positively influence participants through adolescence and into middle adulthood. It did. Internality at ten predicted greater educational attainment than Externality for both males and females twenty-six years later.

Apparently, being Internal helps us to achieve more. Now we need to explore exactly how Internality does that. What is it Internals do differently than Externals that gives them their advantage in achieving academically? For that answer, we return to a concept from chapter 1.

WHY INTERNALITY HELPS US ACHIEVE: THE BIG FIVE

In chapter 1, I pointed out much of Internals' success results from their tendencies to (1) take greater responsibility for their actions, (2) persist longer in their efforts to solve problems, (3) tolerate longer delays of gratification, (4) gather more information, and (5) show greater resistance to coercion than Externals. Nowhere is that more clearly shown than in academic achievement. Because they believe their efforts determine what happens to them, Internals persist when the going gets tough, while Externals don't. Herb Lefcourt, a major voice in the study of Locus of Control, put it this way: "The link between locus of control and cognitive activity appeals to common sense. . . . Without an expectation of internal control and without persistence despite imminent failure, the postponement of immediate pleasures and the organizing of one's time and efforts would be unlikely. . . . Individuals must entertain some hope that their efforts can be effective before they can make the sacrifices that are prerequisites for achievement."[15]

Internals are the "Little Engine That Could" from the picture book familiar to many of us. They are always saying to themselves, "I think I can. I think I can." This attitude drives them forward. Do these assumptions about Internals' tendency to persist and delay gratification apply when it comes to achievement? They certainly do.

Donald Gordon, a colleague of mine during my early years at Emory, had his students look at whether young children's LOC affects how long they will persist on a task.[16] In Donald's study, he presented a group of children with two word racks containing six letters—two vowels and four consonants. He asked the group to make as many words as they could from the letters. Even though it was equally difficult to make words out of each rack, the children were told that with the first word rack, the number of words they could make depended on their skill, while the other depended merely on luck. While these instructions had no effect on the performance of the children generally, Donald correctly predicted that Internals would persist longer than Externals on the task overall. It also should be noted that completing ambiguous and difficult word tasks is probably very similar to what children encounter in their everyday school situations. As Donald and his colleagues concluded: "Since reinforcement in academic environments usually occur at a low rate, students need to persist at academic tasks for relatively long periods of time with little reinforcement. . . . Internal control would give them some degree of independence in non-supportive classroom environments."[17]

Locus of Control differentially affects persistence in children even as young as preschool age. This is what was found in a study completed by Mark McLeod, a bright graduate student who is now the director of the Emory Counseling Center.

In his study, Mark had teachers rate the persistence of preschool students in their classes.[18] The degree of structure provided by the teachers was determined by the philosophy and orientation of the different preschool administrations. In the structured classroom, teachers expected each child to complete specific tasks (e.g., working with a particular letter of the alphabet) before engaging in other activities (e.g., coloring, making collages, looking at books). By contrast, in the unstructured classroom, the children were free to choose among any of the available activities (e.g., playing with blocks, coloring, board games, looking at books) and to switch from one activity to another at their own discretion. Teachers were asked to rate the "persistence" of children on tasks. They were not aware of the children's LOC. Internal children persisted longer than Externals in the unstructured environment, and External children persisted longer than their Internal peers in the more structured environment.

What does this signify? It indicates that beginning very early in the academic life of young children, Locus of Control is already an important factor in determining the best learning environment for individual students. At the preschool age, in lieu of trying to change children to be more Internal, parents and teachers can decide to place them in either a structured or unstructured classroom to facilitate their achievement. Obviously, one size does not fit all when it comes to Locus of Control and academic settings.

REWARDS, ACADEMIC TASKS, AND LOC

Besides persisting longer at academic tasks within a structured rather than unstructured classroom, Externals also appear to stick to assignments longer when the reinforcement they receive comes from others instead of deriving from self-directed motivation. This valuable insight into the actions of Internals and Externals was discovered by Susan Morris and Stanley Messer, who built a "teaching machine" that presented questions in one opening and a space for answering in another opening.[19] After students answered the question, they pushed a lever that revealed both the question and the correct response. Their score was the number of correct answers gathered within forty-five minutes.

Children dealt with the machine in one of two ways. They could be alone with the machine and in control of the entire process of questioning, answering, revealing and correcting the answer, and totaling the points, or they could sit next to the adult running the study and let him or her control the process. In essence, the major difference between the two processes was whether the child or the adult was in charge of scoring and totaling the points.

What the researchers found shouldn't surprise us at this point. Externals persisted longer and got more points when the task of assessment was left to an adult than when they were answering questions from the machine on their own. Internals, on the other hand, did the same whether they were on their own or with the adult. As Morris and Messer concluded, teachers and parents can either put their efforts into making children more Internal, or they can provide externally controlled children with structured assignments that are rewarded externally.

BUFFERING AGAINST NEGATIVE TEACHER EXPECTATIONS

Poor Externals. They have trouble persisting at academic tasks unless outsiders notice and reward them; they seem incapable of looking inside themselves for the encouragement and reinforcement needed to keep working and learning. Externals are susceptible to outside influences, and besides parents, the most important of the outside influences are teachers.

One important way Internality produces better academic achievement is by acting as a buffer against negative factors such as poor teaching. Research shows the teacher–student relationship has much to do with how well students achieve. A good relationship will generate shared excitement in the pursuit of the students' academic goals and be characterized by understandable and clear communication. But bad teacher-student relationships can stifle and even extinguish whatever energy students have available for achieving academically.

I'm guessing you are aware of the influence teachers' expectations have on students' achievement, regardless of the students' actual academic ability.[20]

In a classic study, at the beginning of the school year, one group of teachers was led to believe their students were high achievers, while another group was told their students were low achievers. In reality, the students didn't differ in their academic performance. The teachers and students were left alone for the semester.

At the end of that semester, students with teachers who expected them to do well did well, and students who had teachers who expected them to do poorly did poorly. While the students had not differed from one another in achievement before the study, they did at the end. Teacher expectancies made the difference in how much their students learned.

We can avoid this kind of bias by educating teachers about the dangers of being unaware of their expectations for their students' achievement. Is there anything else that can be done to protect students from teachers' negative expectations? Fortunately, Locus of Control provides an answer.

If you recall, two of the Big Five characteristics of Internality are resisting coercion and persisting in difficult times. These traits prove useful in helping to buffer or neutralize the adverse effects of low teacher expectations.

Prihadi Kususanto and her colleagues gave questionnaires covering Locus of Control, self-esteem, and perception of teachers' expectations to a large group of students.[21] When they analyzed the results, they found negative expectations by teachers were associated with lower self-esteem in Externally controlled students but not in Internally controlled students. If the students were Internal, their self-esteem was unaffected by what the teacher thought of them.

Internality appears to provide protection against the negative expectations of teachers in an academic setting. This is consistent with the idea that Internals resist being unduly influenced by others even when those others have high status. Internal control is an effective way to protect students against the detrimental circumstance of being in a classroom where their teacher does not expect them to do well.

REINFORCEMENT CONDITIONS AND LOC

Besides preferring to work within a structured classroom and being more sensitive to teachers' negative expectations, Externals also appear to be more motivated by external reinforcement than Internals. In another study, Morris and Messer used their teaching machines again. This time, the machines presented arithmetic or grammar questions for the students, but under two different reinforcement conditions.[22]

In the *self-reinforcement condition*, students were told to mark their own answers right or wrong. The experimenter explained the task and then left the vicinity of the machine but stayed in the room in case there were questions. The students were responsible for keeping track of the number of points they received for correct answers.

In the *external reinforcement condition*, the experimenter not only told students how the teaching machine worked but sat alongside them, examined the answers, marked them right or wrong within view of the students, told the students when they had gained a point, and entered the total score in the visible point counter.

While Internals' point totals were the same across both conditions, Externals performed better in the external reinforcement condition. Morris and Messer concluded using external reinforcement can help motivate Externals to persist in solving problems. Just having someone stay around and express interest seems to be what Externals need to improve academically.

STUDENT RETENTION AND LOC

Dropping out of school is a loss for both students and institutions. Retention is a valued goal for colleges for many reasons, not the least of which is that students who drop out take with them an incomplete learning process and deny schools the tuition they need to keep operating. As a result, higher education administrators are always on the hunt for factors that can predict college retention and academic success. One exemplary study has been completed at the University of Louisville.

Researchers Denise Gifford, Juanita Briceno-Perriott, and Frank Mianzo administered LOC tests to more than three thousand incoming freshmen who were attending summer orientation before the start of school.[23] The researchers noted that previous studies had found Externality to be a common characteristic of high school students who dropped out. Looking at past results positively rather than negatively, they concluded minority and lower socioeconomic class students who stayed in school and were successful academically were more likely to be Internal. So they reasoned LOC should also be a significant determiner of a successful first year of college, as measured by grade point average (GPA) and the decision to stay in school.

They were correct: Internality predicted higher academic achievement, while Externality tended to indicate lower academic achievement, as measured by GPA. From these data, the researchers concluded: "Because students who were retained were found to have higher grades than those who were not, and students with a more Internal locus of control had higher grades than those with a more External locus of control, then it is reasonable to suggest that students who obtained higher scores on the locus of control scale (Externals) may be more at risk for dropping out of college."[24]

Gifford, Briceno-Perriott, and Mianzo suggested strongly that to keep their students in school and have them achieve to the best of their ability, colleges need to find and target Externals at the very beginning of the college experience. This action plan makes sense according to Rotter's theory as well because it is at the beginning of a new situation that a generalized Locus of Control will have its maximum impact, and attending college is certainly a new situation for freshmen. The researchers did not precisely describe what colleges should do when they identified Internals and Externals, but they might want to incorporate some of the ideas presented in chapter 10. In general, we already know Externals work best in structured, unambiguous situations; appreciate extrinsic rewards; and enjoy being guided by others. One possible general intervention would entail providing structured, clearly presented study-skill workshops for Externals led by individuals who use praise for progress generously. It would be easy to find out whether such workshops helped students improve their academic achievement and stay in school.

SUMMARY

Locus of Control is very much part of determining if we achieve academic success or not. More than half a century ago, Internality was found to be associated with academic achievement in children. Since then, LOC has held the attention of researchers who have examined its role in all kinds of academic activity. Because of the consistent association of Internality with higher academic achievement, programs have been developed that seek to make individuals more Internal.

In recent years, academic administrators have expressed a greater degree of interest in finding ways to motivate Externals to achieve more. As a result of research findings, we now know Externals are motivated to achieve when they interact with high-status individuals (teachers, coaches, tutors) in structured situations in which extrinsic rewards are available. The recent findings that Externals are much more affected by social attention and rewards than Internals can be used to construct learning situations that encourage the academic achievement of Externals. This means we can offer Externals more immediate help in achieving while other programs are being run to make them more Internal.

School administrators no longer need to sit back and wonder who is going to succeed or fail. Using what they know about Locus of Control, they can devise programs that can give direction and hope to externally controlled students so they, too, can achieve to the best of their potential.

CHAPTER 5

LOCUS OF CONTROL IN ACTION: ACHIEVEMENT IN BUSINESS

"The best way to predict the future is to create it."
—**Peter Drucker**

A college student, a young man with short dark hair, raised his hand and said, "Public relations, eighty thousand." Another, a woman wearing a white blouse and jeans, said, "Me too, about the same." I thanked them both, then asked if anyone else was willing to tell the class if they had a job waiting for them after graduation and what their beginning salary was likely to be. To my shock, almost everyone in my class raised a hand. That's when I realized that this class on the psychology of leadership, my first in the Goizueta Business School at Emory University, was going to be very different from the courses I had taught in Emory's College of Arts and Sciences for four decades.

In my previous classes, a question concerning what seniors were going to do after graduation tended to be answered with great uncertainty and trepidation. Usually, a few students had jobs lined up that didn't pay much, others were going on to graduate or professional school, and still others were returning home to live with their parents and didn't have a clue about what they were going to do. These business school seniors were an entirely different matter. These young men and women were eager to share the good news of their fruitful futures; they seemed confident that great things were indeed coming their way.

You may remember the movie *Wall Street* and its unique central character, Gordon Gekko (played by actor Michael Douglas), who was supposed to represent what big players in finance were like. He said things like, "The point, ladies and gentlemen, is that *greed*, for lack of a better word, is *good*."

If you Google "What is important in business?" you mostly get statements about profitability and growth, and little else. It seems as though the spirit of Gordon Gekko lives on. In fact, this spirit probably had something to do with the Great Recession of 2008, when we all experienced the negative fallout from greed gone wild. However, although money is undeniably a prized goal for many in the business world, I've learned from my business students that success cannot merely be defined by one's financial status. That is to say, *contra* Gekko, lust for wealth is *not* what truly motivates a businessperson.

Teaching business students over the past five years has made me much more optimistic about the future of business than I ever was before. I have learned business students are far brighter and more caring than I thought they were. You may wonder how I, a lifelong academic with no business experience, got an opportunity to teach in the business community. I do, too, because, until recently, having anything to do with business education was the furthest thing from my mind. Here's how it all happened.

Andrea Hershatter, an associate dean of the Goizueta Business School, attended a lecture I gave to one of the many informal clubs in the school. My talk centered on the importance of relationships in life. When I was finished, Andrea thanked me kindly for sharing my thoughts. As she and I walked out together, she told me, "You know, Steve, what you talked about is what our students need to learn. They need to know that interacting with others is the cornerstone of success."

"Oh, really?" I remember saying with incredulity. "Aren't they mostly just interested in making money?"

"Money is only part of it," she responded. "They also want to belong, to be connected, to be liked and respected—and they need to know how to make that happen. Would you like to teach a course for us? You can teach whatever you think is important about relating and try to put it in the business context as much as you can, but do it your way."

I was both honored and surprised that this prominent business school dean thought I had something to offer her students. And I was both surprised and startled that I was even considering saying yes. After I met a few more times with Andrea, the idea became less far-fetched, and, before

I knew it, my first class of second-semester senior business students was sharing their future plans with me.

Once I accepted the offer to teach, I had to wrestle with what exactly to include in the course. I knew I would be dealing with some of the brightest and hardest-working students to be found anywhere in the United States, but I also knew they, in contrast to my previous college students, had little or no background in psychology. Likewise, they were steeped in business principles and practices, while my business experience was pretty much restricted to a bit of consulting I had done with companies like Ralston Purina and General Mills.

I asked myself, what did I know that could help them as they entered their high-pressure business careers? Whatever I chose to teach had to be taught in only fourteen weeks and had to be interesting enough to keep their attention as they got closer to graduation. As I busied myself reading all I could about what was being researched and written about in business, two facts became clear. First, relatively little had been published about relationships and the role they play in the business world. Second, it came to my attention that when writers discussed success in business, the concept of Locus of Control kept popping up. Now these were two topics I knew a little bit about and felt I could share with the students.

LOCUS OF CONTROL AND DEFINING BUSINESS SUCCESS

The time I taught my first business school course and every time thereafter, LOC was a core part of the class. I wanted students to understand the concept and where it came from so we could use that as a jumping-off point to look at what was known about it in their fields of interest, especially leadership at both the managerial and executive levels. But I did not stop there, because I came to discover LOC has much more to offer students in their search for a richer, broader-based definition of success.

In our initial class meeting, I put a very simple formula on the board.

Technical Skill + ??? = Success

After writing the equation, I told the students this course was about filling in the area represented by the question marks. In our initial discussions, we agreed the business faculty had done a great job of teaching students the technical skills they needed. The first part of the equation seemed clear. However, things got a little dicey when we turned to discussing exactly what was meant by the term "success." Students were surprised when they realized this part of the equation isn't as clear as they thought it would be.

Students in that initial class, and in all classes I have subsequently taught in the "B" school, engaged in a healthy debate about the nature of success and about what goes into being "successful." Is success best measured by a monetary value? What about relationships with family and friends? Is being successful the same as being happy? Can money bring happiness? If it doesn't, what else is important? Is having money better than having time? Is marriage, or at least a long-term relationship, part of being successful? What about children? Is it OK to be unethical in the pursuit of money? The questions mounted, and the definition of success became cloudy before sharpening into a larger and clearer image.

In every class, it eventually becomes clear to the students that, though financial rewards are certainly important for feeling successful, so is being satisfied with your job, your life, your friends, your family, and your ethical behavior. At this point, I let the students know Locus of Control is involved not only in the more narrow monetary definition of success but in nearly all aspects of their now-richer definition. It is to those indicators of success I turn next.

INTERNALS AND EXTERNALS IN BUSINESS SITUATIONS: WHAT INDICATES SUCCESS?

When all is said and done, to feel personally successful, we must feel we are being paid fairly for the work we are doing. The following are the most popular ways of gauging success.

LOC and Earnings

Most companies and most employees prefer not to make earnings public, but in those instances where they have, it is clear Internals do better than Externals. That is certainly the case with telemarketers. Ari Kalechstein and I found Internal telemarketers with a high social need to be recognized made increasingly more money over time than any of their peers: after one month of work, $12,500 versus $9,550; after two months, $31,600 versus $20,439; and, after six months, $103,763 versus $75,668.[1]

Internality also was found to be associated with the personal and financial success of midlife American men.[2] Vance Caesar compared the responses of ninety high-income men to those who were less wealthy on scales measuring a number of personality dimensions including their self-esteem and LOC. He found the higher the wealth, the higher the Internality.

Studies from European countries also sound the same tune concerning the expected association between Internality and earnings, although the relationship is stronger for women than men in both Russia and Poland.[3] Similar findings were reported by June Poon, Raja Ainuddin, and Sa'Odah Junit in a study of Malaysian entrepreneurs.[4] Along with data from Rotter's LOC scale, they gathered subjective self-report indicators of a firm's performance. This manner of gathering performance data was used because business owners are not likely to share their financial data. Poon and her colleagues were confident such perceptions of firm performance would be consistent with those gathered by objective measures. As they predicted, Internality and higher firm performance were positively related.

LOC and Earnings When Working with a Team:

Many other studies from the United States and elsewhere show individual Internals are more adept at making money than their External peers, but do they also shine when they work with others as part of a team? Christophe Boone and his colleagues in the Netherlands used an ingenious approach to find out which combinations of Internals and Externals would make up the most competitive teams in a business exercise.[5] They used data from a Dutch multiperiod management simulation called the International Management Competition. This imposing-sounding title simply refers to a study in which teams (fewer than ten members) are put together to see how well they run a fictitious business. Teams must make continual decisions about a number of issues, such as material purchases, wage levels, promotions, and machine capacity. The unusual aspect of this simulation is that teams do not just do something once but are required to work together continuously over time. Teams must keep making day-to-day decisions over the six months the game is played to make best use of new developments as they occur.

What makes this study so relevant to us is that teams were composed of different combinations of Internals and Externals. All teams had exactly the same material and financial starting position and faced identical, fixed-parameter settings. Everything was equal among all players and all teams—except their composition of Internality and Externality.

Here's what they found. Of the forty-four teams that competed, the teams with all Internals and without leaders gathered more information and achieved higher financial performance than any of the other teams. In fact, when even one External member became part of the team, the information-gathering proficiency and financial performance were reduced; likewise, when Internal members were added to External teams, those teams' information-gathering efficiency and financial performance increased. The key to better financial performance in this exercise was having as many Internals on the team as possible!

Interestingly, adding a leader to a team made up largely of Externals did have a positive impact on the team's performance. However, adding a leader to a mostly Internal team reduced performance. Introducing a leader into some groups or teams, it appears, can actually *hinder* performance. Leaders can help External teams, but not Internal ones.

Here's what Boone and his colleagues suggest if you want to build the best teams:

1. Groups that are largely External should be provided with an Internal leader.

2. Teams that are largely Internal should be left alone: don't even *think* of introducing a leader from outside!
3. Overall team effectiveness can be improved by applying what we already know about the kinds of situations Internals and Externals prefer to be in. That is, Externals work better in structured situations with strong leadership, while Internals prefer ambiguous circumstances that allow individual agency.

The important takeaway message from this groundbreaking study is unless you happen to have an unending supply of Internals at your disposal, you should be aware of the LOC orientations of your team members and try to provide a work situation that fits the composition of the team. Teams with mostly External members should be highly structured, while teams primarily made up of Internals should be loosely structured. Following this simple suggestion is one way of giving each of your teams its best chance of success.

LOC AND LEADERSHIP

One day, I decided to hang around the business school and listen in on conversations and class lectures, and I counted the number of times I heard the word "leadership." I stopped counting at two hundred, and that took only an hour or two of eavesdropping. In the business world, success and leadership go hand in hand. (Although I do want to mention an area of interest called "followership" that is gaining momentum. Understanding what makes a good follower makes sense when thinking about leadership because, after all, you can't have one without the other.)

Of the many possible leadership types, two of the most prominent are *transactional* and *transformational*. From what I can tell, transactional leadership has been around for a longer time and focuses on a process of bargains and negotiations between leaders and followers. Transactional leaders are prone to use rewards to motivate followers to meet agreed-upon goals and punishments to prevent negative behaviors like mistakes, delaying tactics, and avoidance. Think Donald Trump.

Although they also can use rewards and punishments characteristic of the transactional leader, transformational leaders are more likely to emphasize the pursuit of a vision in which followers transcend their self-interests in order to accomplish a higher goal. Charisma, intellectual stimulation, and individualized consideration distinguish transformational leaders. They typically present a vision of a high goal and then use whatever means are available to inspire followers to reach beyond themselves to reach it. Think Steve Jobs.

If you think the transformational leader would most likely be Internal, you would be in agreement with Jane Howell and Bruce Avolio.[6] They knew from past research that Internal managers would be "more capable in dealing with stressful situations, place greater reliance on open and supportive means of influence, pursue riskier and more innovative company strategies, and generate higher company performance than Externals."[7] So it didn't take too great a leap of faith for them to predict Internality would also typify the transformational leader.

To find out if they were correct, they studied seventy-eight male managers with at least twenty years of service that represented the top four levels of management in a large Canadian company. The managers completed Rotter's Locus of Control scale, their followers completed measures of leadership behavior, and performance data were obtained from records. Transformational leaders were indeed more Internal and had the highest performance outcomes.

There are other studies that show when it comes to leading, Internals make better managers, soldiers, scoutmasters, and teachers than Externals. As we move from the factory, battlefield, and classroom to the boardroom, we find a similar superiority of Internality in CEOs.

We must once again thank Christophe Boone and his colleagues for giving us a view of how Locus of Control operates at the highest level of leadership.[8] They were able to obtain the cooperation of thirty-nine "small firm" CEOs for their study of LOC and company performance. As was found with other leaders, the higher the CEO's Internality, the better the financial performance of the company. Boone and his colleagues then took their study one step further, taking a closer look at the firms' financial performance before and after they reported the above association. What the researchers discovered was fascinating and has much to say about the impact of LOC on others over time especially when the situation is problematic.

They divided the CEOs' scores into three groups: Internal, average, and External. They wanted to see if the Locus of Control of any of the CEOs would be related to the unprofitable companies that would later end up in bankruptcy. Of the firms that were unprofitable early on, none of the five companies headed by an Internal CEO was bankrupt six years later, but five of the six companies led by an External CEO were. For whatever reason, when the going gets tough, companies headed by Internals were more likely to survive and those directed by Externals to falter. Although we don't know exactly why this happened, we do know that Internals are more likely than Externals to be responsible, persistent, and able to delay gratification and gather information—characteristics useful in keeping a foundering company afloat.

The idea that Internals stay the course in difficult times bodes well for their impact on an organization. Internals have a greater "tribal" commitment to their organization than do Externals. They are fiercely loyal and determined to see things through for the protection and well-being of their people. Because they seem adept at solving problems, having Internals around for the long haul is good for business, regardless of what the business is about.[9]

LOC, WELL-BEING, AND JOB SATISFACTION

Financial success is only a small part of how business leaders measure their worth. Like them, to feel successful, we must enjoy our jobs and feel good about ourselves. So how does Locus of Control fit in here? How much does it have to do with the all-important feelings of contentment and fulfillment? If Internality can make us more money but can't bring us greater satisfaction, how useful is it in the long run?

To answer this question, we need to look at the results of massive studies that have examined workers, managers, and executives from all over the world. What the studies have in common is a quest to identify those sometimes-elusive factors that help us feel better about ourselves.

Work and General LOC and Satisfaction

Let's begin with an investigation, termed a *meta-analytic study*, completed by Qiang Wang, Nathan Bowling, and Kevin Eschleman at Wright State University in Ohio.[10] In a meta-analytic study, the authors do not collect their own research; instead, they gather and analyze the results of other researchers who have published papers about a topic. In this case, the goal of their review was to evaluate whether a scale specifically built to measure LOC in the workplace would predict outcomes better than a general scale. The researchers gathered data from 184 studies that had used more than fifty thousand participants. Through a well-established but dizzyingly complex set of statistical analyses, they were able to show specifically work-related LOC scales are able to predict job satisfaction better than general scales, but a general scale is better able to predict general life satisfaction than a specific work scale.

It is noteworthy that scores on both the specific and general scales were related to satisfaction in two of the most relevant aspects of success, satisfaction with work and with life. In both instances, Internals are more content than Externals.

While it is clear that LOC and satisfaction are connected, this kind of study does not tell us exactly what is going on in the jobs and lives of Internals and Externals that might affect their satisfaction. We could guess from what we have learned about Internals and Externals that the Internals' belief they can have something to do with what happens to them probably plays a significant role.

While impressive, the data from the meta-analysis were largely from participants in the United States. The studies I describe next look at whether the superiority of the Internals in well-being is largely an American phenomenon or a more universal one.

LOC and Well-Being at Work

Paul Spector from the University of South Florida has been one of the most informative and useful contributors to the business community for the past forty years. His research has influenced generations of industrial and organizational psychologists, and he has published some of the most cited and most impactful research in all of psychology. Two of his many studies have direct relevance to the question of Internality's role in job and life satisfaction.

Spector uses the word "well-being" in place of "satisfaction," but it is apparent they mean pretty much the same thing. He accepts the findings showing Internality is associated with positive well-being both on and off the job in the United States, but he questions whether this relationship holds globally. To evaluate this question, Spector chose to focus on managers from a variety of countries.[11] His data came from the Collaborative International Study of Managerial Stress, which was originated by Spector and his colleague C. L. Cooper. This far-reaching study included surveying the responses of a whopping 5,185 managers from twenty-four "geopolitical entities." Along with several English-speaking countries such as Australia, Canada, New Zealand, and the United States, he also surveyed managers from Asia and eastern and western Europe. The managers ranged from entry level to the tops of their organizations; roughly three-quarters of them were men.

When all the analyses were completed, one clear finding stood out: namely, Internality was related to better job satisfaction and higher feelings of well-being across all countries. What is even more impressive is that this association was consistent across managers who came from individualistic cultures (where people are motivated primarily by their own goals and preferences and are independent) and collectivist cultures (where people view themselves as part of a network of social groups and value interdependence).

Spector and his colleagues make an excellent point suggesting Internality may be used differently in individualistic cultures than in collectivist cultures. For example, in contrast to the United States, where Internality may be expressed by directly controlling what goes on in a job, people in a collectivistic culture like Japan might more commonly express Internality in relation to other networks of people working in the same field.

At least when it comes to managers, across countries, cultures, and gender, Internality is securely linked to feeling better about your work and your life. But there's more. In fact, another study, which dwarfs the size and extensiveness of those we have just reviewed, takes us from a consideration of how Internality relates simply to satisfaction, and addresses how Internality is inextricably linked with an overall sense of happiness.

Happiness, Freedom, and Control

Paolo Verme from the University of Turin in Milan, Italy, has written a paper that presents the possibility that Internality is intimately tied to the concept of freedom of choice.[12] He argues that because Internals see themselves as having behavioral choice, they place a higher value on having the freedom to choose. Thus, Locus of Control acts as a regulator of the intrinsic value we place on our freedom of choice, with Externality dampening and Internality increasing the importance of this freedom.

Next, Verme points out how past studies have shown happiness and Internality are related, but income and happiness are related only up to a certain level of income, after which other factors take over. Internality may be one of those factors. To answer the question of whether Internality and freedom of choice are related to happiness, Verme used an enormous data set, the *Values Surveys 1981–2004 Integrated Questionnaire*. It was composed of 267,870 observations on individuals from eighty-four countries. From the 913 variables included in the survey, he developed a freedom of choice and LOC scale. At the end of this study, Verme concludes, "A variable that measures freedom of choice and locus of control is found to predict life satisfaction better than any other known factor such as health, employment, income, marriage or religion across and within countries." If he were going to bet on what variables would best predict life satisfaction anywhere in the world, Verme says, "my money would certainly go on freedom and control."[13]

Summary of LOC and Business Success

It is apparent that in our professional lives, we want to earn what we think we are worth, while doing work we enjoy. It is also clear a successful personal life is one filled with satisfying relationships. Locus of Control is plainly involved in the attainment of these goals.

Before we leave the world of business, I want to share one more important area in which LOC is involved: how we react to change from inside and outside our company.

INTERNALS AND EXTERNALS IN BUSINESS SITUATIONS: HOW THEY REACT TO THE POSSIBILITY OF CHANGE

Business leaders can use what we know about Locus of Control to help employees deal with the uncertainties that characterize change. Change is a fact of life in business, whether it concerns reorganization within a company, acquisition of a company by an outside concern, or an employee's movement up or down the job hierarchy. We need to accept the reality that companies and their managers are always somewhere in the process of planning change, dealing with change already underway, and recovering from change that has been completed.

We know Internals and Externals react differently to the possibility of change.[14] Business leaders can use this knowledge to structure their message to minimize the stress and anxiety generated by proposed changes. Successful transitions are distinguished by high employee commitment to the process, and managers can facilitate this commitment by dealing differently with Internals and Externals within their company.

Internals and Externals may have difficulty with transitions for different reasons. Internals may get caught up in their own confidence to handle change and not realize at times it is best for them to just let go and let the process move forward. In contrast, if what is called for is just letting the process happen, then Externals would be comfortable and effective, but they would be ill at ease if they felt pressured to change themselves and their behavior during the transition. As we will see, Internals are better able to face ambiguity and to help others deal with it. Externals, on the other hand, don't quite know what to do about change and will fight to maintain status quo even when it is not an option. Why? Internals generally behave more positively in response to change and cope better with it because they believe they can, in this new and evolving environment, find ways to affect what happens to them.

To be more specific, Externals are more likely to be frustrated by uncertainty and may respond to it with negative actions. Justin Sprung and Steve Jex use the term "counterproductive work behavior" to describe behaviors such as aggression, interpersonal conflict, sabotage, theft, waste of time and materials, malicious gossip, refusal to cooperate, and even physical assault.[15] These behaviors make sense when viewed as tactics to preserve the status quo.

Why are Externals prone to negative and self-defeating activities? An obvious explanation is they don't know what else to do. Because they haven't previously been collecting information and using it to practice solving problems, they don't have the resources to come up with new and effective ways to deal with change. They are trying to maintain what they are used to because they neither know how to develop new behaviors nor can visualize how they would operate in a restructured job situation. Doing something is better than doing nothing. I grant you Externals are not using a great problem-solving strategy, but it may be the only one they have.

Business leaders have yet to catch on to how important it is for them to address change issues through the Locus of Control lens. We need leaders who will take what is known about LOC and use it to make their companies' transitions smoother and more productive. For example, C. W. Hung and K. T. Hsu describe a situation in which a local insurance company is taken over by a foreign-owned company.[16] The employees of the acquiring company have greater organizational commitment than those of the acquired company. In the acquiring company, employees are in what Sheryl Shivers-Blackwell of Florida A&M University and other researchers would call a "strong situation," where the structure is firm and optimism is high. In this situation, without much stress or concern, LOC should have minimal effect on outcomes.[17]

However, feelings would be quite different in the company being acquired. We call the situation "weak" when the future of employees is unknown and ambiguous. In this kind of situation, Internals and Externals behave differently due to the uncertainty. Internals will be galvanized into action and search the new situation for clues on how to behave. Externals, in contrast, will be frightened by the loss of structure and certainty, resorting to passivity or anti-change behavior to protect the status quo.

Jingqiu Chen and Lei Wang make a plea that those in charge of the change process should understand that whether Internals and Externals support or resist change depends on how it is presented to them.[18] To allay fears and prevent counterproductive behaviors, Externals need to be presented with a detailed, structured sequence of events that describes the path from where they are to where they will be. If possible, they would like no surprises along the way.

In contrast to the fears and trepidations of Externals, Internals are likely to have a more positive attitude toward change. If possible, they look forward to putting their "oar in the water" as change happens and progresses. They are more eager to participate in all aspects of the transition, from its planning to its implementation and, finally, to its evaluation. They would like to be invited to meetings where options are discussed and ideas are exchanged. They'd like a chance to have an impact on what happens during the transition and what the new work situations will be like. Internals will resist being squeezed into an already-decided structure where they will have nothing to contribute. If Internals and Externals are handled appropriately during corporate reorganization, there is a good chance they not only will go along with change but embrace it.[19]

In my reading of the business literature, I find that when Locus of Control is discussed, Internals get the best press. Authors sing the praises of having Internals in their organization. We saw earlier in this chapter how teams made up totally of Internals outperformed all other teams. We have read that even at the highest levels of management, the more Internal CEOs lead the strongest companies.

The usual advice from the authors of this literature is to either hire as many Internals as possible or set up programs for changing Externals into

Internals (see chapter 10 for a description of methods used to change Locus of Control). This advice is difficult to follow for a couple of reasons. First, remember that for the past thirty years, our country has been becoming more External. As a result, Internals are going to be increasingly difficult to find and hire. Second, it is time-consuming and expensive to run programs with the goal of making employees, managers, or CEOs more Internal.

Rather than spending time and resources finding Internals or changing Externals into Internals, we can use what we know about Locus of Control to help us through change. We know Internals make better leaders than Externals, but we also know Externals make better followers. To make change work, we need to organize our change tactics to embrace these strengths.

Followership is the capacity of an individual to actively follow a leader. Without followers, there are no leaders. This is a burgeoning area of study within organizations. For example, retired US Air Force colonel Phillip Meilinger has come up with ten rules for good followership. I'll give you a couple so you can get the general idea.

- "Don't blame your boss for an unpopular decision or policy. Your job is to support not undermine."
- "Make your decision and then run it past your boss. Use your initiative."
- "When making a recommendation, remember who will probably have to implement it. This means you must know your own limitations and weaknesses as well as your strengths."[20]

Every successful organization needs employees who are good followers. These people like working within a structure, and they do their best to meet the responsibilities given to them. They deserve time and attention from anyone contemplating change.

A healthy share of followers are probably External. During a transition, they will welcome structure and the implementation of extrinsic reinforcement. To motivate their efforts, single them out for praise and present them with monetary or other concrete rewards. To help them deal with change, provide clear descriptions of how they fit into the process and what the payoffs are in terms of workload, salary, and vacation time.

Take-Home Message

Internals respond more positively to change than Externals, but using an appropriate intervention can get Externals on board as well.

LOC AND WORD-OF-MOUTH COMMUNICATION

Before closing this chapter, I would like to leave you with one more example of the many ways Locus of Control can be applied to business—in this case, the use of word-of-mouth communication in marketing. Desmond Lam and Richard Mizerski have argued this method of communication is more persuasive and impactful than anything from the Internet, newspapers and magazines, one-on-one sales, or radio advertising. While some think the powerful effects of word-of-mouth communication are largely uncontrollable, Lam and Mizerski's research seems to show otherwise.[21] It suggests if people can identify the factors influencing word-of-mouth communication, they can use that information to guide marketing programs to more specific targets. Locus of Control was the initial factor they evaluated, and in-groups and out-groups were the targets.

In-groups are characterized by strong ties among members and by a sense of "belonging, familiarity, intimacy, and trust."[22] Think family and close friends. In contrast, out-groups are characterized by weaker ties among members and word-of-mouth communication with people who are not family or close friends. Think club membership.

Locus of Control and preferences for in- and out-group word-of-mouth communication were collected from undergraduate business students. Internals were more likely to engage in word-of-mouth communication with their out-group, while Externals preferred to use their word-of-mouth communications with their in-group. This suggests Externals are more risk averse and desire the companionship offered by their in-group members. In contrast, Internals were more action oriented and ready to engage the larger number of people available in out-group contexts.

Based on their results, Lam and Mizerski concluded LOC can be used as a means of targeting market segmentation. For example, because Externals are more likely to engage in promoting word-of-mouth communications with family and close friends, efforts should be made to target important family members to raise awareness of products. In contrast, because Internals are already spreading information about products to a wider, more diffuse group of individuals, a more general promotional effort is needed.

This is an example of how a simple study can produce material that could be useful in business practice. The idea is to connect with people and help them find their own way to being better than they were before we met them. Locus of Control can be used to accomplish that goal.

ANOTHER TAKE-HOME MESSAGE

Business is about competition and achievement, and so is Locus of Control. Internality relates to success in all aspects of individual and team business behavior as well as feelings of well-being across the world. In addition to trying to make employees and managers more Internal, the concept of Locus of Control can be applied by managers and administrators to make employees more comfortable with the stress generated by planned and unplanned business changes. LOC can function as an organizing principle in business practices that touch the lives of employees and administrators. Although the business community is beginning to understand the efficacy of the follower-leader relationship, the role LOC plays in business relationships has gone largely unexplored. It is potentially an incredibly rich area for further research and practice.

CHAPTER 6

LOCUS OF CONTROL IN ACTION: ACHIEVEMENT IN SPORTS

"Persistence can change failure into extraordinary achievement."
—Matt Biondi, Olympic gold medal winner in diving

There are many ways we can achieve, and having an Internal Locus of Control seems to assist all of them. We've seen that, with notable exceptions, Internals outperform Externals in academic achievement situations: they tend to get superior grades, score higher on academic tests, and solve problems with greater efficiency. Internals achieve more than Externals in business as well. They make more money, are better leaders, and find ways to feel better about themselves and what they do. Now it is time to look at another area of achievement to see if Internals are once again more successful than Externals. What role does Locus of Control play in sports?

We have always been interested in who can run faster; jump higher; throw farther; or score more goals, points, or runs. It is through the crucible of competition that this pursuit of victory, or, at the very least, contention, brings the importance of achievement into the picture.

Vince Lombardi, the legendary coach of the Green Bay Packers, introduced his own unique definition of achievement in sports with his famous formulation: "Winning is not the most important thing. It is the only thing!"[1] His intensity was well known, and he coached his Packers to their first two historic Super Bowl victories. But it was his rare gift to connect with his players that made him an extraordinary leader.

Certainly, the path to athletic success is not an easy one for most of us, and, as we know, Locus of Control is evoked whenever we face mental, spiritual, and, in this case, physical challenges. Even the most successful of athletes will fail often in their attempts to reach their goals. NBA superstar Michael Jordan has described the arduous trek toward success as one littered with innumerable crushing failures. Here he compellingly sets forth this seeming paradox: "I've missed more than 9000 shots in my career. I've lost almost 300 games. 26 times, I've been trusted to take the game winning shot and missed. I've failed over and over and over again in my life. And that is why I succeed."[2] Can anyone doubt Jordan is Internal? His persistence to achieve success in the face of failure makes him a terrific model of Internality.

The clear suggestion that athletic achievement is characterized by determination, persistence, effort, and hard work should sound familiar to those of us who have studied Locus of Control in other areas of achievement. Regardless of the pain, heartbreak, and agony of defeat, Internals "grit it out" and persevere in order to gain superiority in competitive circumstances. The obvious prediction we make about Locus of Control and success in sports is that Internals will be more accomplished than Externals.

SPORTS AND EXERCISE IN THE UNITED STATES

Why would I present a chapter on athletic achievement and Locus of Control? Because athletics are as much a part of American life as apple pie and the Fourth of July, which, by the way, is celebrated with road races all over the United States. There is not a holiday that doesn't have a traditional sporting event tied to it, from the Indy 500 on Labor Day to the Rose Bowl football game on New Year's Day. Where achievement is measured by winning and losing and requires us to perform at the top of our potential, there is Locus of Control.

I want to describe where we are with sports in the United States before I get into the specifics of LOC. This will form the background against which I will argue the more Internal we are, the more likely it is we will be fitter, compete more effectively, injure ourselves less often, and recover more quickly from injuries than Externals. First, let's study a snapshot of athletic participation in America.[3]

On any given day, about 15 percent of people fifteen years of age and older are participating in some sport or exercise activity. By "participating," I mean spending at least thirty minutes in the activity. While that sounds like a lot, keep in mind that on any given day, five times that many are spending at least that long sitting around watching television. Participation in sporting activity varies by area of the country, with people in the West being 50 percent more likely to be athletically active than those from the south central part of the United States.

For those who choose to engage in sports, running is the major individual pastime, while basketball is the most popular team activity. Men dominate football, basketball, golf, and soccer, while women prefer yoga and aerobics. Bowling, swimming, surfing, and water skiing are engaged in equally by the sexes. Not surprisingly, younger people (those from fifteen to twenty-four years of age) choose team sports like basketball, football, and soccer more often than those twenty-five and over. Those older than fifty-five prefer walking, but there is no age difference in racquet sports. Finally, because most of us have to schedule our sports activities around work, they generally have to fit into our early mornings, late afternoons, evenings, or weekends.[4]

It takes some effort to stay fit enough to participate in sports, and participation has important payoffs in terms of health and social adjustment. And Locus of Control is right in the middle of it all, affecting whether or not we participate. If we do take part, it affects how successful we will be.

Although fully 91 percent of Americans believe sports are important to child development, the latest statistics show participation of children is on the decline.[5] A household survey sponsored by Sports Marketing Surveys for the Sports & Fitness Industry Association in 2007 found around 2.5 million fewer children are playing organized basketball, soccer, track and field, and baseball than five years ago. Much of this decline can be attributed to parental concerns about the risk of injury and to the emphasis on winning at all costs (according to the espnW/Aspen Institute Project Play Survey of Parents on youth sports issues).[6] It is difficult to be certain how Locus of Control is playing a part in these parental decisions. On the one hand, it could be the decline is due to External parents being overprotective of their children and interceding before they have a chance to learn about how their behavior affects outcomes in an athletic situation. On the other hand, the decline in sports participation could be the result of Internal parents reading the ever-increasing information that shows defective coaching and win-at-all-costs competition in children not mature enough physically or mentally and deciding to keep them out of sport experiences.

It turns out parents are right on target about fearing that more children are being injured now than they were previously. High school athletes have an estimated two million concussions and other injuries and thirty thousand hospitalizations each year. Not only are injuries frequent, but the Centers for Disease Control and Prevention estimate half of all the millions of sports injuries that occur each year are preventable.[7] You will read later that it is the externally controlled athletes who are more likely to be hurt, and when they are hurt, they are likely to take a longer time recovering.

We know Internal coaches connect better with their players by communicating more effectively. It could be External coaches are more likely to drive children away from participating. Although Locus of Control was not assessed in coaches or children, a study showed when coaches had received training in communicating with children, 95 percent of their players returned the next season, as opposed to only 76 percent of players for coaches without such training.[8] It appears training coaches to be better communicators and better able to connect with their players could boost participation and may even make the sport a safer and more enjoyable experience.

LOC AND SPORTS

We know Internals are better at taking care of themselves and are more apt to participate in the kinds of fitness activities that improve their physical well-being. While I focus in chapter 9 on the possible role of Locus of Control in the US obesity epidemic, I want to mention here that America leads the world in the prevalence of overweight and obese children, who, of course, grow up to be overweight and obese adults. Engaging children and adults in sports and fitness activities is one of the most effective interventions we have in our fight to slow down the unhealthy rise in obesity. Just as with academic and business achievement, Locus of Control has much to do with determining who is passive, uninvolved, and not into fitness and sports, and who is the opposite.

Studies show those who participate in sports like tennis, swimming, ice hockey, and running are more Internal than comparable groups who don't.[9] Internals achieve more than Externals in hockey, marathon racing, and children's gymnastics.[10]

Locus of Control research in sports falls into two sets: first, how Internals and Externals prepare to perform in athletic contests, and, second, how each LOC type responds after the contests are finished. Researchers have paid attention to how LOC is concerned with:

1. the frequency of participants' injuries and length of time recovering before returning to competition;
2. the occurrence of superstitious behavior in the form of "rituals";
3. burnout and the psychological functioning of athletes;
4. the ways goals are set and the impact of reaching or failing to reach them;
5. adherence, or lack of it, to training rules;
6. team leadership and relationships to teammates; and
7. ordered or disordered eating as a function of coaching demands.

LOC AND THE FREQUENCY OF INJURY AND RETURN TO COMPETITION

Researchers have found Internal athletes across all ages and sports have fewer injuries than Externals do. Preventing injury is one of the most important goals of all athletes.[11] Sports fans know how injuries can affect the outcome of pennant races and championships. How many of us sit on pins and needles as we watch our favorite players out of action moving their legs, wrists, or necks and wonder if they will be able to return to the game? The simple truth is that injuries prevent athletes from performing to the best of their abilities.

Coaches and participants could use the knowledge that Internality appears to be related to a lesser and Externality to a greater chance of injury. Based on what we have learned about Externals, we should be especially concerned about how they go about training and preparing for athletic competition. What is needed are procedures to neutralize their basic belief injuries are due to luck or chance.

Here's what to do to offset Externals' tendency to be less prepared for athletic performance. We know they respond to structure and extrinsic reward, so it would be important for a coach to be forthright about telling them exactly what they have to do to prepare, including exercises, workouts, and even the kind of shoes or athletic gear they should wear. Any way coaches could bring attention to the progress Externals make would help them stick to the routine asked of them. Internals, on the other hand, just need to know what is required of them and the basis for the requirements. Chances are that they will comply with the coach's game plan.

Not only do they get injured more, but Externals also recover less quickly than Internals for all the same reasons they tend to get injured more in the first place. They do not believe their behavior and outcomes are inextricably linked, and so they are less likely to follow procedures necessary for their recovery. (This is consistent with findings presented in chapter 9 that Externals take a longer time to recover from a wide variety of physical diseases than Internals do.) To recover more quickly and more efficiently, Externals need the same sorts of structure and guidance described above for the prevention of injuries in the first place. They also respond positively to charts and graphs that describe the procedures to be followed and show progress being made.

LOC AND SUPERSTITIOUS RITUAL BEHAVIOR

Sports are a hotbed of superstitious rituals and behavior. While we would expect Externals to be more likely than Internals to show superstitious behavior, that is not always the case. It appears this depends on how the ritualistic behavior is viewed.

Take Michael Jordan, arguably the best basketball player to ever play the game and someone we would expect to be very Internal, judging both from his career and from the quote earlier in this chapter. He wore the same pair of University of North Carolina underwear shorts underneath his uniform shorts for every game on his way to winning six National Basketball Championships. He began this superstitious practice because he thought it first worked for him when his college team won the NCAA national championship. Since basketball shorts were very brief during Jordan's playing era, he lobbied the powers that be to start manufacturing longer playing shorts so his well-worn underwear shorts wouldn't show through. These longer, baggier shorts are still in vogue today.

Strange as this behavior was, there are even more unusual rituals practiced in sports.[12] Take Jason Giambi, an All-Star Yankee baseball player, who decided for some reason to wear a flimsy golden thong in place of his usual underwear whenever he found himself in a serious batting slump. Or tennis champion Serena Williams, who has decided it is imperative that she bring her shower sandals to the court with her for her matches. Once the match begins, she has to bounce the ball five times before her first serve and twice before her second. As proof of the power of her rituals (and perhaps evidence of a self-fulfilling prophecy), Williams has most often lost when her routine has been disrupted in some way (which of course probably reinforces her superstition).

Most superstitions stay encapsulated—that is, they don't spread. When they do spread, they can become compulsions and create havoc. This was the case with baseball player Kevin Rhomberg's superstition, which involved touching. When people touched him, he felt compelled to touch them back. When players on other teams became aware of his ritual, they found any number of reasons to keep touching him in order to throw him off his game. In fact, one baseball game was actually delayed by umpires because opposing players did not listen to their demands to stop touching him.[13]

Two studies show a close connection between superstitious practices and Locus of Control. The first one examined elite athletes from top-ranked soccer, volleyball, and hockey teams in the Netherlands, and the second one looked at Division I and Division III track and field participants from American colleges. In the first, researchers sought to find out if Internals or Externals were more likely to engage in superstitious rituals.[14] They chose members of top-ranked sporting teams because they believed superstitious rituals would be most pronounced at this level because of the added emphasis on winning and keeping your position with the team. It turned out 80 percent of the players practiced some kind of superstitious ritual before a game. These rituals included "putting a piece of chewing gum in a trampled part of the field," "having to see the number 13," "kissing a football shirt," and "smoking a cigarette the morning of the game." Most players felt sure that if they weren't allowed to perform the ritual "things would go definitely wrong."

Perhaps surprisingly, the researchers found that Internals had greater commitment to rituals than Externals. Even though Internals admitted the rituals often had little to do with useful preparation for the game, they saw a "strong link between enacting superstitious rituals and a desired outcome, reduced anxiety and tension." The link was especially strong when the competition was with opponents perceived as equal to or better than the Internals. It appears Internals will adopt rituals as a basic way to reduce the unhelpful anxiety and tension that can color an athletic contest.

Somewhat different relationships were found when investigating superstitious behavior in American college students at Division I and Division III schools.[15] Though Locus of Control was once again a prominent factor in whether or not athletes practiced rituals, in one study it was the External and not the Internal athletes from Division III schools who endorsed superstitious behavior more often. Perhaps the different findings between this and the previous study were due to the inherent difference between professional and collegiate sports. Unfortunately, we do not have information on whether the rituals were done to reduce stress or ensure a victory.

Incomplete though they are, these results suggest the links between Locus of Control and superstitious behavior may vary by sport. The Dutch study used members of teams who must function together simultaneously in a match, while the American sample was made up of track and field athletes whose performances contribute to a team total but who actually complete individually and at different times from one another. The athletic situation—team (Internals more superstitious) versus individual (Externals more superstitious)—differentially pulls for Internals or Externals to engage in more or less superstitious ritual. This area deserves much more study to see if superstitious ritual has an overall facilitating or deleterious impact on performance. It might also be interesting to find out how coaches view the role of superstitious rituals—like petting the bulldog mascot (at the University of Georgia) or touching a large stone (at Clemson)—before the game begins on the performance of their teams of superstitious rituals.

LOC AND THE PSYCHOLOGICAL FUNCTIONING OF ATHLETES

Much of what contributes to the performance of athletes has to do with their psychological state, mental preparedness, and perseverance. It turns out Locus of Control is intimately involved with all these activities and more. For a start, in recent research, high-level tennis players from six different regional tennis leagues were asked to complete self-report questionnaires that included LOC and anxiety scales.[16] The result was that compared to Internality, Externality was related to higher anxiety, especially when matches were most competitive and important. That is to say, when the going gets tough, Externals get anxious.

When we turn to soccer, we find LOC is again related to motivational factors.[17] In the first example, adolescent British soccer players completed a number of tests that revealed that compared to Externality, Internality was associated with higher perceived soccer competence and motivation to compete. The association between Internality and competence was especially high when players were higher in what is called "intrinsic" motivation—that is, they just loved to play soccer for soccer's sake and not for "extrinsic" rewards like medals and awards. The take-home message here: Externals are not as competitively motivated as Internals, nor do they tend to perceive themselves as competent to compete.

In another soccer study, this time using elite Olympic-level female players from Norway, Internality was found to be linked to what was called "high task orientation."[18] When questioned about the soccer match in comparison with other activities in their lives, Internals compared to Externals indicated they were more focused on the soccer match than on any other activity or concern. The take-home message here: Externals are not as focused on the competitive task at hand as are Internals and are not as ready to compete.

Internals gain an advantage over Externals by preparing themselves better for athletic competition. David Le Foll and his colleagues used an imaginatively designed study in an attempt to identify what Internals might do in preparing for athletic competition to give themselves a competitive advantage.[19] They used learning to putt a golf ball as the activity, but what they were most interested in was what the putters did during the three minutes between the teaching sessions. During this down time, the researchers counted how many practice putts the participants made while waiting for the next session to begin. Internals, it turned out, were active and practiced more putts during the rest period than Externals. Even when they were supposed to be taking a break, Internals were engaged in behaviors that increased their chances of being athletically successful. Externals, on the other hand, rested more during the break. The take-home message here is that Internals practice more when they get the opportunity.

From what I've written so far, it doesn't sound as though Externals would be the best teammates. Je Tsai and colleagues would agree with my conclusion.[20] When they surveyed hundreds of college athletes in Taiwan, they found Externals were more likely than Internals to "morally" disengage. In other words, they were more likely not to care about others and not to follow rules. The authors in this case went so far as to call for Externals to receive "moral education to the end of enhancing the quality of sports contests and competitions through fewer rule transgressions and greater moral engagement."

While I wouldn't go as far as recommending that Externals take a course on morals, I do see their findings certainly suggest Externals might be more likely to experience other negative outcomes such as burnout while engaged in sports. Jennifer Black and Alan Smith, for example, looked at senior-level swimmers and found Externality to be connected to higher indications of burnout.[21]

Disordered eating was the focus of another group of scientists.[22] Their study produced complex findings, but one clear result was that Internal athletes were able to protect themselves from developing maladaptive eating behavior. Externals, on the other hand, developed disordered eating habits when coaches and friends were also External and ate "badly." Externals were more likely to be negatively affected by the "bad" eating behavior and Externality of others. Internality in athletes served as a buffer between them and the negative influences of others.

With all this as background, it should not surprise you that when it comes to being liked and seen as potential leaders, Internals win out again over Externals. In one study, the researchers had members of men's baseball and soccer teams rate one another on friendship and leadership. Internals, it turns out, are more often chosen as friends and as leaders than are Externals.[23]

CONCLUSIONS ABOUT LOC AND SPORTS AND A COMMENT ABOUT "FLOW"

I have been involved with sports all my life. My childhood memories are filled with visions of family baseball games. I watched my father pitch in a competitive industrial baseball league and saw my mother shag fly balls in the park at picnics. I was a cross-country and track runner in high school and college and even tried a turn or two at wrestling, although my six-foot-two frame only carried 112 pounds. (I was known as "the zipper" because I looked like one when I stood sideways and stuck out my tongue.) As an adult, I've run age-group track, and I play golf and tennis to the present day. I understand and have experienced the pros and cons of competition versus cooperation in my sports activities, as well as the effects of adopting an Internal or External orientation when I participate.

In light of the research literature, it seems like a no-brainer to conclude that Internality would be the best orientation to have when engaging in athletics, especially competitive athletics. But keep in mind that few of the research studies have considered the role of the fit between individuals' usual level of Internality and the degree of Internality appropriate for the situation. Take the parallel example of students trying to complete an academic assignment that is way beyond their knowledge or capabilities. The reality is that no matter how hard they might try, they are not going to succeed in completing the assignment favorably. It is beyond their resources to do so. However, if their Internality is actually too high, they may believe if they "just try hard enough," they will succeed. As a result, when they inevitably fail, they are likely to blame themselves and feel worthless even though there truly was nothing more they could do to succeed.

A balance between the challenge of the problem and the level of skill we possess is a necessary condition for something called "flow" to occur. Celeste Taylor and her colleagues studied the effect of Locus of Control on this.[24] They used the definition given by Mihaly Csikszentmihalyi, who has studied this phenomenon for two decades and defined "flow" as the experience individuals describe when performing at their best (within the boundaries of their ability at any given time).[25] Flow is a metaphor used to describe those moments that stand out as being the best of a person's life. For flow to occur, not only must there be balance between situational demand and personal skill, but individuals must enjoy the success of completing the task for its own sake and not for outside rewards. When in the "zone," as it is more frequently described by athletes, there is a unique, even magical quality to what is going on that makes a person feel positively superhuman.

I know what Csikszentmihalyi is talking about. I've experienced it in tennis and golf and running. Bill Russell describes this better than I can in an excerpt from his book *Second Wind: The Memoirs of an Opinionated Man*:

> Every so often a Celtics game . . . would be magical. That feeling is difficult to describe, and I certainly never talked about it when I was playing. . . . It came rarely, and would last anywhere from five minutes to a whole quarter, or more. It would surround not only me and the other team, and even the referees. At that special level, all sorts of odd things

happened: The game would be in the white heat of competition, and yet somehow I wouldn't feel competitive, which is a miracle in itself. . . . I never felt the pain . . . nothing could surprise me. It was almost as if we were playing in slow motion. During those spells, I could almost sense how the next play would develop and where the next shot would be taken. Even before the other team brought the ball inbounds, I could feel it so keenly that I'd want to shout to my teammates, "it's coming there!"—except that I knew everything would change if I did. . . . There have been many times in my career when I felt moved or joyful, but these were the moments when I had chills pulsing up and down my spine.[26]

If preliminary research is to be believed, Internality increases our likelihood of experiencing this wonderful state of affairs. Taylor and her colleagues had management students take scales measuring flow experiences, autonomy, and LOC and found a clear and strong linkage between Internality and more frequent occurrences of flow.[27] They concluded there was a "dynamic interaction" between Internality and flow experiences that boded well for dealing with challenges. They noted that Internals would actively seek out strategies to overcome situations of boredom by increasing task complexity or by overcoming anxiety about competition by practicing harder at the skill tasks needed to make themselves better. It was like they were adjusting the temperature—not too hot and not too cold.

The relationship between flow and Internality certainly calls for more study, and not only in athletic activities. Locus of Control is not only involved whenever we find ourselves within an achievement situation but also, as you will see next, when we have to cope with the psychological and physical challenges of life as well.

SUMMARY

Internality is related to successful performance in many sports, but there remain a number of athletic activities in which its effect has yet to be evaluated. As well as looking at how Locus of Control operates in sports like football, it also would be interesting to look at how the concept relates to performance at different stages of an athletic career. I attempted to do this with my comparison of Tiger Woods and Sergio Garcia in an earlier chapter. I made the point that Internality played an important role in Woods's phenomenal success as a professional golfer. Now that he is in the latter years of his career, I believe his Internality, which, based on his recent statements, hasn't changed very much, is now inappropriate for his abilities and may be contributing to his recent difficulties and failures. Perhaps looking at the LOC of other athletes like quarterbacks in football and strikers in soccer would explain successes and failures at all stages of an athletic career.

In any case, it is easy to see how Locus of Control could be significantly involved in the performance of athletes in a sport like golf, which involves so much time spent thinking between athletic moments. I wonder what part LOC would play in determining performance in American football and basketball, where players are required to process their reactions to intense physical effort and at times violent action.

COPING WITH RELATING, PSYCHOLOGICAL DISORDERS, AND PHYSICAL ILLNESS AND INJURY

INTRODUCTION TO PART 3

Not only is Locus of Control relevant to how much we achieve in our schools, at our jobs, and in our sports competitions, it is relevant to how we handle the psychological and physical demands of life. Our LOC is our companion when we reach out and try to connect with others, and it is activated when we are stressed and must cope with failures that come when we are unable to reach our goals no matter how hard we strive.

The next three chapters focus on three different but related areas of coping. In chapter 7, we deal with the challenging task of forming relationships with others. In this chapter, we will see how Locus of Control plays a part in how we form our relationships and what we do when we encounter relationship problems. In chapter 8, I explain how LOC determines whether or not we develop psychological problems that, if not cared for early on, may turn into diagnosable disorders such as depression and anxiety. LOC is also very much involved with our attempts to cope with psychological difficulties once they are present. In chapter 9, we change our focus from psychological matters to physical ones. Physical diseases and injuries are universal events. We've all been ill, and most of us have had to deal with one sort of injury or another. Locus of Control has something to say about how well we react to all these setbacks.

CHAPTER 7

COPING WITH RELATING

"The most significant single ingredient in the formula of success is knowing how to get along with people."
—**Theodore Roosevelt**

Famous people aren't shy about giving us advice about how to interact with our fellow human beings. Take what Carl Jung had to say: "The meeting of two personalities is like the contact of two chemical substances: if there is any reaction both are transformed." Or Benjamin Franklin: "If you would be loved, love and be loveable." Or even Henry Winkler, who played "the Fonz" on the television show *Happy Days*: "Assumptions are the termites of relationships."[1]

Soon, the quotes all began to run together and sound like clichés. I realized I wasn't learning anything new from them. My guess is you've also heard all sorts of "helpful" relationship advice from others and perhaps have even offered a pithy quote or two about the how, what, where, and why of relationships. If what we see on television and at the movies and listen to in our songs is any indication, relationships are one of our major preoccupations. With all the time we spend talking, writing, and discussing our relationships, you would think we would be pretty good at them, but if you did, you'd be wrong. In spite of its importance, we're often surprisingly bad at relating to others.

How bad? One out of every two marriages ends in divorce, a rate that's been about the same for the past two decades.[2] We are abusing one another to the point where each year (1) four million women are physically assaulted or raped, (2) 750,000 children are reported victims of abuse and neglect, and (3) between one and two million Americans sixty-five years of age or older are injured, exploited, or otherwise mistreated by someone on whom they depended for care and protection.[3] Over the past ten years, the numbers have increased, but it is not known whether that is the result of better reporting of incidents or an actual increase.

Unfortunately, our children reflect our relationship failures. A nationwide survey by the Centers for Disease Control and Prevention (CDC) found one out of every three public elementary school children reported feelings of prolonged sadness, hopelessness, and disconnection from others. Feelings of sadness and hopelessness are consistent with the rise in the number of children diagnosed with depression and other psychological diagnoses that have at their very core an inability to relate.

Successfully relating to others turns out to be much harder than it looks, and yet, even though we fail at our relationships more often than we'd like to admit, we still pursue them as though our very lives depended on them. Why? Because they probably do! Forming good relationships is key to having a satisfying and happy life. Simply put, if we are good at relating, we are happy, and if we aren't, we're not. It doesn't matter how bright we are, how much money we have, or how attractive we are—if we can't make relationships work, our lives will be less satisfying. Ed Diener and Martin Seligman, two influential researchers within the area called "positive psychology," completed a study in which they asked students who scored at the top 10 percent of a happiness scale why they were happy. The answer? Having strong ties to friends and family and making the commitment to spend time with them![4]

LOC AND RELATING TO OTHERS

Let me get straight to the point. When it comes to Locus of Control and getting along with people, Externals have a more difficult time of it than Internals. I'm going to spend most of this chapter explaining why I think this is the case and suggest some possibilities for improvement.

To establish our approach to LOC and relationships, I need to introduce you to the model I use to organize my thinking.

The Four-Phase Model of Relationships

Marshall Duke and I introduced our four-stage model of relating in the 1980s, and it has remained our guide for structuring our research and theorizing about the way relationships operate. We have found its very simplicity is helpful in reminding us of what we need to be aware of to make our relationships progress successfully.[5]

We believe all relationships go through a constant repeating cycle of Choice, Beginning, Deepening, and Ending. One of the implications of this model is that the earlier in the relationship process we have problems, the more profound the negative impact. If we cannot get past the Choice or Beginning phases effectively, how can we hope to manage the later phases? It's no coincidence those suffering from the most serious psychological problems have their greatest trouble beginning relationships.

Though different skills are needed to handle each phase, the ability to accurately communicate our feelings verbally—and, even more so, nonverbally—is important to all phases. I will explain why I consider nonverbal communication so vital after I briefly describe each of the four phases of relationships.

The Choice Phase

Although we will meet thousands of people in our lifetime, only a handful ever get close enough to us to be called friends. The long journey toward friendship has to begin with a choice and a commitment to the interpersonal process. Sadly, there are a few people who cannot make that choice to begin relating; it is too difficult a step for them, and the result is that they end up isolated and alone. Fortunately, most of us choose to move to the next step and begin.

The Beginning Phase

Once the choice is made to relate, we have to figure out how to begin and with whom. Luckily, we get help doing this from our culture and our society. We are taught "manners." This is a set of rules for what to say and what to do when beginning a relationship. We are all familiar with the etiquette when meeting someone. We smile, offer our hand for a handshake, and introduce ourselves. This is often followed by making small talk about the weather or some such innocuous topic. We do this so often we forget those times in childhood when we didn't know how to do it. I'm reminded of this when my grandchildren visit and I can hear their parents whispering to them, "Take your hands out of your pockets and look at Grandma's face." "Smile and act like you're glad to see her." "Tell Grandpa what you did today." It always brings back memories of my own manners education.

Those of us who do not master manners are going to face an uphill fight to handle the next stage. People with Asperger syndrome or a nonverbal learning disability have trouble here because they have difficulty mastering the skills needed to enter easily into a new relationship.

The Deepening Phase

If you have successfully managed to begin a relationship, it is now time for you and the person with whom you are interacting to decide if you want to deepen it. All our most valuable relationships are deep ones: life partners, close friends, colleagues with whom we work or play. Deep relationships give life meaning, and research shows if we have close friends, we live longer, recover more quickly from illness, and are happier and more satisfied with life.[6]

Deepening with others is a complex process that is not for the faint of heart, but the payoffs are worth it. How valuable are deep relationships? A study reported in the health newsletter of Harvard University examined data from more than three hundred thousand people and concluded a lack of strong relationships increased the risk of premature death by 50 percent. That's equivalent to smoking fifteen cigarettes a day.[7] It appears one of the best ways to be physically healthy is to have plenty of good relationships.

Books have been written about the deepening process. While there is some controversy about how best to deepen, most agree effective communication has much to do with being successful. Honest self-disclosure, agreement on central issues and attitudes, and the ability to forgive and move on all seem to be important. It is difficult to overstate the importance of nonverbal communication in determining if we can successfully deepen with another. The truest aspects of our emotions are communicated through facial expressions, tones of voice, personal space, touch, and the like.

The Ending Phase

Perhaps the most important and most difficult phase of relating takes place when we end our relationships. Most of us don't like endings and try to avoid the feelings they generate at all costs. Instead of processing what is happening as we end, we get "busy" and "angry" at other things to distract ourselves from our true feelings.

While becoming busier and angrier might make an ending easier to tolerate, it costs us dearly. We miss the opportunity to look back over the life of our relationship to see what we did wrong and what we did right. We miss the chance to thank those who made our time worthwhile and ask them for feedback about how we related to them. We miss the opportunity to consider those relationships that didn't work out and the reasons for their failure.

You would think with all the endings we have in our lives we would be better at them than we are.

I have taught a class on relationships for forty years at Emory. In the seminars, I teach second-semester seniors about the importance of relationships in their lives. We read the research thoroughly and present reports on pertinent topics, but the cornerstone of the course is my challenge to the students to be aware of endings and to make them good ones. Graduation is an ending they know is coming, but it is amazing how easy it is for them to "forget" how many days are left. To help them keep the ending in mind, at each class meeting, I write in really large numbers on the whiteboard how many days are left.

I have them complete ending diaries focusing on what they are doing each week to end well. I'm always impressed by how difficult it is for the students (and the rest of us) to acknowledge an ending when we know it is coming and to put in the necessary effort to deal with it successfully. The core task for the students is to become aware of those people who were important to them during their time at Emory and to tell them that they were important and why. Through this process, students gain information from others about what they may need to know to change when they begin their next set of relationships. Endings are a great time to learn about who we are and how we relate.

APPLYING THE FOUR-PHASE MODEL:
LOC AND THE CHOICE AND BEGINNING PHASES

We find Internals and Externals have different personalities, social skills, and learning preferences that have much to do with how successfully they relate to others. While all four stages are important for the relationship process, in the initial stages of relating, it is our personalities that give others both a glimpse of who we are and the information they will use to decide whether to try to deepen with us.

PERSONALITY: INTRODUCING JERRY

Jerry was getting ready to go on his first date with someone his friend Tyler had set up for him. He looked in the mirror, and a fairly good-looking twenty-eight-year-old man with short brown hair and brown eyes looked back at him. He turned his face first one way and then another and noticed he had a bit of a four o'clock shadow showing. Should he shave? Nah. It just seemed like so much trouble, especially because this date would prob-ably end up like so many of the others where, for no reason, the woman seemed to lose interest in him.

Then his thoughts turned to what to wear. Tyler told him this woman was a fashionable dresser—not snooty, but she was someone who valued looking good. Jerry gazed into his closet. He had a nice assortment of dress pants and shirts as well as his usual collection of nondescript jeans and often-worn shirts. After thinking about his choices, he said to himself, "What difference does it make? She'll either like me or she won't," and pulled out jeans with a stain or two from the time he went out for barbecue with the guys and a faded green polo shirt with a button missing. "At least I'll be comfortable. I mean, clothes don't make the man, especially on a first date."

Although Tyler made a point of telling Jerry not to be late because he had managed to get a table at a good but inexpensive restaurant, Jerry lost track of time. When he looked at his watch, he had a momentary spell of anxiety, but then he told himself, "They'll hold the table." He hurried out the door, but, when he got to his car, he realized he had forgotten his "lucky" silver dollar, so he rushed back into the house to find it. Once he had it in his hand, he calmed down and thought, "Now everything is going to be just fine!"

What is your guess? Is Jerry more likely Internal or External? This should be a no-brainer because, although the description is brief, he is clearly an externally controlled man. How do we know this? For starters, he is ignoring the information his buddy gave him to help prepare for this date and is instead depending on luck or fate to guide his grooming. Next, he shows no insight into his past interpersonal failures—no awareness his behavior could have something to do with why women don't stay interested in him. His dependence on a "lucky" coin rather than his own actions is the final evidence of his Externality. His lack of awareness of the connection between his behavior and its consequences has prevented him from learning what he needs to know to change his self-defeating behaviors into those that would give him a better chance of success. Without awareness, Jerry will continue to make the same relationship mistakes.

Having a positive and pleasing personality would be a great advantage for attracting others and getting the relationship process off to a good start. It is clear Jerry has not presented himself in ways that would necessarily appeal to others. Is this thumbnail sketch of Jerry's personality consistent with what researchers have found characterizes Externals?

WHAT DO THE PERSONALITIES OF
INTERNALS AND EXTERNALS LOOK LIKE?

One simple way to find out about the personalities of Internals and Externals is to have them take personality tests. This was done in one representative study of college students.[8] They completed both a Locus of Control scale and a personality test called the Adjective Check List (ACL). On the ACL, students were instructed to check those adjectives they thought best described them and, in turn, their responses were used to rate fifteen personality characteristics.

Internals scored higher on the personality characteristics of *Achievement*, *Dominance*, *Endurance* (persistence), and *Order* (being organized) than Externals. Externals, on the other hand, scored higher on *Succorance* (being dependent) and *Abasement* (feeling guilty and belittled) than Internals. In other words, Internals see themselves as striving to achieve, lead, be organized, and persist more than Externals do, while Externals report themselves as wanting more to follow and to be taken care of and feeling more guilt than Internals.

Researchers found similar results in another study, in which Internals and Externals completed another personality test called the Life-Style Personality Inventory.[9] Consistent with what was found above, Externals reported themselves to be less likely to compete successfully with others, to more often be hurt by them, and to feel more helpless than did Internals. In contrast, Internals endorsed leadership, helping others, and being cooperative to a greater degree than Externals.

Based on the research, Externals' personalities are just plain less attractive than those of Internals. They have lower self-esteem, less assertiveness, and lower frustration tolerance but are more authoritarian and socially anxious than Internals.

Summary

If personalities are the key to getting off to a good start in relationships, then Externals are at a considerable disadvantage. Although I point out throughout this book that Internality is not always good and Externality is not always bad, the way Externals describe their own personalities suggests they will not necessarily be attractive to others and may not even be attractive to themselves. This is the topic we turn to next.

WHO IS MORE INTERPERSONALLY ATTRACTIVE: INTERNALS OR EXTERNALS?

Another way of asking this question is whether would we like someone who is similar to us or who complements us? Though a half century of research has failed to answer this question satisfactorily, based on how Internals and Externals describe themselves, we would probably predict that Internals would have a better time of it and be more attractive to others than Externals. But let's look at the research.

A popular personality theory suggests we are most attracted to people who are most similar to us.[10] If true, then Internals would like Internals and Externals would like Externals more than they would their opposites on the LOC continuum.

Marian Morry did a series of studies examining the role of LOC and same-sex friendship.[11] She asked students to bring along a same-sex friend to the experiment they were doing. Students then completed one scale for themselves and another as they thought their friend would. Their friend also completed a scale. Morry found students thought their friends' LOC was closer to their own than it actually was. Similarity in orientation between friends only existed in the minds of the students.

Morry and a colleague found out even more in the continuation of the same study.[12] Participants completed their own scale and another one as they thought a close same-sex friend of theirs would that they brought with them. They asked the participants to rate how satisfied they were with the friendship. They predicted the Internality hypothesis would hold: Internals would be liked better than Externals. They found this was true for women; the more External was her friend, the less satisfied she was with the friendship. However, LOC failed to predict relationship satisfaction for men.

Although Internality may be a strong predictor of achievement, it does not seem to be related to whether male participants felt satisfaction with a same-sex friend.

The idea Externals aren't very satisfying to have as friends for women agrees with findings that show Externals make less gratifying spouses because of their tendency to be passive in interactions with their partners. Externals' passivity in response to difficulties hurts them in this area, just as it does in achievement, health, and business.

Was it their passivity that made External friends less satisfying? Morry was curious to find out. She, along with colleague Cheryl Harasymchuk, had participants complete scales for themselves and as they thought a same-sex friend would. (This time, the actual LOC of the friend was not obtained.) In this study, they also had the participants complete a problem-solving survey that described what kind of problem-solving techniques, either passive or active, their same-sex friend used. As before, they found the more External women described their friend to be, the less satisfied they were with the relationship. As Morry and Harasymchuk suspected, same-sex friends seen as more External by women were also perceived as more likely to use what are termed passive problem-solving behaviors. That is, External women who were perceived to solve relationship problems by neglecting them rather than facing them and trying to solve them were not satisfying friends.[13]

However, once again men's findings were different from women's—in fact, they were opposite. For men, the more External they perceived their same-sex friend to be, the more they were satisfied with him. The type of problem-solving approach used by the male friend played no part in determining satisfaction.

While there is still much to learn about the role of LOC in the relationship process, we can thank Morry and her colleagues for finding out some significant things. First, we are likely to see our friends as being more similar to us in LOC than they are. Second, LOC is differentially important in the friendships of women and men. For women, it seems as though they want their same-sex friends to be more internally than externally controlled and to use active problem-solving techniques if relationship issues develop. On the other hand, if LOC plays a part at all for men, they want their same-sex friends to be externally controlled. If we assume Externals are more passive and Internals are more active, then women like their friends to be actively engaged with them, while men desire friends who are more passive and likely to go along with things. However, these are very tentative findings; much more needs to be discovered about the role of LOC and same-sex friendship.

From what we have learned so far, Internals and Externals will attempt to deepen relationships differently. Bear in mind that, by their very nature, transitions are characterized by ambiguity. Participants are leaving the more structured beginning phase and entering into a negotiation about whether to take the relationship deeper. At times like this, Internals are prone to be more driven by information, in contrast to Externals, who are more passive and laissez-faire. Based on these differences, Externals may have a more difficult time deepening their relationships.

A former undergraduate honors student, Neil Blumberg (who is now a well-known forensic psychiatrist in Baltimore), and I were trying to find out who is more interpersonally attractive, Internals or Externals. While we found Internals were liked better initially, we wanted to know if they became even more attractive than Externals during the deepening phase.

Here is what we did.[14] We made audiotapes of male and female individuals representing Internality and Externality. Neil and I spent an inordinate amount of time making sure the tapes sounded cohesive, intelligent, and realistic rather mere stereotypes of Internals and Externals. We used the items from the Adult Nowicki-Strickland Internal External measure and Julian Rotter's scale as a script for our audio presentations to guide the representations of Internals and Externals we recorded and then played for the participants.

In the study, we led the participants to believe we were interested in seeing if they could accurately judge the personalities of others using only a small amount of information. They listened to the recordings and then evaluated the person they heard by using an Interpersonal Judgment Scale (IJS). Three of the IJS items measured interpersonal attraction: (1) liking for the person, (2) working together with the person on an experiment, and

(3) having the person for a roommate. We found regardless of their own LOC orientation, participants liked the Internals better than the Externals. That Internals were more attractive than Externals is consistent with what many others have found. However, when we looked closer at the scores from the IJS, we found the difference between Internals and Externals was due to the lower ratings Externals received on the roommate item. The possibility of a longer-term relationship made the Externals a much less attractive choice.

Summary

In the early stages of relating, Internals are more interpersonally attractive than their External peers, and they become even more attractive when deepening the relationship is a possibility. Externals may be less attractive because of their tendency to be passive and use avoidance tactics when grappling with interpersonal conflict. But does their passivity make Externals less attractive romantic partners?

LOC AND DEEPER RELATIONSHIPS: ROMANTIC LOVE

How do Internals and Externals deal with romantic relationships? Are Internals better liked and more interpersonally successful? Are Externals more open to the head-over-heels type of romantic love consistent with lives governed by fate and luck?

Kenneth and Karen Dion give us insight into the ways Externals and Internals approach romantic love in heterosexual relationships.[15] They argue because we stereotype romantic love as happening through some mysterious unknown external force, Externals might be more comfortable and therefore more likely to experience "romantic love" than Internals. Internals, on the other hand, may be less likely to, due to their aversion to being influenced by outside forces.

For the experiment, college students completed LOC and romantic love questionnaires. Based on their responses, Externals reported having more romantic attachments and viewing romantic love as more mystifying and idealistic than Internals. However, other findings were unexpected. For example, Internal men in a romantic attachment rated it as more passionate than did their External male peers. Not only that, but Internal men, similar to External women, reported their romantic relationships lasted longer than did their opposites in Locus of Control. Apparently, Internals, especially men, play down the "romantic" notions and mystery of a relationship, but once they are in one, they are more likely to remain in it and be passionate about it.

LOC AND DEEPER RELATIONSHIPS: MARRIAGE

Perhaps the most important long-term relationship any of us will hope to have is marriage or a similar long-term commitment. As I mentioned earlier, we aren't doing so well in this department, as reflected by the number of marriages that fail. Does Locus of Control help us to explain why this is happening?

For example, is LOC involved with long-term marriage satisfaction? We can thank Paul Camp for some answers here.[16] He and a colleague asked wives and husbands who had been married for an average of thirty years to complete scales for LOC and for marital satisfaction. His guess was one of two things would characterize satisfying marriages. First, based on the *similarity hypothesis*, he suggested spouses with similar LOC scores would be more satisfied with their marriage than those with divergent orientations. In the second prediction, based on the *Internality hypothesis*, he predicted the more the spouses tended to have Internal scores, the more likely it was they would be satisfied. What he found was the Internality hypothesis predicted long-term marriage satisfaction best: the more Internal the spouses were, the greater their satisfaction with their marriages.

If Internality is associated with marital satisfaction; what about the opposite side of the coin? Is Externality related to marriages ending in divorce? Helen Barnet asked more than one hundred recently divorced couples to complete questions on both LOC and the intensity of their divorce stress.[17] Somewhat surprisingly, she found Externality played a different role depending on where the former spouses were in the divorce process. Externality was related to lower stress before the actual divorce decision but greater stress after the decision was made. I would guess feeling less responsible heading toward divorce might be more comforting and less stressful than dealing with the reality of divorce and realizing the necessity of making a new start once the proceedings are over.

Externality also characterizes marriages that might be in trouble and are heading for divorce. Sylvester Miott and Frank Lira found wives who were dissatisfied enough with their marriages to seek professional help tended to be more External than their husbands compared to groups of wives who did not did seek help.[18] In other words, wives in unstable marriages were more External than their husbands, in contrast to wives in stable marriages, who did not differ in Locus of Control from their spouses. This finding is somewhat unexpected in the sense that you might expect External wives to suffer in silence rather than actively pursue relief from the relationship. Perhaps Internals in a difficult marriage might believe they still could work out the problems Externals have given up all hope on.

Not only is Externality, especially in women, related to marriage difficulties and dissatisfaction, it is also found to characterize marriages in which there is violence and abuse.[19] Victims of abuse, most often women, were significantly more External than either abusive spouses or nonvictims. That abusers were more Internal than those they abused points out that Internality can be used for good or ill in relationships.

While the results of these studies cannot tell us whether Externality is the cause of the marital difficulties or the result of them, it is certainly involved. One way to find out how Externality relates to marital difficulties is to obtain the Locus of Control of couples before they marry and look at what happens afterwards.

This is exactly the experimental design used by Lilly Dimitrovsky and her colleagues.[20] A month or two before they were to be married, couples took an LOC scale as well as measures of how satisfied they were with the relationship and how depressed they felt. Six months after they had taken their vows, couples again completed the marriage satisfaction and depression scales. While couples' LOC scores were not associated with their self-reported relationship satisfaction or personal depression before they were married, they were six months after the ceremony. Women who were External before they were married became significantly more depressed six months after they were married. Not surprisingly, they also were less satisfied with their partners. There were not significant effects for men.

Based on this preliminary study, being External before you are married, especially if you are a woman, increases the chances of the marriage starting off on the wrong foot. We don't know if the relationships would right themselves with more time or in exactly what way Externality would have this negative effect, but it is apparent Locus of Control plays a role in the emotional state of the marriage.

THE ROLE OF NONVERBAL COMMUNICATION

Externals appear to have more difficulty than Internals at most every point of the relationship process. They have less attractive personalities, are less satisfying friends, and use less effective means of handling relationship problems when they occur. Why do they have such a hard time connecting with others? I may have an answer that, if true, holds great promise for developing ways to improve the relationship lives of Externals.

I believe what is causing Externals so much trouble is that they aren't as good at using nonverbal language as Internals are. As I will explain later in this section, nonverbal language is essential to the smooth running of the relationship process. In fact, it is so basic that those who can't use it properly often end up feeling helpless and confused and as though they have no impact on what is happening to them. In other words, they end up feeling External.

By "nonverbal language," I mean the accurate sending and receiving of emotional information and cues in facial expressions, tones of voice, personal space, touch, postures, gestures, odors, and objectics (what we put on ourselves, such as tattoos, jewelry, glasses, clothing, and hair arrangement).

When I introduced the four-stage model earlier, I mentioned a key to successful progress through the stages was being able to accurately communicate our own feelings and clearly read those of others. While relationship communication takes place both verbally and nonverbally, I've come to believe nonverbal communication is the more important of the two. In fact, I believe this so strongly I have written three books and published more than fifty research articles in support of my conviction that nonverbal communication is the "language of relationship."[21] Let me tell you how I came to this conclusion.

Initially, my awareness of the importance of nonverbal language came from my own observations of the clients in my professional practice. First, I noticed my clients seemed oblivious of what they were conveying nonverbally. They were surprised and, at times, even embarrassed when I pointed out their clenched fists or angry facial expressions were very much at odds with what they were telling me verbally.

Second, during my consultations at schools treating severely emotionally disturbed adolescents, I couldn't help but notice the whopping nonverbal errors they made when interacting with others. The words might be appropriate, but the nonverbal communications were not. I especially remember a young man—let's call him Jeff. He was one of my favorites. I always went out of my way to interact with him when I consulted at his school. During the semiannual school picnic, Jeff and I played right field together. We never made an error, largely because no one ever hit the ball to us.

The teachers wanted to surprise me by having Jeff greet me when I arrived for my consulting visit. He learned the appropriate words to say when greeting someone in the morning. Sure enough, when I walked in on a Tuesday morning, Jeff, who was over six feet tall and easily weighed two hundred pounds, walked right up to me, stood about an inch away from my face, and said, "Good morning, Dr. Nowicki. How are you?" I was used to the nonverbal gaffes of the students, so, rather than pulling away, I stood my ground. We were quite a sight, Jeff and me, standing in the hall with our noses about to touch. I said, "I'm fine, Jeff. Thank you for asking. Now could you take one step back? That's about the distance you stand when talking with people." He did so, and I thanked him for his warm greeting, said goodbye, and continued to the front office.

Interactions like this one made me very aware of nonverbal errors and the impact they can have.

Marshall Duke and I have studied the phenomenon of nonverbal language for years and have coined a term to refer to those who have difficulties in this area: *Dyssemia*, from *dys*, meaning "inability," and *semia*, meaning "signs."[22] The term refers to individuals who have difficulties with nonverbal signals and signs. They can have receptive Dyssemias (trouble reading the cues of others) or expressive Dyssemias (difficulties sending their own cues accurately).

WHY NONVERBAL COMMUNICATION CAN MAKE OR BREAK RELATIONSHIPS

Verbal and nonverbal languages are both complex, learned, and developmental, and they involve predetermined rules of usage. However, there are major differences between the two modes of communication, and it is those differences that make nonverbal communication so important in relating to others.

First, nonverbal communication takes place more out of our awareness than verbal communication. Most of the time, we are not aware of what we are sending and receiving nonverbally. We may be conscious of the words we are saying, but we have little awareness of what we are sending through our facial expressions and tone of voice. In fact, it is very difficult to bring our nonverbal messages into awareness and keep them there. I have studied nonverbal language for years, but most of the time, I am unaware of it going on while I live my day. If you want to see what I mean, the next time you meet someone, slow down and think about how you and they are standing, your facial expressions, and your tone of voice. Now, try to keep track of all those cues as your interaction continues. My guess is that you will find it difficult, if not impossible.

Even if by some miracle you can keep yourself aware of what is going on nonverbally, you can't make what you've learned public. You cannot comment on what is going on nonverbally between the two of you because it is considered rude. That is the reason why when someone is standing too close for your comfort, you don't mention it. Instead, you move away to a more comfortable distance. Try telling someone he has a sad face even though he just told you he is happy, and see what happens. It is rude to offer your insight into how he is feeling. You can test this out for yourself, but don't say I didn't warn you.

A second trait that distinguishes nonverbal communication from verbal language is it is more continuous. We can stop using our words anytime we wish, but we lack the same control over the nonverbal parts of our communication, which continue to send and receive information about who we are and how we feel whether we want them to or not. As Paul Watzlawick has put it, "You cannot not communicate nonverbally!"[23]

A third difference is this: Make an error nonverbally and it has a negative emotional impact. In contrast, make a verbal mistake and it has a negative intellectual effect. If we use the wrong grammar or syntax ("I ain't seen it"), people may see us as uneducated or perhaps not very smart. Verbal gaffes can be seen in spoken and in written communications, such as church bulletins: "Don't let worry kill you, let the church help," or, "Thursday at 5:00 PM there will be a meeting of the Little Mothers Club. All wishing to become a Little Mother please see the minister in his study."

However, nonverbal blunders can be much more costly emotionally. Think of how we feel when someone stares at us for more than a second or two. What would our reaction be to a stranger coming into a movie theater that is almost completely empty and sitting down next to us? Both of these are examples of nonverbal rule mistakes. Rather than perceiving the strangers who make these errors as ignorant, we are likely to be frightened by them.

Marshall Duke and I call the combination of these three nonverbal language deficits the Dyssemic Core.[24] Because of them, if we make nonverbal errors, we will have a negative emotional impact on others, produce it continuously, and possibly not be aware of the deleterious effect we are having. You are correct if you see this as having a potentially devastating effect on our attempts to relate to others.

CAN RELATIONSHIP DIFFICULTIES BE ASSOCIATED WITH DEFICITS IN NONVERBAL COMMUNICATION?

The answer once again is yes, for both children and adults. Let me give you some examples of what I mean. When Marshall Duke and I were first introducing our nonverbal ability tests (the Diagnostic Analysis of Nonverbal Accuracy, DANVA) to the psychological community, we were sure there would be an association between Externality and poorer performance in identifying emotions in faces and voices.[25] We reasoned if individuals made mistakes reading the nonverbal cues of others, they would have difficulty interacting with them. However, because they were not aware they were making nonverbal errors, they would have no explanation for their failures. In fact, after many such failures, it would seem there was no connection between their efforts to relate and what they were getting back from others. If that sounds familiar, that is because we are describing someone who is externally controlled. The very real possibility is nonverbal difficulties are related to Externality.

To evaluate this hypothesis, children took our LOC and nonverbal ability tests.[26] We also gathered academic achievement and popularity information. As we suspected, compared to Internals, Externals were less accurate in identifying emotion in faces and voices, less successful academically, and less popular, to boot.

Additional studies showed External adults also were less adept at identifying emotions in faces, voices, and postures. Not only did they have more trouble reading nonverbal cues than Internals did, they also had more trouble expressing their emotions nonverbally. Howard Friedman, the current editor of the influential *Journal of Nonverbal Behavior*, and his colleagues used a test they developed called the Affective Communication Test (ACT) to confirm this.[27]

Why are Externals less accurate nonverbally than Internals? One possibility is they are less motivated to process the information. It could be they are as adept as Internals but just don't care enough or aren't energized enough to do anything with it. Deborah Richmond, an undergraduate student, and I evaluated that possibility.[28] We noted tests of nonverbal communication have standard instructions that are fairly innocuous and straightforward. We wondered what would happen if we changed the instructions to be more motivating or to provide a more effective strategy to use in identifying emotion in facial expressions. We ran students through the three different kinds of instructions and found—much to our disappointment—Externals remained less accurate than Internals regardless of what instructions we gave them.

Undaunted, I thought perhaps Externals' nonverbal deficits resulted from an inability to process nonverbal information as quickly as Internals. We have to keep up with what is being communicated in rapidly changing facial expressions, or we will run into interpersonal problems. To test this possibility, my doctoral student Eileen Cooley, who is now a professor at Agnes Scott College in Atlanta, and I wanted to know whether Externals were slower than Internals in discriminating emotion in faces—a deficit that would be absent when they were asked to discriminate emotion in words.[29]

Two pairs of emotion words (e.g., happy/sad, angry/mad) and two pairs of emotional facial expressions were flashed on the video monitor. Participants pressed a button as quickly as they could to indicate whether the pairs were the same or different.

As we thought, Externals and Internals did not differ in how fast they could discriminate between two emotion words, but Externals were significantly slower than Internals when trying to discriminate facial expressions. Externals seem to have a specific deficit in discriminating nonverbal but not verbal emotion cues.

This result may help us understand a little better why Externals have a harder time using nonverbal information effectively during an interaction. Remember, while both verbal and nonverbal cues are being sent quickly, the nonverbal ones are more continuous. Even if your interaction partner and you have stopped using words, the air between the two of you is filled with nonverbal cues being sent and received. Think of the havoc that might result if you were too slow to pick up new nonverbal cues because you were still stuck processing the old. A facial expression showing sadness could have changed to one signaling anger, but if you are slow to discriminate, you might miss the change and respond to sadness when that is no longer appropriate. Think about how facial expressions last only for a second or two and are continuously changing, and you can see how being slow to discriminate would be especially troublesome if two people were working through an emotional issue.

SUMMARY

There is evidence Externals have difficulties at most every stage of relating to others. They have more trouble beginning, deepening, and ending relationships than Internals. Even other Externals aren't attracted to Externals. It may be that part of their problem relating to others is they are not as skilled nonverbally as Internals. There is evidence they are slower at discriminating facial expressions, which could interfere with ongoing interactions. If so, then one possible way of helping Externals cope with the stresses of relationships would be to improve their nonverbal processing performance. Programs are available for that and offer hope for Externals who hope for an easier time connecting with others. Interventions could be streamlined by testing to find whether difficulties lie in a specific nonverbal channel, like faces or voices, or in particular emotions, like happiness, sadness, anger, or fear.

CHAPTER 8

COPING WITH PSYCHOLOGICAL DISORDERS

"Even the easiest parts of life are difficult. Trying to find out who we are and where we fit in the world can be exhausting and demoralizing. I know at times I've felt as though I was crazy. It is a wonder that we all aren't insane."

—**written to me by an unknown student**

DEFINING WHAT IS "ABNORMAL"

The task of determining what is psychologically "normal" and what is "abnormal" is not as easy as one might think. The line that divides the two states is clearer for physical disease than it is for psychological disorders. In psychology, at times, abnormality seems to be more in the eye of the beholders than in the individuals themselves. Religious zealots handling poisonous snakes because they believe their faith will protect them from injury would be seen by many of us as peculiar, but does it rise to an accepted definition of a diagnosable disorder? How about the case of a heavily armed person who bursts into a movie theater and opens fire on the crowd, killing thirteen people and wounding many more? Afterward, he appears disoriented and mutters something about people out to get him. Is this unusual act enough to earn him a diagnosis? A jury of James Holmes's peers didn't think so; they concluded he was sane and sentenced him to prison for thousands of years.[1]

The uneasy truth is, although most of us feel we can "tell it when we see it," there is no widely accepted definition of abnormality. We are uncomfortable around those whom we believe are behaving abnormally, and we want to put space between them and us as quickly as we can. But is our discomfort enough of a reason to give people a diagnosis that may well stay with them for the rest of their lives? I don't think so.

As a clinical psychologist, I have followed the hunt for a satisfactory definition of abnormality for a very long time. Mental health professionals have used three different perspectives in their search for the cause, explanation, and definition of abnormality: the *biological*, the *psychological*, and the *systemic*.

The biological explanation assumes the causes of abnormal behavior can be found in the physiological functioning of our bodies and/or what we may inherit from our parents. The psychological perspective, in contrast, suggests our abnormalities come from defective learning, thinking, and memory. The systemic belief traces abnormal functioning to what happens to us as we live with families and in other communities that transmit culture.

Although all three approaches have had some success in explaining and understanding where abnormal behavior comes from, they have largely failed to answer our most pressing questions regarding the cause and treatment of abnormality. Because of this, most mental health practitioners use a combination of the three approaches to guide their thinking and practice.

Marshall Duke and I have wrestled with the problem of definition more than most. We have published textbooks on abnormal psychology and grappled with the uncertainties of determining what is and is not abnormal in our clinical practice.[2] Often, we find ourselves in the uncomfortable position of not having an appropriate diagnosis for our clients' difficulties and needing to use one that only approximates what is going on.

The tenuous nature of diagnosis in the area of psychological abnormality has been the norm for as long as I can remember. The manual we psychologists and psychiatrists use to diagnosis individuals has expanded from a few score diagnoses in the mid-1960s to the hundreds of diagnoses available now. Apparently, more and more of our behaviors and practices are now seen as worthy of being diagnosed as abnormal. At the same time, over the years, I also have seen major disorders like "neuroses" take up significant space in the diagnostic manual for decades and then suddenly disappear from one version of the manual to the next.

Some diagnoses are less controversial and have remained largely unchanged over the years. These are the disorders we will look at most closely in this chapter and evaluate through the lens of Locus of Control.

LOC AND ABNORMALITY

In the previous chapter, I've shown how Locus of Control is tied to our success or failure at every stage of relating to others. I've pointed out how Externals experience difficulties at the beginning, deepening, and ending stages of relationship and how this results in their having lower self-esteem, being less popular, and feeling lower levels of well-being. Sometimes, Externals' relationship problems develop into something serious that can incapacitate them and contribute to the development of a psychological disorder.

The involvement of Externality in psychological abnormality did not come as a surprise to Julian Rotter. He was a fully trained and practicing clinical psychologist who believed LOC was intimately tied to psychological adjustment and maladjustment. From the very beginning, LOC was found to be a factor in psychological difficulties. A decade or so after publication of the Rotter scale, Bonnie Strickland, my colleague who was so instrumental in the early days of my study of this concept, reviewed what was known up to that time. After evaluating the hundred or so studies that had been completed, her general conclusion was pathological difficulties were indeed linked to Externality.[3]

For the rest of this chapter, I will bring you up to date on what we have found since Bonnie's analysis. I'll begin with what I believe to be one of the most damaging of all psychological problems: depression and the closely related disorder of suicide. Failure to connect with others in meaningful ways can have deadly consequences.

LOC AND DEPRESSION AND SUICIDE

I must begin with some worrying news. As I mentioned in Chapter 1, whether it is better diagnosing or some combination of factors causing an increase in the actual incidence of depression, the number of people diagnosed with depression has increased at an alarming rate during the past three decades to where, in our lifetimes, about one out of five of us will have depression severe enough to warrant a diagnosis. The problem is even worse for women, who are diagnosed at twice the rate of men in the United States and in most other countries of the world.[4]

To be diagnosed with a "depressive episode," we must have a change of behavior that includes either depressed mood or loss of pleasure for most of the day every day for two weeks, accompanied by a variety of less crucial but still important symptoms such as "fatigue, feelings of worthlessness and/or guilt, sleep disturbance, trouble concentrating, [and] thoughts of death."[5]

All the above feelings and behaviors are familiar to everyone, but those without a diagnosis of depression usually experience them briefly and with less intensity than those with such a diagnosis. That depression doesn't incapacitate people or interfere with their everyday lives, as the diagnosable form did to the young woman whose story follows.

A DESCRIPTION OF POSTPARTUM DEPRESSION

I think the "blues" began right there at the hospital. I felt unable to relax at all. Now that I was a mother, I had many important duties. I didn't feel sure I could live up to these responsibilities. . . . After we were home for a while, I began to feel like a shell. I did the same thing every day. While the baby was awake, I was his servant, and when he was asleep, I cleaned and checked on his breathing. Nothing could upset my routine.

Although it's called postpartum "blues," I remember feeling incapable of being blue. I just felt profoundly empty. There was no feeling for anything. I was quite sure that I didn't and couldn't love my husband or child. The very worst day was when our baby was baptized. It was a bright spring day. I remember that a shaft of sun shone in from the porch that morning, and I somehow saw it as a symbol that there was light and life somewhere, but I would never be part of it. . . . Soon I began to think I'd probably die.

How might Locus of Control be involved with this woman's depression? Would you be able to guess whether she is more likely to be Internal or External? Which would hinder and which would enable the development of depression? I think solid arguments could be made for either speculation.

The argument for Internality suggests if she were Internal, she would be prone to feel responsible for what happens to her and thus be vulnerable to suffer the negative consequences of her belief in Internality. In fact, this argument—that Internality and depression would co-occur—was made by some early LOC theorists.[6]

On the other hand, in her review, Bonnie Strickland made the case for Externality.[7] She reasoned if this woman were External, she would feel powerless about changing what was happening to her and be helpless to affect her future in a positive way. The result would be that Externality and depression would be associated with one another.

Both explanations have merit, but the argument has been resolved by studies showing, with rare exception, that Externality, and not Internality, is linked with depression. Unfortunately, the studies didn't reveal whether Locus of Control causes depression or vice versa, but we do know Externality and depression are linked, in that they have both increased at a remarkable rate over the past three decades. The rise in Externality parallels the rise in the number of people diagnosed with depression. As if that news weren't bad enough, as Externality and depression have risen, so has the rate of suicide, especially in adolescents and young adults.

LOC AND DEPRESSION: THE BRISTOL STUDY

While there is no clear proof Externality "causes" depression, let me describe a study that clearly shows how it can increase the probability for depression in children from disadvantaged backgrounds. Iryna Culpin and her colleagues at Bristol University in England seized the rare opportunity to use information gathered from a longitudinal study of thousands of children and their parents.[8] They set out to discover why some people develop physical and psychological disorders and others do not.

Past research shows that living in "bad" circumstances (e.g., being poor, living in inadequate housing, moving often) before the age of five put children at higher risk of developing depression later in life. But not all children raised in these conditions end up being depressed adults—a significant number don't. Why? What protected some children from depression, and what pushed others toward it?

Culpin and her colleagues found disadvantaged children who had experienced social adversity early in life and were more External in adolescence were the ones who developed diagnosable depression disorders as young adults. Externality appeared to be the impetus driving socially disadvantaged children into full-blown depression as young adults.

On the other hand, and on a much more positive note, children who were from the same background but were more Internal than their peers did not develop depression. As Externality appeared to facilitate the children's slide from negative childhood experiences into depression when they became adults, Internality somehow neutralized the impact of a disadvantaged childhood and led children into a more positive adjustment as adults.

Let me give you an example of how this study's findings played out in the real-life situation of two girls I happen to have known.

WHICH CHILD WILL BE DEPRESSED AS A YOUNG ADULT: LATIKA OR LANEY?

Latika and Laney were childhood acquaintances. They were classmates in the second grade for a short time, but then first Latika and then, a few months later, Laney had to change schools because their single moms had found better jobs in a different part of their large Midwestern city. Both girls were average students who got mostly Cs in school with an occasional

B or D. Latika had two older brothers and a younger sister; Laney also had three siblings, but they were all brothers, one older and two younger. Latika's mother was divorced, while Laney's father had left two years ago to find work and never returned. Both had moved so many times they could not keep track. Life was difficult for the two girls; there was little money for extras, and both had to do a lot of work around the house, especially babysitting. They never quite knew what tomorrow might bring.

As "fate" would have it, they once again found themselves in the same sixth-grade classroom. One day, they decided to have lunch together to talk about what each was doing and were surprised at how similar their lives seemed. Their teacher was a younger woman who thought girls should be involved in activities, especially sports. She loved to tell stories about her own experiences playing soccer and basketball in high school and how she continued to play sports now just for fun. Both Latika and Laney loved to hear the stories because they really liked their teacher. When she announced to the class she wanted to start a sixth-grade soccer team for girls, Latika and Laney jumped at the chance to join in. For the next four weeks, the girls practiced with the team when they could get away from their chores at home. Neither was a terrific player, but they weren't bad either, and both loved the pure joy of running around and playing with a team where everyone had a role. This was something neither had experienced before. After four weeks of practice, they had a chance to play against a sixth-grade team from another school. It was a great game, and they won on a last-minute goal from one of their teammates. Everyone hugged and giggled, and some girls even cried.

The teacher told the girls how proud she was of them and that she had arranged to play another game in a week's time. Latika and Laney couldn't wait. Then the news came to Latika that her aunt had invited her and her family to come live with them in a different part of the city. Two days later, Laney's mother told her she was leaving her present job to take a new one that would take them out of this school district and into a new one. There were many tears when they told each other and the teacher that they would have to leave the school and the team. And then, like so many times before, they were on the move to new places and new schools, but with the same old feelings of being jerked around by powerful forces beyond their control.

One thing turned out to be different, however. While Latika's move took her too far away for additional contact, the teacher kept in touch with Laney. When Laney arrived at her new school, she was surprised and delighted to hear her previous teacher had been communicating with her new one. She wanted to know if Laney would like to continue playing soccer and, if she did, if she would like to join a team her previous teacher was going to be coaching on weekends. Laney dearly wanted to do this, and soon a plan was arranged. Laney's mother and her teacher/coach helped organize Laney's life so she could meet her responsibilities at home and play on the team as well. To make this happen, Laney's previous teacher agreed to go out of her way to pick her up and bring her back from practices and games. Via this arrangement, Laney experienced stability and predictability as well as new relationships with her peers in a team setting. Even though her family continued to live on the edge, Laney was learning she could gain control over circumstances of her life. She began to know what it was like to balance her chores, schoolwork, and outside activities. Her positive experiences with youth soccer led to an invitation to play on her high school team. Here, she made more friends and learned even more about what she could and could not control about her life. Throughout this time, the relationship with her teacher grew into a mentoring one that Laney treasured. She appreciated her teacher's support during all those times when she felt discouraged about the things going on at home.

The story of how Laney found a way to avoid becoming depressed even though she was living a socially disadvantaged life is consistent with what was found by Culpin and her colleagues. Helping individuals like Laney learn to be more internally controlled may be one way to prevent depression in children from disadvantaged backgrounds. The authors of the study concluded that programs calculated to change LOC orientations to more Internal could help reduce the risk of developing depression.[9] Although they did not suggest which change programs to use, I will offer some possibilities in the final chapter.

LOC AND DEPRESSION: OLDER ADULTS

If Locus of Control can interact with children's background to affect the likelihood of depression, might it also have the same effect in older individuals? This is an important question because depression among the elderly is at epidemic levels and exacts high emotional and financial costs. Is Externality the culprit here, too? Our answer comes from a review done by Norwegian scientists who looked at just about every study they could find that involved depression and coping in older adults.[10]

The review arrived at this conclusion: if you want to help older adults who are trying to cope with their diminishing physical and cognitive functioning, make them as Internal as possible. As is the case with children from difficult backgrounds, it appears Externality assists in the growth of depression in older adults. However, Internality blocks it. In the words of the study's authors, "Conclusively, the ability of an older person to retain good coping resources in terms of a strong Sense of Control and high Internal control seem important for mental health and in the understanding of depression late in life."[11]

LOC AND DEPRESSION CAUSED BY PHYSICAL DISEASE

As I will cover in more detail in chapter 9, physical illnesses are associated with depression. One example is sickle cell disease.

One out of ten people living in Jamaica carry the gene for sickle cell disease, an illness that can strike at any moment, sapping patients' energy and bringing waves of unrelenting pain. Would experiencing this illness bring about depression and increased Externality? To answer this question, Roger Gibson and his colleagues asked adult sickle cell patients to complete LOC and depression scales. A particular type of Externality, "powerful others," was associated with depression in these respondents.[12]

The researchers reasoned patients may have felt this way because they had been largely ignored by medical staff in the planning, design, and implementation of their own pain management procedures. Patients often felt left out of decisions regarding medication, admission, and discharge. When the patients gained a more active role in their healthcare, their depression lessened.

USING LOC AGAINST MATERNAL DEPRESSION

Before we leave the discussion of depression, I want to share another potential way to modify the damaging effects of this condition. Not surprisingly, children of depressed mothers are also often depressed and anxious. Lisa Coyne and Alysha Thompson thought Locus of Control might play a role in modifying the negative impact on preschool children.[13] They found the children of more Internal depressed mothers reported fewer symptoms of anxiety and depression than the children of depressed mothers who were more External. That is, although depressed mothers were more External than nondepressed mothers, those depressed mothers who were not as External as other depressed mothers had children who had fewer indicators of depression and anxiety.

How exactly did the mothers' Internality translate into better adjustment for their children? The authors' best guess was Internals are more prone to cope with stress by using cognitive problem-solving skills rather than emotional problem-solving skills. Cognitive problem-solving skills reflect a more active, engaged, and focused approach, rather than the more passive avoidance characterizing emotional problem-solving skills. Mothers who were more prone to meet problems head-on despite their depression helped their children avoid becoming depressed and anxious themselves.

Based on the findings of this study and many others, Externals can cope better if they can learn to use cognitive problem-solving skills. Here is the way cognitive problem-solving usually goes.

1. Stop, slow down, and think: is there a problem?
2. If there is a problem, what is the possible conflict that is causing the problem?

3. Why is there a conflict?
4. Think of possible solutions.
5. Reason through how each of your solutions would work out.
6. Which solutions are possible for you with the time and resources you have?
7. Choose what you are going to do.
8. Do it.
9. Evaluate how it went.

In contrast, emotion-focused problem solving tends to follow these steps:

1. Deny there is a problem to avoid the upset that admitting there is one would generate.
2. Distract yourself by getting involved in other activities.
3. Write about what is bothering you in a journal or diary.
4. Meditate to reduce your emotional upset.
5. Find food to eat that is comforting.
6. Suppress feelings that are upsetting.

Can you see why cognitive problem-solving is more effective than emotion-focused approaches in reducing feelings of powerlessness and depression? Coyne and Thompson call for programs to teach parents to cope better with their children by using cognitive problem-solving skills. Better parenting would result in better-adjusted children, regardless of diagnosed disorders.

LOC AND DEPRESSION: A SUMMARY

Research findings reveal a close relationship between Externality and depression. While Externality may, on its own, generate feelings of depression, it most often does its damage by interacting with other negative conditions such as social disadvantage and physical disease. Researcher after researcher has recommended that one way to deal with depression is to make people more Internal. Because there is no practically applied and accepted way to do that, a more realistic suggestion is to teach the use of cognitive problem-solving skills to cope with difficulties produced by depression.

LOC AND SUICIDE

Not only has the frequency of depression increased at an alarming rate, so has that of suicide. In fact, the suicide rate has gone up each of the past dozen years to where it now is, at its highest level. The latest statistics reveal more than forty-one thousand known suicides took place last year, or one every 12.8 minutes. Gender differences abound regarding suicide. For example, although three times as many women *attempt* suicide than men, *four times* as many men actually complete suicide.[14]

Suicide has claimed the lives of many famous people: Ernest Hemingway and his granddaughter, Margaux; Marilyn Monroe; Cleopatra; Brutus; Virginia Woolf; Philip Seymour Hoffman; and Nero, to name just a few. But it is clear you don't have to be famous to experience enough unbearable psychological stress and pain to be driven to choose this drastic way of "problem solving." People contemplating suicide feel at wits' end, as though they have run out of options and have no other ways to deal with feelings of shame, sadness, and pain—a description that reflects feelings of Externality.

A frightening statistic is that suicide rates for adolescents have risen over the past thirty years, and now, the age of those at the high risk is between eighteen and twenty-four.[15] If that isn't enough of a warning, a recent Centers for Disease Control and Prevention survey of elementary school children found one out of three admit to feelings of prolonged sadness, hopelessness, and disconnection from others. Perhaps even more distressing is that one out of ten of the children reported thoughts of attempting suicide.[16]

Is LOC in the form of Externality involved with this rise in suicides? An answer comes from William Evans, Patsy Owens, and Shawn Marsh, who, in an extensive survey of eighth-grade students from four western states, found a significant link between an increased risk of suicide and Externality.[17] It appears Externality and heightened risk of suicide may go hand in hand, and not only in adults but in younger people as well.

Because we know Externality plays some role in suicidal thinking and behavior, perhaps changing Externality would be an effective way to lower suicidal risk. But any intervention needs to keep in mind Externality also plays a part in the unique aspects of the suicidal state: (1) its brief duration, (2) its state of ambivalence about living or dying, and (3) its dyadic nature.

People are seriously suicidal for a relatively brief period of time. During this time, they feel the most External and unable to consider any other way to solve their problems. It is here cognitive problem-solving techniques would be most useful by suggesting other options that can be worked on after the critical period has passed.

Recognizing suicidal people are ambivalent about their decision but see no other options reminds us relationships are the key for all of us. Knowing Externals feel most comfortable with structure, we can offer ways to organize their lives after they get through the crisis. Cognitive problem-solving skills are especially useful at this point.

The third unique feature of the suicidal state is the realization it is not an individual act, as maintained by some, but actually a dyadic one that has far-reaching consequences. An individual's suicide affects the lives of many other people. Externals who have tried to connect with others and failed may have a difficult time realizing they and others remain linked. Helping them understand they do have power to affect others' lives in positive as well as negative ways can stimulate dialogue and lead to new ways to solve problems. This helps to remind them they can exercise Internality at this crucial juncture in their lives.

APPLYING WHAT WE KNOW: SUICIDE PREVENTION CENTERS

I spent time in a twenty-four-hour crisis suicide prevention center as part of my training to become a clinical psychologist. I witnessed the following one evening at the center:

Late one evening, just after a routine call, a man phoned and told the counselor who answered he was going to kill himself. The counselor, a woman in her late forties, used all her considerable therapeutic skill to try and talk this man out of suicide. She did keep him talking, and the more she found out about him, the more it became clear to her this was a serious threat to kill himself. She knew he had a loaded gun next to the phone.

The call seemed to go on forever, but it probably didn't last more than fifteen minutes. Police and hospital authorities were notified and put on alert. Suddenly, the caller's tone of voice changed. He sighed, wished the counselor good night and good luck, and declared he was going to shoot himself. We held our collective breath and waited to see what happened next. At this point, the counselor broke down sobbing and forcefully told the man he must not kill himself, that people would help him work his way out of his difficulties, and that she cared too much about him for him to die. With tears streaming down her face, she begged this man to live; showing him he was connected with others. In response to this unplanned approach, the caller lost his resolve to kill himself, and he told the counselor where he was.

Not all calls to prevention centers end so happily, but more do than you might think. This story shows the importance of (1) being available during the crisis time leading up to a suicide, (2) keeping contact with the part of suicidal persons that wants to live, and (3) using that connection to deliver the message they are not alone and their lives are meaningful to others. At the end of this kind of problem-solving process, everyone should feel more Internal.

LOC AND ANXIETY

We now move to what could be called depression's psychological cousin, anxiety. We all know how it feels to be anxious: the sweaty palms, the thumping heart, the feeling of dread that something bad is going to happen, and, most of all, the tension that doesn't allow us to relax. Being a college professor, I see anxiety in my students every examination day. I am all too familiar with anxiety, as well, when I approach my dentist's office. I had terrible dental experiences when I was a child, and I've never completely gotten over my fear of going to the dentist. The smell of the dental office as I get near it can trigger anxious feelings.

In times like these, I have to remind myself that in spite of my discomfort, anxiety can be a good thing. It prepares us to deal with what might come next. Scientists call it our "flight or fight" response: if we anticipate danger, should we attack and overcome it, or should we get the heck out before we get hurt? With some reflection, I think most of us would agree that without this early warning system, we would be in big trouble.

The problem with our anxiety is that sometimes it gets out of hand. Sometimes we are anxious when there really doesn't seem to be any reason. We are prepared for fleeing or fighting when neither is called for. It takes a lot of energy to be anxious; excessive anxiety saps our physical and mental strength and leaves us less, not more, able to handle our everyday challenges.

The Anxiety and Depression Society of America points out that anxiety disorders are the most common mental illness in the United States and affect one out of every five adult Americans (just ahead of depression). In spite of the availability of effective treatments, both pharmaceutical and psychological, fully two-thirds of those with anxiety disorders fail to receive treatment, which leads to them being more likely to visit their physicians (five times more likely than those without anxiety) with a variety of physical complaints (that are generated by too much anxiety) or to being admitted to a psychiatric hospital (six times more likely than those without anxiety). The costs of dealing with anxiety run into the billions, but they do not even begin to touch the amount of mental anguish suffered by its victims and those around them. As is the case for depression, there are many more girls and women who are anxious than there are boys and men.[18]

About half of those diagnosed with depression also have a diagnosable anxiety disorder. Actress Heather Locklear is a prime example. She was hospitalized in 2008 to get help with the dual diagnosis of depression and anxiety. She is not the only celebrity who has had trouble with anxiety. Johnny Depp, Kate Moss, Kim Basinger, and Emma Stone from show business; All-Star baseball player Joey Votto; and professional golfer

Charlie Beljan are just a few who have experienced a panic attack, a particular kind of anxiety disorder in which the anxiety is so intense people feel as though they are going to faint or maybe even die. Charlie Beljan even had a panic attack while playing in a tournament.

It is important to note anxiety did not prevent these famous people from becoming successful. And they are not the only ones who have overcome anxiety to have a good life. My guess is thousands of other businesspeople, teachers, actors, contractors, and others are leading successful lives despite their anxiety.

When we consider anxiety involves feeling powerless to handle potential threats from outside as well as fearful emotional responses from within, it is no wonder anxious people have been found to be more External than nonanxious ones at all ages and in both genders.[19] These findings seem especially true for children; studies have found Externality to be related to anxiety in typical children as well as in children referred to a clinic for behavioral problems.[20]

When considering the LOC-anxiety association, we need to be clear as to whether we are referring to what is called "trait anxiety" or "state anxiety." Trait anxiety means we carry anxiety around with us all the time. State anxiety, on the other hand, is created by the situations in which we find ourselves. Whether we are generally high or low in trait anxiety, when driving on an icy mountain road, most of us would experience state anxiety brought on by the dangerous situation. Some of us have unique individual situations that make us anxious; for me, it is dental offices, and for others, it may be heights, presenting in front of people, or taking academic tests. But LOC plays a role in state anxiety as well.

In a study completed using children attending school in Hong Kong, where academic pressure to succeed is already high and increasing, it was found Externality was related to higher state anxiety measured just before the children took their most important academic test.[21] When children were made more anxious by the possibility of failing an important examination, it was the Externals who turned out to be the most anxious. One would guess the performance of External children wasn't helped by the anxiety provoked by the testing situation.

LOC AND COPING: INTERNALITY

We know from past research with depression that Internality functions as a buffer against the negative impacts of this disorder. I'm pleased to tell you Internality works in a similar way to offset the harmful effects of anxiety. Monica Nanda, Beth Kotchick, and Rachel Grover showed the positive impact of Internality in children who have hostile, controlling parents.[22] Hostile controlling parents more often have children who develop "internalizing" problems like anxiety. What Nanda and her colleagues wanted to know was if children's Locus of Control played a role in how they adjusted to the negative effects of controlling parents. As the researchers hoped, they found that children who were more External and had hostile, controlling parents experienced higher anxiety than those who were more Internal. Internality in children was able to soften, deflect, or somehow dilute the effects of harsh parenting more than Externality was. One way to help children deal with stressors, such as living with hostile, controlling parents, is to facilitate the growth of their Internality—which, in turn, will make it easier for them to develop, find, or otherwise gain information that will help them adjust.

LOC AND ANXIETY: A BETTER WAY TO MEASURE LOC IN ANXIOUS PEOPLE

Carl Weems and his colleagues were afraid general scales of Locus of Control were not picking up the specific control issues associated with anxiety. To see if that was true, they built a scale that would only include items specifically related to anxiety-control beliefs.[23] They gave this scale, a general measure of LOC, and a self-report anxiety test to 117 elementary school–age children and found their measure was indeed more highly related to anxiety than the general one. Having more specific measures of LOC should be a great help in studying anxiety and in suggesting where and how to intervene.

LOC AND POST-TRAUMATIC STRESS DISORDER

It was a lovely spring morning in Atlanta. My wife, Kaaren, and I had gotten up early, finished our breakfast, and, almost in unison, said, "Let's take a walk into Decatur." I live just off the campus of Emory University in a beautiful forested area. We can walk in almost any direction from our house and find ourselves in nice neighborhoods with lovely gardens. Getting to Decatur takes about a two-mile walk that ends at our favorite coffee shop, Java Monkey.

We left the house early, about 7:30. We wanted to beat the Atlanta heat, which even in springtime can be difficult to contend with. We decided the beginning part of our walk would be silent, a quiet time for us to enjoy our surroundings without commenting on them. At the appointed time, our silence ended, and we began a conversation about our plans. Would we have bagels or croissants with our coffee? What would we do with the rest of the day?

It was then we noticed that a car that had passed us had turned around and was slowly driving in the direction we were walking. We were on a residential street about six blocks from Decatur. A woman was standing in her yard holding a baby, and I could hear the drone of power mowers cutting grass. It looked serene, but I was suddenly on alert. I turned to Kaaren and said, "I think we are in trouble." She was confused and asked if I was joking. At that moment, the car stopped, and two teenagers got out and approached us with their hands inside their shirts. Kaaren thought they were going to ask directions, but by then, I knew differently. I remember feeling unreal and calm, saying, "Don't fight. Give them what they want." But Kaaren did fight, especially when they ripped her wedding rings off her hand. There was an older man standing by the car staring at us while this was going on, and I can remember him yelling at us not to look at him. The woman with the baby was maybe fifty yards away, and she began to shout, "What's going on? What are you doing?"

I'm not sure, but that could have saved us from further harm. The boys left, got into the car, and drove off. The woman with the baby invited us into her house and called the police. That led to a wild ride around Decatur with a policeman trying to track down the small green Corolla and the three men who had assaulted us. Our search was fruitless, and the officer gave us a ride home.

For many days and weeks after the attack, I had nightmares about people attacking my family as I stood by, unable to do anything to stop them. I know rationally that I did the best thing for our safety by not trying to be a hero, but even as I write this, I find myself getting angry at those men who hurt my wife. I have played out variants of a scenario in my mind in which I take on the young robbers and beat them within an inch of their lives.

About three months after our attack, Kaaren and I again had an early breakfast, put on our hiking shoes, and took a walk to Decatur. It was the first time since the mugging we had the nerve to retrace our steps. We laughed nervously as we came closer and closer to where we were robbed, and when we got there, we looked at each other, hugged for a long moment, and said, "Let's get some coffee."

Post-traumatic stress disorder (PTSD) has worked its way into our consciousness via news reports of combat veterans who have returned home physically safe but psychologically disabled from the traumas they have experienced. We also know an inordinate number of women have been assaulted and raped, an experience that leads some of them to develop PTSD.

According to the National Institute of Health, PTSD is an anxiety disorder that can develop after exposure to a terrifying event or ordeal in which there was the potential for or actual occurrence of grave physical harm. Traumatic events that may trigger PTSD include violent personal assaults, natural or human-caused disasters, accidents, and military combat. People with PTSD have persistent frightening thoughts and memories of their ordeal, feel detached or numb, may experience sleep problems, and can be easily startled.[24]

The National Center for PTSD points out that experiencing a trauma is not as rare as you might think. They estimate about six of every ten men and five of every ten women experience at least one significant trauma in their lives. Only a small percentage of those go on to develop PTSD at some point in their lives. So why do they go on to develop PTSD after a trauma, while most of the others do not?

The most obvious answer to this question is the severity and duration of the trauma determine who will develop PTSD. However, as so often happens, the obvious answer is not the correct one. Matt Kushner and his colleagues concluded that severity and duration account for a surprisingly small percentage of the PTSD that develops.[25] In light of this, they suggested that individual traits of the trauma victims themselves may well determine who does and who does not develop PTSD and, if they do develop PTSD, how severe it will be. And that, of course, brings us to Locus of Control.

Because the core of the definition of PTSD is being faced with a threat we cannot control, it seems likely Externality is involved. But exactly where in the time span of the trauma and its aftermath does Locus of Control have its effect? Will it happen immediately after the trauma, or will it take a week, a month, or maybe a year? Will our pretrauma LOC have an effect on how we handle the aftermath?

Men are most likely to develop PTSD after combat and women after being sexually assaulted. Karen Karstoft and her colleagues looked at the effects of combat exposure in Israeli soldiers one, two, and twenty years after the Lebanon war.[26] They found External LOC, along with overuse of emotional problem-solving techniques, predicted the severity and chronicity of PTSD in these combat veterans. The LOC effect was strong enough for the authors to recommend using Externality to predict which soldiers would show chronic long-term PTSD.

As a reaction to combat trauma, Externality apparently has a constant long-term relationship with the severity of PTSD symptoms. Does that occur in other types of trauma-related PTSD as well? Weiqing Zhang and her colleagues provide some answers to this question in their study of the reactions of adolescents who experienced a severe earthquake in China.[27] They point out that though there is some suggestion PTSD symptoms are common in adolescent earthquake survivors, this has not been studied longitudinally. Victims were assessed at three and seventeen months after the earthquake.

The single most powerful predictor of PTSD symptoms at three months and second-strongest predictor at seventeen months was Externality, especially in regard to the factor of chance. At both time points, Externality was a significant and constant predictor of PTSD symptoms beyond the amount of earthquake exposure. It and passive emotional problem-solving behaviors were the most negative factors seventeen months after the traumatic episode. On the flip side of these findings, the authors point out an Internal LOC was a strong protective factor against PTSD symptoms. Internality and cognitive problem-solving skills are crucial in coping with natural disasters like earthquakes.

Matt Kushner and his colleagues extended the study of LOC in the development of PTSD by not only including women who were rape victims and but also women who had experienced nonsexual assault, such as simple assault, robbery, and aggravated assault.[28] In an interesting twist to the usual assessment of LOC, they obtained three types of control: (1) perceived control during the attack, (2) perceived control over a future attack, and (3) perceived control over negative events in general. Remarkably, only general control was significantly related to the severity of the PTSD. Neither victims' perception of control during the assault nor their expectation for control over a similar assault in the future were related to PTSD severity.

Although the most frequent cause of PTSD in women is sexual assault there also is evidence that physical assault from an intimate partner can also be devastating. Georgia Noon completed her dissertation by examining women who were battered by an intimate partner during the previous year.[29] First, she found the majority of the abused women met criteria for a PTSD diagnosis. Second, she found Externality was related to the severity of the PTSD disorder. She concluded battered women are at risk for PTSD and that Externality is a significant factor in the development of PTSD symptoms.

It appears that, at least for women who have been assaulted, Externality is associated with severe psychopathological reactions. Women who generalize their Externality in this manner seem to be changing their basic assumptions about the fairness and safety in the world in general.

One thing is clear about Locus of Control and PTSD. If you are External before experiencing a trauma, and if you are External after the trauma, you are at greater risk for developing PTSD. Internality appears to operate as a protective factor throughout the process.

SUMMARY: LOC AND PSYCHOLOGICAL DIFFICULTY

Together, depression and anxiety affect nearly half of us in the United States. One constant Locus of Control theme emerges: Externality is associated with depression, suicide, and anxiety. Another theme is that Internality can act as a shield against the negative impact of both depression and anxiety. Both themes are found when looking at other severe psychological disorders such as schizophrenia, for which a fifteen-year follow up of patients showed Externality was related to fewer periods of recovery and to both depressed mood and psychosis.[30] Another study showed Externality at age eight predicted the development of psychotic-like symptoms in early adolescence.[31]

I think we would be hard-pressed to find a psychological difficulty that hasn't been related to Locus of Control in some significant fashion. We've seen how the concept is involved in the development and maintenance of PTSD, regardless of whether the initiating trauma is combat, rape, or natural disaster. PTSD is related to LOC because it is, by definition, a disorder in which loss of control has devastating consequences.

I could go on and mention Internet addiction and other disordered behaviors, but I think the point is made.[32] LOC needs to be part of the discussion of how psychological disorders develop and are maintained, tolerated, and treated. Though it appears better to be Internal than External, it is not clear exactly how Internals gain their advantage. Certainly the use of problem-focused rather than emotion-focused techniques is one probable reason for Internals' successes. Still, I suspect there are other factors involving Internals' tendencies to persist, gather information, and delay gratification that have yet to be explored in other studies.

CHAPTER 9

COPING WITH
PHYSICAL ILLNESS AND INJURY

"Lack of activity destroys the good condition of every human being, while movement and methodical physical exercise save it and preserve it."

—**Plato**

Everyone has heard or read stories about elite athletes who gain the world's attention and admiration for their outstanding feats of physical speed, ability, or strength. But for me, such accomplishments pale in comparison to someone like the athlete described by sportswriter Rick Reilly in his articulate and moving column simply entitled, "The Runner."[1]

THE RUNNER

Even though he has run in every high school cross-country meet since his sophomore year, Ben has never won a single race. In fact, Ben has never finished ahead of any other runner on his own or his opponent's teams. And yet, crowds of peers and adults stick around for hours at times at every meet to see and cheer his finish. You see, Ben has cerebral palsy. The disease plays havoc with his attempt to walk, let alone run. He must twist and contort his legs and arms strangely to first get and then keep his body moving. His gait being more like a shuffle means that any little undulation of the ground could cause him to fall. And because cross-country means traveling across rocks, tree roots, and streams, fall he does, over and over again, but each time he falls, he drags himself up and starts moving again. At the end of every race, his body is banged up and bloody, but he perseveres and finishes to the shouts of encouragement and joy from his ever-present fan club.

Ben is a hero to all who know him and an inspiration for all of us to do our best and to find out the limits of what we can do. In Ben's words, he does it "because I feel like I've been put here to set an example. . . . Anybody can find something they can do . . . and do it well. I like to show people that you can either stop trying or you can pick yourself up and keep going."

I do not know Ben personally, but I would be very surprised if he were not internally controlled.

HOW IMPORTANT IS PHYSICAL FITNESS?

That the key to our physical health and athletic performance is being fit shouldn't be surprising. Physical fitness has been an object of increasing focus of public policy over the past two decades. We've all seen and heard the numerous public service ads from the President's Council trumpeting the need for us and our children to be fit. Scientists have been producing studies the results of which reinforce the links between being out of shape and being susceptible to physical illness or injury. You would think the public outcry for physical fitness, coupled with the scientific evidence tying fitness to health and happiness, would have gotten us off our collective couches and away from our computer screens and to the gym—that we should be champing at the bit to get ourselves in shape. If anything, however, over the past twenty years, we and our children have gotten less, not more, fit.

How bad is it? I already gave a preview in my introductory comments to the chapter on athletic achievement. We know that only one out of twenty adults reports doing the recommended thirty minutes of physical activity per day, and merely one out of five adolescents and adults meets the minimal guidelines for both aerobic and muscle-strengthening activities.

So what are we doing in place of the walking, running, and biking that ought to be occupying our time? The answer is disquieting. The time we and our children should be engaged in doing healthy things, we instead are spending in front of some kind of screen—watching television, using a computer, or playing a video game. Recent surveys show we are spending an average of 7.5 hours a day, or about half of our waking hours, sitting and gazing at one kind of hazily lit monitor or another.[2]

As if all this sedentary screen time weren't bad enough, it also seems that during the time we are sitting and watching our video displays, we also are eating poorly. Most of us eat less than the recommended portions of healthy foods such as vegetables, fruits, and whole grains and more than the recommended levels of saturated fat, refined sugars, and salt. Wrap your head around this: Americans eat thirty-two more pounds of fat a year now than they did fifteen years ago and almost double the healthy level of salt.[3]

Wait, it gets worse. In spite of all the negative press associated with eating salt- and fat-laden fast foods, the number of fast food restaurants has doubled over the past twenty years, and our average daily caloric intake has risen by six hundred calories. Knowing this, it follows that the states with the greatest proportion of overweight people, Alabama and Kentucky, also have the highest number of fast food restaurants in America.

The poor eating habits and lack of physical activity have combined to produce what some have called an obesity epidemic. Things have gotten so bad that it is estimated half of all adults in the United States will be obese within a decade. Our children are following us down the path to obesity. Over the past twenty years, obesity has doubled in children between the ages of two and five, quadrupled between ages six and eleven, and tripled between ages twelve and nineteen.[4]

Our reduced physical activity and unhealthy eating habits have made more of us obese, and our obesity, in turn, has made us more vulnerable to a host of life-threatening diseases, including diabetes, heart disease, high blood pressure, cancer, and ulcers. Our unhealthy lifestyles are threatening our physical and mental health as well as that of our children. To prevent this, we need to change.

LOC AND PHYSICAL FITNESS

How can Locus of Control help us understand how we got into this physical fitness mess, and, more important, how can it help us get out? For starters, I believe LOC can explain why when it comes to fitness, so many of us engage in self-defeating behaviors. You know where I'm going with this, don't you? The core definition of External LOC is believing and acting as though we have little to say about our futures. I don't imagine it is an accident that both our physical fitness and our Internality have tanked over the past thirty years. Our increasingly External perspective dictates that we become less motivated to persist at the things we need to do to be fit. Why? Because, in large part, we don't see the link between our actions and our fitness levels or the subsequent greater likelihood of negative physical consequences including obesity, high blood pressure, and illness. We are paying an enormous price for our higher Externality in the form of poorer health, lower quality of life, and the development of life-threatening diseases.

To support my claim that there is a link between Externality and poor fitness, I need to take us to the beginning of the fitness process, to how Externals think and feel about fitness and what they do when faced with the choice of whether to participate in fitness activities or not. From what you already know about Locus of Control, I don't think you are going to be astounded by what I tell you next, but I may have a surprise or two in store regarding the reasons for men's and women's exercise choices.

Let's begin with how Internals and Externals think and feel about fitness.

DO EXTERNALS HAVE MORE NEGATIVE ATTITUDES REGARDING PHYSICAL FITNESS ACTIVITY THAN INTERNALS?

No matter who we ask—boys, girls, men, or women—the answer is the same. Externals plainly have a greater distaste for fitness activities than Internals do.

Not only do Externals show limited enthusiasm for the idea of starting an exercise, fitness, or activity program, they also are more likely to leave it after they begin. You might think once Externals experienced the positive effects of exercise, they would want to continue, but (as you will see later) they don't. This holds true whether the fitness program takes place in a community center, health club, school, or corporation. So not only does being External make you less likely to begin exercising, it also makes you more likely to quit.

Many have tried to overcome this sad state of affairs for Externals but failed. One such example was an innovative physical fitness program created by researcher Jaqueline Hooper to be "implemented and marketed . . . to attract individuals who are sedentary, smoke, are unable to cope with home-mediated stress and have an external locus of control."[5] However, her program failed to decrease the usual 50 percent dropout rate, and, not surprisingly, she found out those who dropped out were more External than those who stayed.

While it makes some sense that Externals do not volunteer for exercise and fitness programs as often as Internals, it is more difficult to understand why, once they are in one, they don't stay. Swedish psychologists Peter Hassmén and Nathalie Koivula may have found one possible explanation: Internals and Externals differ in how they perceive the amount of effort they are exerting when they exercise.[6]

Fifty typical female university students, none of whom were athletes or were participating in outside exercise programs, rode in place on stationary bikes at a pace of sixty revolutions a minute for sixteen minutes. At the end of each four-minute segment, the participants' heart rates were recorded, as were their perceptions of how hard they were exerting themselves, on a scale from one to ten. Past research has shown a firm relationship between our heart rates and how hard we perceive our exertion to be. Depending on how hard the cyclists said they were working, they could correctly estimate their exertion, underestimate it (state a lower level of exertion than their heart rate indicated), or overestimate it (state a higher level of exertion than their heart rate indicated).

What the experimenters did next produced valuable insight into why

Externals are more prone than Internals to dropping out of exercise programs. At the end of each four-minute segment, the power level of the cycling machine was ratcheted up, and the cycling task got progressively harder. Early on, during the first two four-minute segments of cycling, you couldn't tell the difference between External and Internal women; their perceived exertion was right on target with their heart rate. However, in the more difficult and straining third and fourth segments, differences between Externals and Internals emerged and grew larger with greater exertion. External women overestimated their exertion, while their Internal peers remained on target. In other words, External women perceived they were working much harder than they actually were, based on their heart rate.

If this tendency to overestimate physical effort also happens for other activities that make up physical fitness programs, it seems clear Externals may drop out of fitness programs simply because they perceive they are working harder than they really are. They are misreading physiological information generated by their own bodies during exercise and gathering erroneous messages about how long they might be able to sustain their efforts. In turn, this suggests one simple way to help Externals remain in exercise programs is to improve their ability to read the physiological cues generated by their bodies by continuously presenting heart rate and other cardiovascular functioning information through monitors. Another possible suggestion is to provide them with games and activities that would distract them from their cardio exertions.

DO MEN AND WOMEN HAVE DIFFERENT ATTITUDES ABOUT FITNESS?

Simply put, women and men exercise and diet for different reasons. In hopes of uncovering possible triggers and sustainers of obesity, Deborah Cobb-Clark, Sonja Kassenboehmer, and Stefanie Schurer asked thousands of women and men about their exercise and eating behaviors.[7] They looked at exercise from an economic perspective in which they saw the effort to be fit as an investment that can be valued more or less by different people.

Using an economic metaphor, the study concluded Internals showed they were willing to invest more in their fitness behaviors than Externals by being healthier eaters and more enthusiastic exercisers. What is impressive about the Cobb-Clark study is the sheer size and representativeness of the participants involved.

Additional digging into the mountains of data revealed one of those interesting qualitative gender differences, here separating Internal men and Internal women as to their reasons for investing in fitness: "Men with an internal locus of control seem to expect higher health returns to their investments in diet and exercise than do their more external counterparts. . . . Women with an internal locus of control appear to adopt healthy habits because they derive greater satisfaction from those activities."[8]

I take this to mean Internal men expect to get more bang for their buck from dieting and exercise in terms of physical outcome, while Internal women are more satisfied with feeling better about themselves and their involvement with a healthier lifestyle. Though Internality is the same motivational force driving both genders into fitness activities, men and women may be exercising for completely different reasons that have yet to be discovered.

Not only is this true in the United States and western Europe but also in the rest of the world. Jane Wardle, Anne Haase, and Andrew Steptoe, who have studied international views of health for many years, found both consistencies and differences between men and women in how they decided if they were overweight or underweight.[9] They obtained the body mass index (BMI, a measure of weight-to-height ratio) of nearly twenty thousand university students from twenty-two countries. Women overestimated perceptions of being overweight at the lower BMI indices, in contrast to men, who underestimated being overweight at the higher BMI indices. In other words, women who weren't overweight more often thought they were, and men who were overweight more often thought they weren't. Perceptions of being overweight and attempts to lose weight were lowest in Mediterranean countries and highest in Asian countries. In fact, women from Asia, especially Japan and Thailand, were more concerned with their weight than women from anywhere else in the world. It is easy to see how such perceptions might influence how we exercise and eat.

OUTCOMES OF FITNESS PROGRAMS FOR MEN AND WOMEN

If the reason Internal males "invest" in exercising is because they expect to be rewarded by increased physical performance, then it follows that they should outperform External males on fitness tests. To explore this possibility, I was fortunate to be able to call on Tom Johnson, an Emory colleague and friend, who was at that time not only a professor of physical education but chair of the department. Because of his vocation, Tom had a longtime interest in the role of Locus of Control in physical health and fitness and athletic performance. As the winningest soccer coach in Emory history, he had often applied the concept to the roles and responsibilities of different team members. From his perspective, he reasoned he wanted his defensive halfbacks and goalies to be the most Internal because they controlled crucial aspects of the match.

Tom and I, along with physical education professor Dan Adame and Emory doctoral graduate Steve Cole, completed a series of studies that illuminated the role of LOC in exercise and fitness performance. We reasoned that while Internality was a great motivator, its ability to energize people toward their goals would be affected by how much they valued those goals. This is a fundamental idea first offered by Julian Rotter way back in 1954. It made sense to us that if the goal being pursued by Internals was highly prized by them, it would energize them all the more to perform at their best.

We, and others, had previously shown Internals, especially Internal men, performed better on fitness and exercise tests than Externals, but what we did not know was how much the varying value of physical fitness would affect their performance. To find this out, we asked 435 students to complete LOC scales and to report how much they valued not only their physical fitness but also their physical appearance and physical health.[10]

We were not surprised when we found Internals who greatly valued physical fitness also performed higher than anyone else. What we also noted was that the best performance of Internal men who valued personal fitness highly came when they were completing their fitness tests (which included sit-ups, grip strength, and a 1.5-mile run) in front of female examiners. Interestingly, Internal women were not similarly affected by the gender of the examiner and performed at about the same level regardless of who gave the test.

This finding brings up an interesting possibility. Perhaps many Internal males who value fitness goals exercise so intensely simply to attract the attention of the opposite sex. Such motivation would fit nicely within evolutionary theory, which assumes women are attracted to powerful men who can protect them.

LOC AND SMOKING

I smoked a pipe in graduate school in a vain attempt to look older and more sophisticated. I didn't know then that tobacco was the greatest single cause of preventable death and disease in the United States. I only knew everyone who was cool smoked. I remember returning to college in the fall and seeing guys from the tobacco companies standing at the entrance to the student union, handing out free packs of cigarettes. We all took them and practiced how to light and hold them while blowing smoke through the sides of our mouths. Most of us smoked in high school as well, but it just seemed even more important to smoke in college. It was part of being a "with it" college student.

Today, smoking has maintained its number-one ranking as a cause of preventable death and is responsible annually for nearly a half million deaths and $157 billion in lost work and medical expenses. This is true even though the number of people smoking has declined considerably over the past three decades to about one out of every five Americans, of whom a disproportionate number come from the lower socioeconomic classes.[11]

Breaking the smoking habit is tough. Of the more than half of smokers who try to quit their smoking addiction annually, only 5 percent are able to remain successful at the end of a year.[12] As Christine Sheffer and her colleagues point out, it can be a mystery for those of us who do not smoke why our family members or friends give up the prospects of long-term health, relationships, and monetary savings in favor of smoking and coughing a lot.

Sheffer attempted to treat smokers with a variety of the most potent present-day psychological treatment methods that focus on changing the way smokers think. Externality was the major psychological factor that separated out those who would fail "stop smoking" programs. Not only were smokers more likely to be External to begin with, but the higher the Externality, the less successful they were in maintaining abstinence after the treatment stopped.

LOC AND EATING

Unlike exercise and fitness, which we can avoid if we wish, we all have to eat. But what we eat has long-term consequences for our health, and Locus of Control has consequences for what we eat. For more information, we must return to Cobb-Clark and her Australian colleagues. They asked more than seven thousand men and women questions that revealed whether LOC was associated with healthy eating habits. They used a scientifically accepted set of criteria called the Healthy Eating Index (HEI) that includes (1) eating fruit seven days a week; (2) eating vegetables seven days a week; (3) avoiding (eating less than once per month) fatty, high-cholesterol foods such as fried potatoes, French fries, hot chips, or wedges; and (4) avoiding milk fat by drinking skim or low-fat milk.

I don't think you are going to be surprised by the finding that Internality was associated with much higher HEI scores than was Externality. But I think you will be surprised the highest association between Internality and healthy eating was in the oldest age group (55–69) for men and in the next-youngest age group for women (40–54).[13] Perhaps there is a recognition as we age—at least, if we are Internal—that we are not immortal and eating well will give us a better chance at good health and more years of life.

Other researchers have confirmed Internals have healthier habits and behaviors. Steptoe and Wardle, some of whose work I have referred to earlier, examined the practices of nearly three thousand university students in eighteen countries and found Internals were more likely to exercise, eat breakfast regularly, brush their teeth daily, eat fiber, limit salt, and avoid fat.

They concluded being high on Internality and low on chance Externality reduced risk of becoming obese as much as having social support did.[14]

SUMMARY

What can we conclude about Locus of Control and its relation to exercise, physical fitness, and other healthy behavior? It seems clear Internals not only value exercise and physical fitness more than Externals, but—likely because of that—are more physically fit. Internals are less likely to smoke than Externals to begin with, but if they do smoke, they are also more able to stop than Externals. Internals are also more likely to eat healthy foods, including more fruits and vegetables, than Externals. Since lack of exercise, physical activity, smoking, and eating unhealthy foods have all been linked to obesity, which, in turn, has been identified as a significant risk factor in heart disease, diabetes, and high blood pressure, there appears to be a strong connection between Externality and any number of unhealthy physical outcomes. It turns out being External is a risky business—so risky, in fact, that on average, Externals live four to seven years less than Internals.

But if you are External, do not lose hope. There is good news if you are willing to consider becoming more Internal. German and American psychologists Frank Infurna, Nilam Ram, and Denis Gerstorf collaborated on a study of how changes in perceived control over a sixteen-year period affected mortality over the following nineteen-year period.[15] They gathered information from more than two thousand adults at four different time points: 1986, 1989, 1994, and 2002.

Here's the good news. If, during the sixteen-year period, LOC changed toward Internality, as opposed to remaining the same or moving toward Externality, it translated into the participants living longer and feeling better. In other words, Externality is not cast in stone, and if people are able to become more Internal, they actually appear to gain a shot at a longer life. Now that is something to think about if you are considering lighting up your next cigarette, having a giant piece of cheesecake, and telling yourself, "Whatever will be, will be."

LOC AND COPING WITH PHYSICAL DISEASE

Up to this point, we have been dealing with Locus of Control as a risk factor for the development of serious, debilitating physical illness. Now we turn to the real thing: physical diseases and the role LOC plays in them. Much of what we know in this area comes from the work of Kenneth Wallston and his colleagues at Vanderbilt University's School of Nursing, who constructed the most frequently used health LOC scales.

Wallston has devoted his life to the study of health LOC and how it affects both the development of disease and the response to disease once it has occurred. His devotion to the community good is shown by the fact that he has made the scales he constructed freely available to the public.[16] It should be noted that (1) the items only relate to health and (2) the scale measures two types of Externality, chance and powerful others. The scale has been used so extensively it would be impossible to do it complete justice in this brief space, but I want to present some findings representative of Wallston's and others' work in the area of physical health and disease.

Not surprisingly, those with physical diseases such as diabetes, Parkinson's, sickle cell disease, asthma, and epilepsy tend to be more External.[17] The general impact of a chronic and debilitating disease can make us feel as though we have lost control over our bodies, our health, and most everything else. However, it is crucial to note that once we suffer from a disease, are injured, or undergo surgery, LOC has a significant role in determining how well or how poorly we deal with our difficulties.

Coping well can be a tricky business. When we are ill or injured, we do lose some control over what is happening to us, but we also can make the mistake of thinking there is nothing we can contribute to making ourselves better. We may forget we remain in control of many aspects of how we live with our difficulties and what we do to recover from them. However, we also face the possibility of making the opposite mistake; that is, thinking we have complete control over our recovery and can cure all our ills if we just try hard enough. When we can't and suffer setbacks, we blame ourselves, feel like failures, and become depressed.

The best way to manage ourselves when we are ill or injured is to apply the *Balance Rule of Coping*. This means matching our own personal LOC with the control available to us in the situation. Even if having a disease or enduring an injury makes us more External for a time, it does not make us totally helpless. Using the Internal control expectancies that are left can help us cope and recover. I know this from my own personal experience of having a heart attack and bypass surgery.

COPING WITH A HEART ATTACK AND
SUBSEQUENT SURGERY AND RECOVERY

Bristol, England, can be an enchanting place, especially in an area called Clifton, where seventeenth- and eighteenth-century houses abound and where Bristol University is located. I've often traveled to Bristol during my academic career to work on various research projects involving, among other things, Locus of Control. Since 1991, a unique study of the anteced- ents of physical and mental health called the Avon Longitudinal Study of Parents and Children (ALSPAC) has been underway. Its scientists have followed and tested all children born in 1991 and 1992 in the Bristol envi- rons, as well as their parents. Because my tests were used to measure LOC in both parents and children, I have been very much involved in the study. Over the years, I have become good friends with many of my colleagues in Bristol, including Dr. Jean Golding, the originator of ALSPAC and its chief cheerleader and fund-raiser.

Jean is one of the most remarkable people I have ever met. Her name is linked with almost all the major British longitudinal investigations. The contributions her studies have made to improve the health of children, especially regarding sudden infant death, are staggering and have been recognized by the British government in the form of an honorary degree and an Order of the British Empire. But she has done all this while battling the return of chronic painful symptoms from a childhood bout of polio that would have stopped anyone else in their tracks.

It was from visiting Jean during the summer that Kaaren and I were preparing to return to the United States. We were having a party to thank Jean and her staff for all their help during our stay. It was about four in the afternoon, and everything seemed in order, so I told Kaaren I was going to walk down the hill from our apartment to say goodbye to a colleague who was unable to attend our farewell party.

Looking back, I remember I was not feeling at the top of my game. Things were spinning a bit for me, and my stomach was unsettled, but I chalked that up to the chaos of packing and getting ready to leave. I saw my colleague briefly, said my goodbyes, and left the office. Bristol is a hilly place with many steep ups and downs, and as I started up the hill toward my apartment, I felt very, very odd. I began to sweat and, for some reason, could not continue walking and had to sit down on the steps of the geography department. As I sat there trying to marshal my energy to stand up, I suddenly thought, "I'm having a heart attack!" But, just as quickly, I dismissed this absurd idea. How could I be having a heart attack? I don't smoke, I work out, and no one in my family has heart issues. So I stood and began to walk up the hill again. This time, I only got about twenty steps in before I had to sit down. This time, the message was loud and clear: I was having a heart attack.

What followed was a blur. I do remember receiving kind and supportive care from the doctors and nurses at the Bristol Royal Infirmary hospital, and eventually, I was flown home to Atlanta. On my return, I met my cardiologist, Laurence Sperling, who also happened some years before to have been a student in my undergraduate abnormal psychology class. I comforted myself by remembering he was one of the brightest and best of my undergraduate students and always paid attention during my lectures. I was convinced my life was in good hands. When he returned with the test results, he told me my condition was too serious for medication, and he recommended I have quadruple bypass surgery. I was stunned.

I remember the day I met my surgeon. He and his senior nurse came in, wielding charts to show and videos to play that would describe in great detail what was going to happen to me. As he began to explain what would occur during the surgery, he must have picked up on nonverbal cues from me because he quickly stopped his explanations, put down the remote for the video machine, leaned forward, looked at me directly, and said, "I just want you to know that I am very good at what I do. I have done hundreds of these operations, and you will do just fine." With that, he asked if I had any questions and, after answering the few I had, shook my hand and left.

The surgery was successful, but my recovery was difficult. During the first ten days, I experienced much pain and felt very depressed. I was told to walk a bit, but mostly I just sat and felt helpless. When I went to see Dr. Sperling on the tenth day after surgery, he did all the appropriate tests and proclaimed I was doing fine. But I wasn't feeling fine, and I told him so.

"So," he said. "I think it is time for Dr. Nowicki to get moving again to help himself get better. Would you be willing to participate in a rehab program I'm starting?"

"So soon?" I countered. "Is it safe?"

"We'll be monitoring you all the time, and there are trained nurses and aides present. I think it is important for you to be doing something that you feel is contributing to your recovery, rather than just sitting around waiting to get better. What do you think?" He was telling me it was time to reclaim my Internality over what I could do.

"OK," I said, and the very next morning, I found myself walking on a treadmill under the watchful eyes of the rehabilitation staff. It was scary, and it was wonderful. I remember how relieved I felt that I was finally doing something to reclaim my former life. After many weeks of feeling as though I was at the beck and call of luck, fate, and chance, it felt great to reassert my intention to be Internal again.

Looking back on my experience and how I coped with it, I'm impressed by how much my Locus of Control fluctuated during the course of my illness and recuperation. I often wonder how my recovery would have gone without the push from my cardiologist to enter rehab and my own decision to stick with the treatment program once there. I also wonder what happens to so many heart bypass survivors who decline the offer of a rehabilitation program and are left to reclaim their lives on their own. Me, I am eternally grateful for my choice. So grateful, in fact, that I remain in the program some ten years later.

I think most everyone who is dealing with serious illness or physical injury faces the same challenges I did and has difficult choices to make about how to cope with what is happening to them. I may be biased, but I think applying the Balance Rule of Coping to find the correct balance between personal and situational control is at the center of how well we recover from illness, surgery, and injury.

Diabetes

According to the latest National Diabetes Statistics Report of the Centers for Disease Control and Prevention (CDC), the number of new cases of diabetes has more than tripled from a total of 493,000 in 1980 to more 1,700,000 in 2012. Putting together the number of new cases with those that have already been diagnosed in the past leads to this astounding conclusion: one out of ten Americans and one out of four adults who are sixty-five years of age or older has diabetes. It is the seventh leading cause of death in our country.[18]

Type 1 diabetes is usually diagnosed during childhood or adolescence and is the result of an autoimmune attack on one's own ability to create insulin. We suffer when there is no insulin in the system to transfer glucose from properly digested food to the bloodstream into cells for future use. Those with type 1 diabetes must have injections to provide the insulin that allows the glucose transfer to take place and keep us alive. Usual symptoms of diabetes are increased thirst, pains in hands and feet called neuropathy, and increased glucose in the blood.

In contrast to type 1 diabetes, type 2 diabetes can occur at any age and is the result of fat, muscle, and liver cells becoming less sensitive to the effects of insulin. This forces the pancreas to secrete more insulin to offset the loss of sensitivity, and if it can't keep up, patients develop the typical symptoms of diabetes listed above.

Diabetes is a really major problem, and it becomes an even bigger one when people with the disease fail to comply with treatment protocols. Before we become critical of failures to comply, understand the medical procedures are complex and painful, consisting of insulin injections, glucose monitoring, diet modifications, exercise, and monitoring of blood pressure and cholesterol levels. Only two-thirds of patients who know they have type 2 diabetes comply with care that could help them control the disease they have. If research is to be believed, one of the reasons for the lack of follow-through is that some patients fail to see a connection between their compliance and controlling their disease. In other words, they are External. A quick glance at the websites for the American Heart Association presents numerous self-reports of diabetes patients and their struggles with understanding the power their own behavior and attitude have for a healthier life.

The patient Marcy W is a vivid example of the power of recognizing the connection between lifestyle choices and health outcomes. She describes how she had never paid attention to doctors who told her that her weight, eating habits, and lack of exercise would lead to her premature death. Then, one day, a particular doctor "looked her in the eye" and told her she would not live to be fifty. Somehow, the intensity of this feedback helped connect her to own ability to make herself better. From that day on, for three years, Marcy fought to change her lifestyle and become the master of her own fate. She is thankful for what she has been able to accomplish and has this message for people trying to control diabetes and create a better life for themselves: "I would tell anyone struggling with diabetes this: . . . Small changes do add up to big, big results. Don't ever give up. It's worth everything to keep trying."[19]

Researchers back up the supposition Internals do better with treatment routines than Externals and, as a result, recover more quickly and proficiently.[20] An interesting wrinkle in treatment approaches comes from a study in Italy that experimented with comparing compliance checks (completed individually by medical personnel) with group evaluations (accomplished by staff workers meeting with a number of patients).[21] Over a two-year period, individual visits to patients took place every two to three months for type 1 diabetes and every three to four months for type 2; group visits took place at about the same pace. All compliance interactions were calculated to motivate patients to stick with treatment and to offer them the opportunity to discuss coping strategies. The group approach worked far better than the individual one. Group meetings led to increased Internality and adherence to treatment than individual conferences. In a statement that reminds me of the Balance Rule of Coping, a patient put her experience this way: "It is important because you acquire awareness. I now feel ready to take care of myself."

High Blood Pressure

If you don't have high blood pressure, you probably know somebody who does. The CDC estimates that one out of three of us has high blood pressure, somewhere around seventy million adult Americans.[22] Of these, about half treat their affliction with medicine, exercise, diet, or some combination of all three. That's the good news, but, obviously, the bad news is there are thirty-five million with high blood pressure who don't engage in procedures that would be helpful. The number of people at risk is even larger than that because in addition, one out of three Americans has what is termed *prehypertension*—that is, blood pressure that is high but not high enough to warrant an official diagnosis of a disease.

Often called the silent killer because of its lack of noticeable symptoms, high blood pressure is a significant risk factor in seven out of ten heart attacks, eight out of ten strokes, eight out of ten cases of congestive heart failure, and about half of all kidney disease diagnoses. High blood pressure is a gateway to a remarkably rich variety of ways of killing ourselves, and yet there are millions who don't even know they have it and other millions who know they have it but fail to treat it.

Locus of Control has a lot to do with acquiring the disease called high blood pressure and, once it is acquired, with how it is treated. Can you guess what kind of LOC is associated with high blood pressure? I hope you guessed External. And who is least likely to follow through with treating their high blood pressure once they are aware they have it? Yep, Externals again.

Studies from outside the United States have also found similar associations.[23] In addition, Tantina Hong and her colleagues at Duke were impressed by the ability of Internality to predict adherence in a large group of veterans, as measured by remembering to take pills, noting symptoms, and keeping track of medications.[24] Hong's study calls for more emphasis on the exploration of how LOC can be used to improve adherence to blood pressure (and perhaps other) medication.

Other Diseases

This same LOC effect in coping with the impact of disease connection is often found in a great variety of other physical diseases. Parkinson's, sickle cell disease, epilepsy, and asthma may not be as preventable as obesity, heart disease, and diabetes, but though those suffering from them all are understandably somewhat External, their LOC still has much to say about how well they are dealing with their disease. Even in the group of External patients, the less External among that group are better able to cope with their disease. By coping, I mean they are better at doing the things they need to do to make themselves better and more comfortable. Let me give a few for instances.

Daniel Cukor, Howard Newville, and Rahul Jindal found compared to their more externally controlled patient peers, kidney patients who were more internally controlled were less depressed and more likely to take their medicine when it was prescribed.[25] Lawrence Halimi found better adherence for Internal as opposed to External sufferers of severe asthma.[26]

Locus of Control also has something to say about the problem of depression that often develops in someone trying to cope with a chronic illness. Marilia Zampieri and Elisabete de Souza found as Parkinson's disease progressed and physical and motor symptoms worsened, patients also had to battle depression and its negative effects on their treatment.[27] In this situation, patients who were more Internal adhered to treatment better, showed more initiative in obtaining information about their health status, and were more engaged with activities that promoted a better quality of life, such as physiotherapy and exercise. And they also were less depressed.

That this same association is found in other chronic illnesses such as sickle cell disease and epilepsy suggests LOC may be a significant factor in how effectively patients deal with and recover from chronic and/or severe ailments.

LOC AND COPING WITH SURGERY

Many millions of us will undergo surgery this year, and our attitudes and expectations regarding our role in recovery have much to do with how well we cope afterward. Surgery most often produces stress and anxiety before-hand and depression afterward as we struggle to get well again. We've either experienced this pattern ourselves or have seen it in others close to us. I shared my own bypass surgery experience with you earlier in the chapter. During that experience, I saw firsthand how much my LOC con-tributed to or hindered my recovery. It should be no surprise LOC becomes important in the challenging situation of a disease severe enough to require surgery.

That certainly has been true in the case of recovery from a variety of coronary surgeries. For example, Svein Bergvik, Tore Sorlie, and Rolf Wynn looked at how long it took patients to return to work after coro-nary surgical procedures.[28] When they examined all possible factors deter-mining when patients were well enough to return, they found it was the patients' Locus of Control that played a significant part—and yes, you guessed it: the more External the patients were, the longer it took them to return to work.

Locus of Control has also been found to play a significant role in influencing weight loss and quality of life after bariatric surgery. *Today Show* host Al Roker, actor and comedian Roseanne Barr, *MasterChef* host Graham Elliot, author Anne Rice, and Governor Chris Christie of New Jersey have all gone through a surgical procedure to control their weight.[29] Governor Christie has had a long-running battle with his weight and, in 2013, decided Lap-Band surgery was called for. Although he has not said how much weight he has lost in the years since his operation, his recent comments suggest that it was a success. According to Christie, "It's the best thing that I've ever done for my health. And I look back on it now and wish I'd done it years ago." In response to questions regarding how his doctor thought he was doing, Christie said, "Let me put it to you this way: My cardiologist has donated to my federal PAC, so that probably should tell you everything you need to know."[30]

If past research is to be believed, then chances are Christie is Internal because Internals seem to do better after such surgery than Externals. Compared to Externals, Internals lost more weight and had a higher quality of life. In other words, they were just plain happier than Externals.[31]

If statistics are to be believed, more than a million people will have knee or hip surgery this year. Surprisingly, the greatest increase is in the forty-five- to sixty-five-year-old age group. And the reason for increased rates among this age group is not what you might think, according to David Ayers of the Department of Orthopaedics and Physical Rehabilitation at University of Massachusetts Medical School. Although people tend to assume most knee replacement patients are active Baby Boomers who have hurt themselves by participating too hard in sports and other activities, the reality is different. Knee replacement patients tend to be ages forty to sixty-four and actually fairly unhealthy, with higher rates of obesity and more comorbidities than the over-sixty-five group.[32]

Dealing with the recovery from knee, leg, or foot surgery, especially for those who have neither valued physical exercise nor engaged in healthy activity for decades before their surgery, can create problems, especially if patients are External. Internals have been shown to recover better from anterior cruciate surgery than Externals.[33] They seem to recover better from surgery because they set more realistic goals regarding exercise and other healthy behaviors than Externals.

CAROLINE AND HER PATELLA TEACH US A LESSON IN INTERNALITY

Our Locus of Control is triggered when we find ourselves in situations characterized by novelty, ambiguity, difficulty, and stress. If not much is going on in our lives and we are handling whatever is going on without too much effort, then our Locus of Control is largely dormant and does not play much of a role in how we behave. However, when the going gets tough, when we have a thorny problem to solve or find ourselves in a new and potentially grave situation, our Locus of Control "wakes" and becomes a player in how we decide to solve the problem. Physical injury that requires surgery and long-term care is one of those situations that stimulates us to behave in our customary Internal or External way. Certainly, that was exactly what happened to Caroline when she had her first incident.[34]

Caroline was a self-proclaimed sports junkie at thirteen years of age. She played basketball, softball, soccer, and field hockey and dreamed of being a star swimmer in college. Her dreams turned into nightmares beginning with what she thought was a freak accident while playing basketball. She remembers falling, screaming for help, and noticing her leg was twisted in an impossible direction. She hadn't broken it but had dislocated her kneecap.

Caroline did not need surgery and, after physical therapy, happily returned to playing sports. But over the span of two years, even though she was wearing a brace, she continued to suffer painful dislocations of her patella—five in total. This is when she and her doctors realized she needed "quality of life" surgery that would allow her to carry on typical activities but not sports.

The surgery was invasive, and the recovery took a year. Caroline felt supported by friends who visited often and who painted her toenails as well as just hanging out and talking. It was difficult: "There were many nights where I felt so sorry for myself that I just wanted to lie in bed and cry. But I told myself that it had to get better eventually."

Caroline learned she had to make compromises, like wearing her knee brace to the prom. Even though she felt better, she knew playing sports again was impossible, so she became the manager for the field hockey team.

All was going well until during her junior year of high school, she "wiped out" in the cafeteria and had to undergo additional surgeries. Once again, she worked herself back into shape and made some additional decisions. As Caroline puts it, "Now that I don't have sports, I have realized that I need to rely on academics more, so keeping good grades is very important to me. I plan to study occupational therapy in college." She has volunteered at a hospital where she could work with children to help them "find happiness no matter what life has thrown at them."

She sums up her experiences so far in this way: "It's not easy to lose things that you love to do, like I loved sports. But I have found a love for new things that are within my capabilities. Although I can't do as much as I used to, I have found other important things in my life."

Caroline's final thought for us is not to take anything for granted because you never know when something might be taken away. She says, "It's been a great lesson because it lets me know that I can really achieve anything if I put my mind to it!" Can anyone doubt that her Internal approach to dealing with her problems helped her negotiate the turbulence of a challenging adolescence? It is a lesson from which all of us can learn.

PART 4

APPLYING WHAT WE KNOW ABOUT LOCUS OF CONTROL

INTRODUCTION TO PART 4

Welcome to the final chapter of the Locus of Control story.

It is here we focus on how to apply what we know about this concept in regard to reaching two general goals: first, developing "appropriate" Internality, and second, modifying learning situations to maximize the potential success of Internals and Externals when we do not have the time or resources to change their orientation.

These are important objectives. Why? Because all else being equal, being appropriately Internal leads us to do better in school, work, sports, and relationships. Internality also helps soften the jolts of physical and relationship difficulties; at the same time, it provides us with an effective coping strategy and a way of forging forward, even when times are tough.

Of course, things are rarely completely equal, so our Internality must be tempered with an awareness of its appropriateness for a given situation. Here's a quick example of what I mean. When my grandson, Soren, was about three years old, his ball rolled under my car. Without even a moment of hesitation, he went to the back of the car and began pushing with all his might, thinking if he just pushed hard enough, he would be able to move the car and retrieve his ball. His Internality at that point, though impressive, was inappropriate for the situation. Like Soren, we, too, can find ourselves in situations in which being extremely Internal is simply the wrong way to handle things.

Earlier in the book, I used the phrase "Balance Rule" to refer to the match between our own personal control and the demands of the situation. I'm certainly not the first person to believe balancing our motivation with the nature of the task is important. Eminent theologian Reinhold Niebuhr is often given credit for penning the earliest form of the Balance Rule. With some minor changes, Niebuhr's formulation became the Serenity

Prayer often used in Alcoholics Anonymous and other twelve-step programs: "God, grant me the serenity to accept the things I cannot change, courage to change the things I can, and the wisdom to know the difference." This simple but profound statement encapsulates a central human truth, one that applies particularly to the insights afforded by our investigations into the effect of Locus of Control in our lives. Keep this in mind as you read the last chapter.

CHAPTER 10

CHANGING LOCUS OF CONTROL OR MODIFYING THE SITUATION

"There are two primary choices in life: to accept conditions as they exist or accept the responsibility for changing them."
—**Dennis Waitley**

Scientists have learned a great deal about the factors involved in the development of Internal and External control expectancies. On the other hand, there is still much we need to know if we are to provide parents and teachers with information they can use to guide the development of appropriate Internality in children. Because so much of what we know has come from the research on antecedents covered in chapter 3, I want to restate that information here.

THE CONTRIBUTION OF THOSE WHO STUDIED ANTECEDENTS OF LOC

Researchers who have studied antecedents of Locus of Control have highlighted the prominence of caring adults (parents and teachers) in providing the proper conditions for the learning of Internality. These researchers point out the importance of adult personality and attitudes in creating situations in which children can learn about themselves and what they can do.

We have learned for Internality to develop sufficiently, children need an appropriately safe environment in which they can feel secure, nurtured, and supported. Within such settings, they are encouraged to explore and interact with their surroundings to gain awareness of what they can and can't control. To learn how Internal they are, they must have their behavior consistently and contingently reinforced by others.

On the other hand, Externality takes root when children have guardians who are overprotective—thus allowing children fewer opportunities to learn their limits—or who are inconsistent, unpredictable, or outright hostile in their parenting. The result is that children become too anxious and constricted to explore at all.

Though what I've described applies primarily to the development of Internality or Externality in children, this principle can also be applied to adults. Adults, like children, find themselves in environments in which their Internality is either nurtured or discouraged.

Very little of what is known about antecedents has made its way into the change programs I'm going to describe next. Change researchers rarely mention parents and teachers as instrumental. They don't reveal what the children are experiencing at home or in the classroom, let alone emphasize a warm, caring, and supportive environment. Most of the time, researchers isolate children and study them separate from the enduring, meaningful context in which they live. I'm not sure why this is the case. It could be for the sake of experimental control, or it may reflect a lack of understanding of how important these elements are. The same criticisms are unfortunately true about change programs involving adults as well.

WAYS TO MODIFY LOC: ONLINE MEDIA

Magazines, newspapers, and the Internet are filled with Locus of Control "experts" willing to share their "knowledge" about this concept and how to assist in bringing about greater Internality. The increasing number of websites concerned with LOC demonstrates how thoroughly it has trickled down into our everyday world.

Website "advisors" tend to follow a consistent pattern in their presentations. First, they usually give a brief, cursory definition of Locus of Control. This is followed by a sentence or two explaining if you want to be a success, then being Internal is good, and being External is bad. Often, this assertion is followed by a brief list of LOC "style questions" for the reader to complete, inventions of the writer or bits and pieces out of context from someone else's test. When you finish the test, you then can read words of guidance on what you need to do in order to get yourself or your child an Internal LOC. Sometimes, to give the presenter a halo of importance, an expert is quoted.

In brief, there is no shortage of advice from online media. Hints or suggestions for becoming more Internal can include most anything: setting goals or monitoring your "self-talk" or learning to breathe better or taking more walks or eating the right kind of foods or any number of other things.

While none of the suggestions seem harmful, and some may even be reasonable, they all lack one thing: scientific backing to properly attest to their value. But what really bothers me about these so-called experts is the way they misrepresent what LOC is and what it will take to change it. Most media pundits give the impression it is a simple phenomenon that can be easily and quickly modified merely by undertaking a few undemanding tasks. Changing orientations, to them, is as easy as changing a pair of shoes that doesn't quite go with your outfit. I can't tell you how many days I have wished they were right on this score, especially when I'm trying to help an External client in therapy or to find ways to save a high-risk External child who is on the brink of self-destruction. At those times, I truly wish modifying Locus of Control were as simple as these "experts" suggest it is.

It's not easy to gain appropriate Internality—not by a long shot. Consider the time it takes for our LOC to develop, the years of interaction and feedback. Old habits aren't unlearned without a struggle. But the good news is LOC can be changed. It just takes the right kind of effort and time. We just have to apply what we know. If we make the commitment to change, we can transform our lives. I know this to be true because I have seen it happen many times over.

WAYS TO MODIFY LOC: DEFINING WHAT IT IS AND WHAT TO CHANGE

Here are a few basic ways in which Externals differ from Internals. Internals expect to play a part in what happens to them; Externals don't. Internals learn from both their failures and successes; Externals learn from neither. Internals gather information for use in the present and the future; Externals see this as a waste of time. Being Internal not only helps us deal with our present difficulties, it also better prepares us for those difficulties yet to come.

WAYS TO MODIFY LOC: HELPING PEOPLE BECOME MORE INTERNAL

I hope you can understand why I and others who seek to modify Locus of Control usually favor Internality. Internals are the kind of people who wake up in the morning feeling as though they have the tools and energy to handle whatever the day is going to bring. It must be disconcerting to feel External and believe you do not have access to ways to affect what is going to happen to you.

Certainly, Externality often helps to soften failure and to protect our self-esteem when we disappoint ourselves and others, but this defensive Externality comes at a high cost: it prevents us from examining our actions to see if what we did might have contributed to our difficulty. Externality prevents us from learning from our mistakes because, by its very definition, the mistakes were not of our doing but the result of luck, fate, chance, or powerful others.

Efforts to modify LOC have taken place at the individual, school, and community levels with children, adolescents, and young and older adults. Unfortunately, the results have proven be somewhat disappointing. While there have been some successes, we should be doing better.

APPROACHES TO CHANGING LOC: ATTENDING CAMP

Many people attended summer camp as children. I was not one of them. My mother led me to believe camps were frightening places where unpleasant things happened to you. Ergo, if I did not straighten up and behave as she wanted me to, I might be "sent to camp." My fear was that once sent away, I might never be heard from again.

Think how I felt when I learned camps were places children actually wanted to go. Based on what I now know, I'm not in the least surprised researchers have looked at experiences at camp or in camplike settings as a potential means of instilling Internality. Most of the studies have focused on disadvantaged children with the assumption camp would be a corrective learning experience for them, away from their negative and unresponsive home environments.

Early in my career, I served as an evaluator of an Atlanta Public Schools outdoor camp program for inner-city children.[1] The program was a five-day-long camp experience with all the usual sporting and recreational activities. The counselors were asked to reward the children whenever they saw them behaving appropriately. At the last meeting on Friday afternoon, each child was given a faux–Native American camp name, and the counselors told the group about a behavior-reward sequence that earned the name. For example, one youngster was given the name of Swift Arrow because he quickly cleaned up for himself after meals.

My LOC test was administered at the beginning and end of each five-day camp. Children were significantly more Internal at the end of the camp experience than the beginning. Unfortunately, with a lack of comparison groups, there was no way of knowing what exactly about the camp experience was responsible for the change. No additional follow-up was done, so we do not know whether the changes toward Internality were maintained after the children returned home.

That was not the case in another study that used a camp experience to make changes in, among other things, children's LOC. In this camp experience, the goal was to use physical activities to bring about change in children with asthma.[2] The campers did gain Internality, which, impressively, was maintained when they were retested a month later. Unfortunately, there was no comparison group.

SUMMARY

Camp experiences do move LOC scores toward Internality, but the changes are generally not maintained, and the exact mechanisms responsible have not been identified. This rather lukewarm evaluation does not mean such experiences are not valuable and could not be used to modify LOC. (Keep in mind camp sponsors weren't explicitly setting out to change this LOC but simply wanted children to have a positive experience. LOC changes were a convenient way of documenting that effect.)

What is lacking in the camp study approach is a conscious attempt to tie together the children's behavior and the hoped-for outcomes of such an experience. The camps did seem to provide the warm, nurturing, and supportive environments necessary for learning the contingencies connecting behavior and consequence. What they lacked was an intentionality of approach in teaching children specifically about the connection between behavior and consequences. In other words, camps may be an excellent circumstance in which to apply programs for changing Locus of Control but, thus far, this has not been done.

APPROACHES TO CHANGING LOC: SCHOOL-BASED APPROACHES

As with camps, schools seem like ideal places to set out to change children's Locus of Control. Schools, after all, are where academic achievement takes place, and we already know the close relationship that exists between LOC and academic success or failure. Unfortunately, few of the studies that have looked into change in this trait have actually focused on academic settings. Rather, such change has merely been seen as a peripheral consequence of altering other school-related behaviors. Researchers in this area usually favor their own pet theoretical perspective and seldom mention anything about research done on antecedents of Locus of Control.

School-Based Changes: Children

Loretta Autry and Michael Langenbach completed a study in which they were trying to increase constructive behaviors (like engaging in the activity specified by the teacher) and decrease disruptive behaviors (like talking out of turn or making inappropriate noises) through the use of behavioral monitoring (teachers giving rewards) or self-monitoring (students rewarding themselves).[3] Their program lasted thirteen days. During this time, children became more Internal using both approaches. Both systems of rewarding succeeded in making students more aware of their behavior and caused them to feel as though they were in charge of acquiring rewards. The greater awareness of that connection, in turn, led them to become more internally controlled.

This type of systematic application of rewards and punishments has successfully changed LOC in both a rural, predominantly white group of students and an inner-city African American population. The longer children remained in the studies, the more Internal they became.

Rather than focus on rewarding specific behaviors, some authors, such as Simona Trip and her colleagues, have taken the approach of attacking the "irrational and dysfunctional" belief inherent in Externality.[4] The authors believe teaching children to think rationally will increase the chances of their being healthy, clear-thinking adults. Through stories, games, and play, students in Trip's study were taught to reduce their dependence on absolute statements and widen the number of choices they had available to them. Students receiving the "rational emotive education" intervention met one hour a week for thirteen weeks. The impact on the students' Locus of Control was "mildly" successful. The two comparison groups that received other experiences once a week, for thirteen weeks or had no intervention at all actually became more External. In contrast, the students in the rational emotive education group stayed about the same. As a result of the changes, at the end of the thirteen weeks, the rational emotive children were significantly more Internal than the other two groups. However, it is difficult to be impressed by a change program whose most positive outcome is making students stay the same.

One researcher reported he successfully changed LOC, but, unfortunately, there are questions about the research that make it difficult to accept what he found. Russ Hill published a book in 2011on how to change Locus of Control based on a study he had completed forty-four years earlier.[5] In the book, he describes what he calls a "validating field study" of three groups of fifth-grade students from ninety-nine classrooms in Philadelphia. When compared to other comparison groups, the students receiving his program apparently became more Internal. But the strange thing about this "field study" is that although it appeared to be highly successful, the results were never published, nor has anyone replicated the study with other groups of students. Hill's book describes the approach he used in some detail, so I hope others will use and test his framework. Until then, his approach and his findings, although theoretically promising and practically detailed, must be considered speculative and regarded with caution.

School-Based Changes: Adolescents

Marshall Duke and I were consultants on a study that applied the Effective Learning Program (ELP).[6] The ELP was developed by Sherleen Sisney, an educator and school consultant, and her colleagues in response to an initiative from the Governor's Scholars Program in her state. It essentially is a program designed to prevent high-risk students from dropping out of high school by helping them understand they must repair their disconnect between actions and consequences in the classroom. The ELP instructors utilized a team-teaching approach to maximize interdisciplinary learning opportunities while modeling the effect via relationship building in order to persuade these students to stay in school.

The program was centered on junior- and senior-level students with a smaller-scale program of classes available at the sophomore level. Ideally, ELP students participated for both their junior and senior years of high school. Thirty-eight students considered at risk for dropping out of high school received the intervention. In addition, regular education students from the same high school and ELP-eligible students who did not receive the ELP intervention served as comparison groups. As had been hoped, a significantly greater percentage of ELP students graduated (92 percent) compared with the comparison group of at-risk students (32 percent), all of whom met the goals instituted for the ELP program.

In terms of LOC, the ELP students became significantly more Internal each succeeding year, in contrast to the students in the at-risk comparison group, who became significantly more External each succeeding year.

The ELP program was successful both in cutting down on dropout rates for at-risk students and in moving them toward greater Internality. However, this program also falls short because it fails to point out what exactly led to its rate of success.

Certainly, the teachers who were trained to (1) make students aware of their External behavior and speech and (2) help them construct and practice more Internal ways of thinking, talking, and behaving are strong candidates for the mechanisms of change. Unfortunately, monitoring and measuring the actual application of the intervention was not reliably done, so we cannot draw sound conclusions. What we do know is the ELP program in its entirety worked at what it was built to accomplish; however, we cannot identify the specific parts of the program that brought about specific changes in the students.

School-Based Change: College Students

Changing LOC can happen at any age. We now turn to attempts to intervene with college students. John Roueche and Oscar Mink devised what they called a "counseling for Internality" strategy to help alienated students learn to be more Internal by focusing on their verbalizations.[7] Counselors helped the students become aware of how their Externality was reflected in their speech and how their External speech affected how they thought.

These counselors were trained to challenge and confront students' External statements and then help replace them with Internal ones. For example, an External statement such as, "I'll never be able to understand this textbook," would be challenged, and the student would be encouraged to replace it with a more Internal one, such as, "If I just take it at a page at a time and reach out to the teacher if I run into problems, I'll be able to understand what I'm reading." Counselors also positively rewarded students' Internal statements verbally by making affirming statements such as, "I like what you just said." The main goal of counseling was for students become more fluent in speaking in Internal statements.

Students from nine community colleges took part for three semesters. Although findings were complex, it was clear participation in the counseling intervention made students more Internal, with white students changing the most, African American students the least, and Mexican American students somewhere in the middle. Unfortunately, the findings were never published in any journal, nor did there seem to be any follow-up in the form of other colleges adopting this approach.

In contrast to Roueche and Mink, who zeroed in on changing speech as a vehicle for changing Locus of Control, Mark McLeod and his colleagues evaluated the ability of a study-abroad experience to make college students more Internal.[8] Today's college students often participate in programs that take them from their home school and place them in a foreign city, school, or environment for varying lengths of time. To read the publicity put out by the programs, you would believe the experience could only be positive and life-changing for all involved. However, most colleges do not evaluate the effect of these experiences on students' personalities or academic performance.

McLeod and his colleagues (of whom I was one) assessed students' LOC before and after their semester study-abroad experience in Europe. Compared to typical students who spent the same semester in the United States, students who went abroad became more Internal and, impressively, maintained their Internality a semester after they returned. As with the camp studies, the authors admitted they could not identify the mechanisms responsible for changes toward Internality. They did offer some possible candidates based on the results of focus groups they held when students returned from their trip. Perhaps the most common refrain heard from the students was that they felt they could take some risks in meeting people from other cultures because they felt "secure and supported" by the study-abroad program; a refrain that echoes the description offered by antecedent researchers for the development of Internality.

SUMMARY

School-based intervention programs have had some success in making individuals more Internal. However, their greatest failing is the inability to identify the mechanisms responsible for change. Making students aware of the connection between how they are speaking and what they are doing appears to be helpful in generating changes toward Internality. Behavioral modification techniques hold some promise, but finding and identifying key mechanisms for changing LOC remains a difficult and elusive task.

We need well-organized studies that focus on directly changing LOC and that use observable, clear, and measurable procedures that could be adopted by others. Most interventions are brief. Researchers seem unaware changing this trait might take a concentrated effort over an extended period of time. It is no accident that the longer participants stayed in change programs, the more progressively Internal they became.

In addition, change programs should include important people in the life of the participants, such as teachers, parents, and perhaps even friends of participants, because such relationships are instrumental in the development and maintenance of LOC. Until we include and evaluate these additional elements, our attempts may not be as effective as they could be.

APPROACHES TO CHANGING LOC: COMMUNITY-BASED APPROACHES

Besides camps and schools, there have been attempts to change Locus of Control at the community level as well. Generally, researchers have taken two approaches: seek to make the community more receptive to attempts at being more Internal, or concentrate on fostering the growth of a particular set of skills that can be used to increase the community's Internality.

Frank Knapp Jr. and Lawrence McClure were invited by a state housing authority to develop a program to make the community environment more stimulating and improve the lives of individuals living in a housing project.[9] The researchers sought to accomplish these goals by giving the participants "tutorial assistance, values clarification workshops, psychological coun-seling, referral services and constructive activities." From an LOC perspec-tive, a major flaw in this program is that the invitation to intervene did not come from the people living in the housing project but rather from an outside power, the housing authority—not the best way for residents to feel they had something to do with making the intervention happen.

Researchers attempted to improve quality of life of the residents by making the environment more receptive to residents' attempts to change their lives. If the environment were more open and responsive, then (it was reasoned) residents' Internal behaviors would be more likely to be rewarded.

While the authors of the study had good intentions, the fact that dif-ferent interventions were used with different age groups and at different times and the spotty participation of the residents compromised the success of the project. In spite of these shortcomings, however, there proved to be some positive results. Participating adults became more Internal over time, but, as is so often the case, the researchers were not certain why this happened. While they speculated the problem-solving workshops they ran could have had a positive effect, they provided no evidence to support this speculation.

Still, I have to at least respect the honesty of the researchers, who sum up their study with the following quote. "A generally positive program and evaluation were achieved despite vague goals, global treatments, prema-ture termination and nonrandom selection of experimental and comparison housing units." Not exactly what you want to hear if you are trying to adopt an intervention to use clear and structured methods calculated to change the Locus of Control of your participants.

The next study I'm going to describe is a breath of fresh air compared to the ones we've been looking at so far because it clearly describes what the authors wanted to do, what they did, and what they found out. And it was successful in changing LOC!

Frederic Wolinsky and his colleagues wanted to provide older adults with a "cognitive training experience" (Advanced Cognitive Training for Independent and Vital Elderly, ACTIVE) in hopes it would reverse the trend toward Externality in people over sixty-five years of age.[10] They were building on previous findings from a national representative study that suggested personal control had a positive impact on health and functioning as far as two decades forward.[11] What they found out was that, compared to same-age control group participants who participated in a different program, older adults who had experienced the ACTIVE training program improved their reasoning ability and speed of processing and became more Internal. They concluded that cognitive training that targets reasoning and speed of processing can improve the cognitive-specific sense of control over one's life.

Wolinsky and his colleagues' results are impressive. Before research began, he and others involved with this large and multifaceted study spent time identifying cognitive factors they reasoned were related to Internality and then targeted them for improvement. What is striking is, while the program took place over a five-year period, the actual training included just ten one-hour sessions for most participants. By targeting and improving cognitive factors associated with Locus of Control, the researchers were able move the participants toward Internality while most same-age peers were moving in the opposite direction, toward Externality.

SUMMARY

Some community attempts to change LOC suffer from the same shortcomings found in camp and school studies—that is, participants generally become more Internal as a result of an experience, but the researchers cannot identify the factors responsible. In contrast, Wolinsky and his associates' study provides a model for others to follow. The researchers used a theoretical perspective to identify what should be changed in order to change LOC, followed by an intervention to alter the identified abilities. Then, they showed the program worked. What is especially useful to us is that we know exactly the reasons for the successes reported in the program. If anyone wanted to replicate the intervention program, they could—and they should.

OVERALL EVALUATION OF APPROACHES TO CHANGE LOC

Studies have shown a variety of different approaches can move External children, adults, and older adults toward Internality. While we don't always know the specific actions that bring about change, we do know raising awareness of how we think and act, illuminating connections between our actions and their consequences, encouraging sensible goal setting, rewarding Internal speech and behavior, using praise and encouragement, and creating safe and secure situations are all aspects of the process toward making us more Internal.

There are two approaches to applying what we know about Locus of Control. The purpose of the first is to change orientations from Externality to Internality. In contrast, the second is to accept significant numbers of individuals are External and use what we know about what motivates them to structure experiences that will assist them to be successful.

CHANGING YOUR OWN LOC

Here are some ways to increase our awareness of the connections between what we do and what happens to us and move us toward Internality. Be reminded any process of change will take a significant amount of time and diligence to produce positive results.

1. Generate choices. To offset their propensity to rigidly adhere to the idea we only have one choice about how to behave, Externals should pinpoint a recent, stressful situation that has often occurred in their lives and make a list of all other possible choices for action in that situation. Don't worry about the worth of the choices or the possibility of their success; just come up with as many choices as you can and write them down.

This is called *lateral thinking*, a term first coined by philosopher Edward de Bono, who found this kind of exercise frees our mind of rigidity and helps prepare us for change.[12] After we have made our list, we can ask friends or colleagues to join us in this exercise to help generate more choices. Getting input from others often opens our eyes to new options we may not have thought of on our own.

2. Set sensible goals. Externals are notorious for failing to set any goals or for setting them unrealistically. I have one particular External friend in mind here. Last January, he set a goal to become fit by Valentine's Day. When I asked him what he meant by "fit," he said, "I'll have lost fifty pounds and be able to spend an hour on the Precor machine at level ten resistance!" He was absolutely convinced he would be able to do this even though he was seriously overweight and had not been to a gym since last year, when he made a similar set of goals he failed to reach. I have to relate that he failed again.

Externals need to formulate small, realistic goals that can actually be achieved. Setting smaller goals increases the likelihood of success so that we can be aware of and rewarded for the connection between our effort and outcomes. Researchers call this method *Goal Attainment Scaling*. Rather than setting just one big goal, it is best to describe a continuum of goals anchored at one end by no progress and at the other end by complete success. With those two extremes in place, a person may begin setting up immediate and intermediate goals between them.

For example, in the case of my External friend above, while we would accept his initially stated goal of losing fifty pounds, we would also do well to generate a series of goals. How much weight loss would he consider to be at least somewhat satisfactory each week over the six-week period between New Year's and Valentine's? One pound? Five pounds? Ten pounds? Let's say he decides that the satisfactory weekly goal was three pounds, while the ultimately satisfactory goal was fifty pounds. By setting more realistic goals, he has a higher probability of experiencing success and gaining awareness of what he is doing to garner that success. Smaller goals also allow us to better map out what we need to do to achieve them. This is a sure recipe for moving toward Internality.

3. Speak Internally to ourselves, then to others. Another way we can begin to behave in ways that will move us toward Internality is to examine our self-talk. We know Externals spend too much of their time talking themselves into failure. Their inward speech is sprinkled with absolute statements that are often negative and fail to tie together cause and effect. Remember Sergio Garcia, the professional golfer trying to explain why he

lost? In his press conference, he declared unknown, uncontrollable negative forces prevented him from winning. This type of explanation provides
no road map for doing better the next time.

To become aware of the extent of your Externality, record yourself
talking about a problem you are having, whether at work, at school, or in
your social life. Afterward, count the number of absolute, negative, and
repetitive statements you make. Write each one down and come up with
a relative, positive, and different response to say out loud and write down
in a notebook. Such exercises can help you become more aware of your
self-talk, which is often used in a self-injurious way, resulting in enhanced
Externality. It can provide you with the beginnings of the new verbal language of Internality.

4. Write in a journal. James Pennebaker, at the University of Texas,
has developed an intervention that has received considerable research
support.[13] He found the simple act of writing about a vexing issue can
produce positive changes in ourselves if continued over a period of time.

According to Pennebaker, the reason expressive writing works so well
is that it forces us to slow down and reevaluate the life circumstance on
which we are focusing. Writing also requires us to produce some degree
of structure for our thoughts. Putting thoughts and emotions into words
helps us become more aware of how we think. Awareness is important for
us if we wish to change our LOC. Writing about our problems demands a
different representation of the events in our brain and in our memory, and
those changes force us to look at ourselves and what we are doing in a new
and different way.

If we were to apply Pennebaker's intervention to changing Locus of
Control, we would direct participants to write about how it feels to be
External and then what it would be like to be Internal in a variety of academic, personal, social, work, or sports situations. They would write for
thirty minutes twice a week. Within a week or two, participants' stories
would tend to change from largely reflecting helplessness and passivity to
reflecting strength and activity. Their behavior afterward would soon cor-
respond to this positive change of attitude.

5. Evaluate. We must understand we are always choosing how to behave from among a variety of options we have available. Externals are not aware they have choices; they believe they only have a few. Becoming aware of the fact of the existence of options is one of our first steps to thinking and acting in more internally controlled ways.

As we become aware we have many options to choose from, we also become more aware we must take responsibility for the choices we make. Constant evaluation of our choices is a crucial part of the process of thinking and acting more Internally. Evaluation helps us to highlight the most advantageous choices and discard those that are encumbering and self-destructive.

To assist in the evaluation process, we can use charting and journaling activities to help identify and track our Internal and External behaviors over time. To gain a fresh perspective, we should ask others to observe us and give feedback about our behaviors. For maximum effect, we ought to cue others into specific behaviors we have identified as candidates for change. It may also be useful to post a chart on the refrigerator or in a note-book and keep track of the behaviors being targeted.

Each day, we should complete a journal entry in which we describe what we thought about and what we did during the day and the good and bad things that happened to us. This daily journal writing differs from the more concentrated single-issue writing Pennebaker suggests above. In this writing task, we shouldn't think too much about what we are writing, but simply write things down "fast and furious." At the end of each week, it may be useful to look back to see how many absolutes and negatives characterize the writing and to highlight each entry suggesting Externality. As we write more like Internals, we begin to think and behave more like Internals, and we'll no doubt find fewer examples of External behavior or thought in our writing.

Proper expectancies are the real payoff and endpoint for those hoping to become more Internal. With correct personal and situational expectancies, we can know what to do and when to do it, thus achieving the greatest likelihood of success for our academic, business, or interpersonal goals. This method has proven to be effective for changing LOC, but it takes time to make it happen properly for ourselves.[14] Coincidentally, one way of telling we are acting more Internally is by our persistence at completing the writing.

These recommendations can be summarized into what I call AGREE (Awareness, Goals, Responsibility, Evaluation, and Expectancy), a program of practical and easily applied procedures I have used in my own life and my personal counseling practice. Let me take you briefly through its main aspects.

AGREE

A is for *awareness*. Awareness of your own LOC and the degree of Internality/Externality suitable for your situation helps guide your intervention. If you have the opportunity, take scientifically recommended LOC tests. A great way to get an even better reading of your awareness is have people close to you complete the test as they perceive you. Notice where you and they disagree. Talk to them about the differences. This way, you might even be able to get ideas of what you might need to focus on to change.

G is for *goals*. Set goals that are practical and allow you to easily assess if what you are doing is moving you toward success. If you have become more aware of a difference between what you thought your LOC was and how others saw it, you may have a good idea of what you have to work on.

Goal Attainment Scaling will help you avoid the common mistake of setting up unrealistic goals. For example, if, through testing, you became aware you were seen by others as more External than you thought you were, you want to do something to change toward Internality. However, since we know changing LOC takes time and persistence, it would be a good idea to set up intermediate goals that would reflect progress toward the greater Internality you are seeking.

R is for *responsibility*. With increased awareness and the setting of more realistic and reachable goals, you will be ready to be responsible for choosing how you will change your LOC expectancies. This is the time for making lists about what you want to change and how you are going to do it. Don't be ashamed to post your lists; they will keep you aware of what you need to accomplish. When you fail, as you will at times, examine the reasons it happened. Continue to become aware of the connection between the way you act and what happens to you.

Identify your external control expectancies which usually involve blame, weakness, rigidity, chance or fate and wishful thinking. Practice speaking in Internal ways. Say positive Internal statements out loud to yourself, then in a whisper, and, finally, silently until they sink in. These suggestions are consistent with what Sean Connolly offered in his counseling model for changing LOC expectancies.[15]

One of the major ways to change the way we think about things is to write about them. The major goal here is to change from External to Internal ways of communicating to yourself at first and to others later. Following Pennebaker's procedure, you would need to write about how it feels to be External and then what it would be like to be Internal. Pick out those important personal and social situations in your life and then write about how you would behave as an Internal and as an External in them. For example, write how you would behave at a social gathering, or in class, or at a meeting. As suggested by Pennebaker, this formal, focused writing should be done twice a week for thirty minutes at a time.

E is for *evaluation.* Constant evaluation of your choices is a crucial part of the AGREE process. Evaluation assists you in creating and highlighting the most advantageous behavior-outcome sequences while also helping you discard those behaviors that are encumbering or self-destructive. The charting and journaling activities discussed above will be helpful in the evaluation process as well. To give you a fresh perspective, I also suggest you seek out others to observe you and provide you feedback about your behaviors.

E is for *expectancies.* Proper and realistic expectancies are, to repeat, the real payoff and endpoint of the AGREE process. With correct personal and situational expectancies, you will know what to do and when to do it so that you may have the greatest likelihood of meeting your academic, business, or interpersonal goals. Retaking the LOC tests can be useful here to evaluate your progress in gaining appropriate Internal control expectancies.

HOW TO MAKE EXTERNALS MORE MOTIVATED
AND INCREASE THEIR CHANCES OF SUCCESS

We now turn from a focus on changing Locus of Control to one in which we accept we have neither the time nor the expertise to make that happen in many situations. In such instances, we use what we know about LOC to help motivate Externals to succeed. One such situation is presented next.

Imagine you are a substitute teacher and you have just found out you are going to take over a third-grade class for the rest of the year. The teacher you will be replacing has had to have emergency surgery, and though she is recovering well, she won't be returning until the following semester. From all you've heard, this class is going to be a challenge. It's not that they differ intellectually from the other third-grade students, but, compared to their peers, they are at the bottom of the barrel in academic achievement. Based on the general report from the principal and individual reports you've read about each student, you've come to one firm conclusion: you are inheriting a class of externally controlled children who aren't achieving up to their potential.

How are you going to approach this class? You do know you are internally controlled yourself, and you are aware of the research showing better student achievement is correlated with greater Internality of teachers.[16] What sorts of teaching methods and disciplinary practices will you employ with the students? You do know something about what motivates Internals and Externals. Perhaps you can use this to improve the academic performance of your soon-to-be students.

You don't have the time or resources to institute a full-blown program to make your students more Internal. Even if you did, your reading of the LOC literature shows you it will take more than a quick fix to accomplish anything substantial. You are, after all, a schoolteacher with twenty-four students; you don't have much spare time. How are you supposed to launch a full-scale, intense program to change your students' LOC? You realize that is impossible to do. How, in short, can you motivate Externals to achieve up to their potential? What do you know that you could begin to use come Monday, when you are scheduled to meet your class for the first time?

The above scenario reflects a dilemma faced by someone responsible for motivating a group of people who are External, whether such a group is found in a prenatal class for expectant parents, a foreign-language seminar, or an instructional learning class for patients about to undergo some kind of surgical procedure. If you are attempting to instruct or motivate a group of people who are External, what can you do to help them accept your guidance so that they can be successful?

MOTIVATING EXTERNALS:
USE STRUCTURE AND PLENTY OF IT

Externals are more comfortable in a highly structured situation, while Internals prefer to have less structure and more freedom to choose what they do. Knowing this, the teacher could start the day by presenting the students with a detailed plan for what they are going to do and the work they will be expected to perform during each class period. Externals will be more comfortable knowing this information. "Free play" sounds good to many of us, but not to Externals. Teachers should even structure and guide "free play" by providing a limited number of choices. The day should begin with a meeting in which the day's activities are presented, posted, and referred to often. The end of the day should include a summary of what was done, what to do for homework, and an idea of what will be coming tomorrow.

In contrast, Internals prefer less structured activities. They like to make their own structure and decide on their own how to spend their time within that framework. If given a chance, they would probably opt for free time whenever possible. The best way to teach Internals is to inform them of a goal, point them to the materials needed to accomplish that goal, let them know when the task has to be completed, and then let them complete it on their own. If you discover you have some Internals among the Externals in your class, you might "cull" them out and provide them with a less structured approach than you have for your External students.

MOTIVATING EXTERNALS: HAVE THEM COOPERATE RATHER THAN COMPETE

Internals always seem ready to compete when the situation calls for it, which is why they do so well in school, business, and athletics. Not so with Externals. When Externals face a competitive situation, they seem to shut down and stop trying. I once did a study that tested how Internals and Externals responded to instructions either to compete against or to cooperate with a same-age partner. Internals achieved the same whether they were competing or cooperating, and, overall, they performed better than Externals. But Externals responded to competitive and cooperative conditions differently, and we can use that difference to help them perform better.

You may remember in one of my studies that when Externals were asked to cooperate with another child, they performed almost twice as well as when they were asked to compete. In fact, in the cooperative condition, they outperformed the Internals. Externals appear to be more sensitive to situational demands than Internals, but what is it about cooperative situations that leads them to perform better? One informed guess is that they are responding to social cues. In the study, the cooperative instructions emphasized that each child's score was important to the final outcome, that the other person was depending on what the child did. Perhaps that was enough to motivate the Externals to improve their performance.

In any case, what can our teacher use from this study to motivate her External students? Cooperation, that's what. She would be clever to set up tasks and projects in which students work together rather than compete against each other. To build on that approach, rather than posting or publicizing which individual students did the best, she could call attention to how the class did as a whole. In fact, she could have students cooperate and draw up a chart that would show the class's progress from week to week. A key to motivate Externals is to place them in cooperative situations.

MOTIVATING EXTERNALS: USE EXTRINSIC REWARDS

Past research shows that compared to Internals, Externals are less likely to work at a task just for the sheer satisfaction of doing it and succeeding at it. If a task becomes difficult or failure looms, Externals are more likely to give up because they think there is little they can do to change matters.

Externals are prone to give up hope of succeeding, whereas Internals are more likely to think they can tinker with their options to improve their chances of future success. For an example, we can look back to the study by Susan Morris and Stanley Messer I discussed in chapter 4. In that study, students completed tasks while receiving either self-reinforcement or external reinforcement. Externals receiving external reinforcement, either social praise or concrete rewards like candy, performed the best. Externals tend to be motivated to succeed under these conditions because they are not sure what will happen in the future and don't trust delaying their rewards until then.

External rewards are an important resource for our teacher to possess as she contemplates dealing with the hypothetical class considered here. Although there are those who call the use of such rewards bribery, rewarding someone for doing the right thing is not bribery. Rather, bribery is when you reward someone for doing the *wrong* thing. Giving external rewards to Externals to achieve a desired performance is not an illegitimate or dishonest strategy but simply giving students what they need in order to succeed.

MOTIVATING EXTERNALS: USE SOCIAL CUES AND PERSONAL CONTACT

Because they feel at the mercy of forces outside of themselves, Externals respond positively to friendly overtures and attention. This, in turn, explains why even when Externals succeed on a task, they may follow this with seemingly bewildering behavior. First, if given a choice to do the task again or not, they usually will choose *not*; second, if they do the task again, there is a good chance they won't perform as well as the first time. Why that happens is a matter of conjecture, but it seems as though luck or chance might be at work. That is, if they succeeded once by chance or luck, they may believe they have used up their good luck on the task and want to try their "luck" at something else.

SUMMARY AND CONCLUSION

We live in an exciting age. We can do so much more now than we could when I was a child. I marvel at the technological advances that surround me. And yet, with all our progress, we are more depressed, anxious, and uncertain than ever before. I began this book with the unsettling finding that over the past three decades, we have been steadily moving toward Externality. This news becomes even more disconcerting in light of the fact that nearly everything in this book strongly suggests Internality is what we need to perform at our best and be satisfied with life.

We need to turn the tide of Externality to Internality. We must do a better job guiding our children while allowing them to err and explore, not overprotecting them into Externality. We understand the conditions that facilitate Internality's growth. They aren't difficult to create at home, at school, and in the workplace, if we put our minds to it. I wanted to make you, the reader, more aware of the importance of Locus of Control in our lives. I have sketched out ways to change our LOC and to establish appropriate conditions to increase Externals' chances to succeed. We can do both if we put our minds and hearts into it.

I concluded the first chapter by sharing the interaction I had with my granddaughter, Hannah Ruth; I told you how I wanted to give her something she could take with her and use to watch over herself when I was no longer around to watch over her. The little, wispy girl who fed the ducks and geese is gone. In her place is an energetic, funny, loving, and challenging fourteen-year-old. I must admit there are many things I miss about her being three—her dependence on me to hold and protect her among the most poignant losses. But, as far as I can tell, that's the price I have to pay for having my wish for her be granted. Hannah Ruth is all things Internal. She is strong and persistent. She works hard and continues to learn the connections between her behavior and what happens to her. My Hannah Ruth is no longer an External three-year-old who needs me to protect her but an adolescent girl growing into an enchanting young woman who, with the help of her parents and teachers, has grown in Internality with each passing year. That is what should happen with all children.

Hannah Ruth's Internality is a powerful tool she can use to watch over herself. She does not need me to watch over her and shield her from danger as much as I did before, and for that, I am thankful. But, like parents and grandparents everywhere, the truth is that I will always be watching over her and her brother from a distance.

NOTES

PREFACE

1. Stephen Nowicki and Julia Roundtree, "Correlates of Locus of Control in Secondary School Age Students," *Development Psychology* 4, no. 3 (April 1971): 477–78.

CHAPTER 1: LOCUS OF CONTROL: WHAT IT IS AND WHY IT IS IMPORTANT

1. Stephen Nowicki and Marshall P. Duke, "Foundations of Locus of Control Research," in *Perceived Control: Theory, Research, and Practice in the First 50 Years*, ed. Frank Infurna and John W. Reich (New York: Oxford University Press, 2016).

2. Monica Nanda, Beth Kotchick, and Rachel Grover, "Parental Psychological Control and Childhood Anxiety: The Mediating Role of Perceived Lack of Control," *Journal of Child and Family Studies* 27, no. 21 (August 2011). Also, Duane Ollendick, "Parental Assessment of Children's Personality Characteristics," *Journal of Personality Assessment* 43, no. 4 (July 1979): 401–405.

3. Frank Infurna et al., "Long-Term Antecedents and Outcomes of Perceived Control," *Psychology and Aging* 26, no. 3 (July 2011): 559–75.

4. Christophe Boone, Bert De Brabander, and Johan Hellemans, "CEO Locus of Control and Small Firm Performance," *Organizational Studies* 21, no. 3 (July 2000): 641–46. Also, Christophe Boone, Bert De Brabander, and Argen van Witteloostujin, "CEO Locus of Control and Firm Performance: An Integrative Framework and Empirical Test," *Journal of Management Studies* 33, no. 5 (September 1996): 667–99.

5. Paul Spector, "Locus of Control and Well-Being at Work: How Generalizable Are Western Findings?" *Academy of Management Journal* 45, no. 2 (March 2000): 453–66.

6. Catherine Gale, "Locus of Control at Age 10 Years and Health Outcomes

and Behaviors at Age 30 Years: The 1970 British Cohort Study," *Psychosomatic Medicine* 70, no. 4 (September 2008): 397–403.

7. Marilia Zampieri and Elisabete de Souza, "Locus of Control, Depression and Quality of Life in Parkinson's Disease," *Journal of Health Psychology* 16, no. 6 (November 2011): 980–87. Also, Roger Gibson et al., "Locus of Control, Depression and Quality of Life among Persons with Sickle Cell Disease in Jamaica," *Psychology, Health and Medicine* 18, no. 4 (July 2013): 451–60; Laurence Halimi et al., "Severe Asthma and Adherence to Peak Flow Monitoring: Longitudinal Assessment of Psychological Aspects," *Journal of Psychosomatic Research* 69, no. 4 (July 2010): 331–40.

8. Lisa Coyne and Alysha Thompson, "Maternal Depression, Locus of Control, and Emotion Regulatory Strategy as Predictors of Preschoolers Internalizing Problems," *Journal of Child and Family Studies* 20, no. 6 (November 2011): 873–83.

9. Adam Bryant, "Charisma? To Her It's Overrated," Corner Office, *New York Times*, July 5, 2009, B2.

10. Paola Verme, "Happiness, Freedom and Control," *Journal of Economic Behavior and Organization* 71, no. 2 (August 2009): 146–61.

11. Herbert Lefcourt, *Locus of Control: Current Trends in Theory and Research* (Hillside, NJ: Erlbaum, 1976).

12. Jean Twenge, Liqing Zhang, and Charles Im, "It's beyond My Control: A Cross-Temporal Meta-Analysis of Increasing Externality in Locus of Control, 1960–2002," *Personality and Social Psychology Review* 8, no. 3 (July 2004): 308–19.

13. Dan Adame and Tom Johnson, "Locus of Control of College Students Over Time" (unpublished research paper, Emory University, Atlanta, GA, 2008).

14. Gerhardt Peters, "Voter Turnout in Presidential Elections: 1828–2012," *American Presidency Project*, accessed October 9, 2015, http://www.presidency.ucsb.edu/data/turnout.php.

15. Peter Flegal et al., "Prevalence and Trends in Obesity among US Adults, 1999–2000," *Journal of the American Medical Association* 303, no. 3 (January 2010): 235–41. Also, "Child Obesity Facts," Centers for Disease Control and Prevention, last modified August 27, 2015, http://www.cdc.gov/healthyschools/obesity/facts.htm.

16. William Evans, Patsy Owens, and Shawn Marsh, "Environmental Factors, Locus of Control and Adolescent Suicide Risk," *Child and Adolescent Social Work Journal* 22, no. 3 (August 2005): 301–19.

17. Ronald Kessler et al., "The Epidemiology of Major Depressive Disorder: Results from the National Comorbidity Survey Replication," *Journal of the American Medical Association* 289, no. 23 (June 2003): 3095–105.

18. Kurt April, Babar Dharani, and Kai Peters, "Impact of Locus of Control Expectancy on Level of Well-Being," *Review of European Studies* 4, no. 2 (June 2012): 124–37.

19. Jim Litke, Associated Press, "Sergio Hits New York Dragging 0-for-39 Baggage," *Fox News*, June 16, 2009, http://www.foxnews.com/printer_friendly _wires/2009Jun16/0,4675,GLFJimLitke061609,00.html.

20. Ibid.

21. Robert Lusetich, "Stop the Spin Cycle, Tiger: Just Admit You Are Completely Lost, and Get a Head Guru," *FOX Sports*, July 22, 2015, http://www .foxsports.com/golf/story/tiger-woods-british-open-golf-majors-pga-close-to -being-done-072215.

22. Christopher Devine, "Tiger Woods' Decline Is Mind-Blowing, Greg Norman Says," *Sporting News*, February 8, 2015, http://www.sportingnews.com/ sport-news/4635048-tiger-woods-decline-is-mind-blowing-greg-norman-pga-tour.

CHAPTER 2: A LITTLE HISTORY OF LOCUS OF CONTROL

1. "TFA on the Record," Teach for America, accessed January 26, 2016, https://www.teachforamerica.org/tfa-on-the-record.

2. Adam Bryant, "Charisma? To Her It's Overrated," Corner Office, *New York Times*, July 5, 2009, B2.

3. Julian Rotter, *Social Learning and Clinical Psychology* (Englewood Cliffs, NJ: Prentice-Hall, 1954). Also, Rotter, "Generalized Expectancies for Internal versus External Control of Reinforcement," *Psychological Monographs* 80, no. 1 (Whole no. 609, January 1966): 1–28.

4. Bonnie Strickland, "Obituaries: Julian B. Rotter (1916–2014)," *American Psychologist* 5 (May 2014): 545–46.

5. Rotter, "Generalized Expectancies."

6. Stephen Nowicki and Bonnie Strickland, "A Locus of Control Scale for Children," *Journal of Consulting and Clinical Psychology* 40, no. 1 (February 1973): 148–54. Also, Nowicki and Marshall Duke, "A Locus of Control Scale for College as Well as Non-College Adults," *Journal of Personality Assessment* 38, no. 2 (April 1974): 136–37; Nowicki and Duke, "A Preschool and Primary

242   NOTES

Locus of Control Scale," *Developmental Psychology* 10, no. 6 (November 1974): 874–80.

7. Rotter, "Generalized Expectancies."

8. Ibid.

9. Stephen Nowicki and Wendy Segal, "Perceived Parental Characteristics, Locus of Control Orientation, and Behavior Correlates of Locus of Control," *Developmental Psychology* 10, no. 1 (December 1974): 33–37.

10. Klaus Schneewind, "Impact of Family Processes on Self-Efficacy," in *Self-Efficacy in Changing Societies*, ed. Albert Bandura (New York: Cambridge University Press, 1995), 114–48.

11. Ibid.

12. Heinz Ansbacher and Rowena Ansbacher, eds., *The Individual Psychology of Alfred Adler: A Systematic Presentation in Selections from His Writings* (New York: Basic Books, 1956).

13. Brittney Beck and Kenneth Brown, "Birth Order and Locus of Control," *Psi Chi Journal of Undergraduate Research* 8 (June 2003): 128–32.

14. Stephen Nowicki, "Birth Order and Locus of Control" (unpublished manuscript, Emory University, Atlanta, GA,1995).

15. Julian Rotter, "Some Problems and Misconceptions Related to the Construct of Internal versus External Control of Reinforcement," *Journal of Consulting and Clinical Psychology* 43, no. 1 (February 1975): 56–67.

CHAPTER 3: HOW WE GET OUR LOCUS OF CONTROL

1. Susan Bullers and Carol Prescott, "An Exploration of the Independent Contributions of Genetics, Shared Environment, Specific Environment, and Adult Roles and Statuses on Perceived Control," *Sociological Inquiry* 71, no. 2 (April 2001): 145–63.

2. Duane Ollendick, "Parental Locus of Control and the Assessment of Children's Personality Characteristics," *Journal of Personality Assessment* 43, no. 4 (July 1979): 401–405.

3. Rachel Freed and Martha Tompson, "Predictors of Parental Locus of Control in Mothers of Pre- and Early Adolescents," *Journal of Clinical Child and Adolescent Psychology* 40, no. 1 (January 2011): 100–10.

4. Erin McClure-Tone, Stephen Nowicki, and Stephanie Goodfellow, "The Impact of Paternal Locus of Control on the Social and Academic Adjustment of Children," *Journal of Genetic Psychology* 173, no. 1 (January 2011): 3–22.

5. Julian Rotter, June Chance, and E. Jerry Phares, eds., *Applications of a Social Learning Theory of Personality* (New York: Holt, Rinehart and Winston, 1972).

6. John Carton, Stephen Nowicki, and Ginger Balser, "An Observational Study of Antecedents of Locus of Control of Reinforcement," *International Journal of Behavior Development* 19, no. 1 (January 1996): 161–75.

7. Theodore Chandler et al., "Parental Correlates of Locus of Control in Fifth Graders: An Attempt at Experimentation in the Home," *Merrill-Palmer Quarterly* 26, no. 3 (July 1980): 183–95.

8. Reed Yates, Kevin Kennelly, and S. H. Cox, "Perceived Contingency of Parental Reinforcements, Parent-Child Relations, and Locus of Control," *Psychological Reports* 36, no. 2 (February 1975): 139–46.

9. Frank Wichern and Stephen Nowicki," Independence Training Practices and Locus of Control Orientation in Children and Adolescents," *Developmental Psychology* 12, no. 1 (January 1976): 77.

10. Karrie Shogren et al., "Locus of Control Orientations in Students with Intellectual Disability, Learning Disabilities, and No Disabilities: A Latent Growth Curve Analysis," *Research and Practice for Persons with Severe Disabilities* 35, nos. 3–4 (Fall 2010): 80–92.

11. Elaine Clark et al., "Striving for Autonomy in a Contingency-Governed World: Another Challenge for Individuals with Developmental Disabilities," *Psychology in the Schools* 43, no. 1 (January 2004): 143–53; Esther Cohen, Gail Biran, and Adi Aran, "Locus of Control, Perceived Parenting Style, and Anxiety in Children with Cerebral Palsy," *Journal of Developmental and Physical Disabilities* 20, no. 5 (September 2008): 415–23.

12. Kate Bayless, "What Is Helicopter Parenting?" *Parents*, accessed January 27, 2016, http://www.parents.com/parenting/better-parenting/what-is-helicopter-parenting/.

13. Shirley Lynch, David Hurford, and Amy Kay Cole, "Parental Enabling Attitudes and Locus of Control of At-Risk and Honors Students," *Adolescence* 37, no. 147 (Fall 2002): 528–49.

14. Herbert Lefcourt, *Locus of Control: Current Trends in Theory and Research* (Hillside, NJ: Erlbaum, 1976).

15. John Carton and Erin Carton, "Nonverbal Maternal Warmth and Children's Locus of Control of Reinforcement," *Journal of Nonverbal Behavior* 11, no. 1 (January 1998): 77–86.

16. Stephen Nowicki and Klaus Schneewind, "A Cross-Cultural Comparison of German and American Students in Social Climate Antecedents to Locus of

Control Orientation," *Journal of Genetic Psychology* 141, no. 2 (February 1982): 277–86.

17. Erin Tully et al., "Family Correlates of Daughters' and Sons' Locus of Control Expectancies during Childhood," *Early Child Development and Care* (forthcoming).

18. Albert Osborn and Janet Milbanks, *The Effects of Early Education: A Report from the Child Health and Education Study* (Oxford: Carendon, 1987).

19. Don Gordon, Richard Jones, and Stephen Nowicki, "The Development of a Measure of Intensity of Parental Punishment within Rotter's Social Learning Theory," *Journal of Personality Assessment* 43, no. 5 (October 1979): 485–96.

20. Mary Ainsworth et al., *Patterns of Attachment* (Hillsdale, NJ: Erlbaum, 1978).

CHAPTER 4: LOCUS OF CONTROL IN ACTION: ACHIEVEMENT IN SCHOOL

1. Allie Birdwell, "Students Spend More Time on Homework," *US News and World Report*, February 27, 2014, http://www.usnews.com/news/articles/2014/02/27/students-spend-more-time-on-homework-but-teachers-say-its-worth-it.

2. National Center for Education Statistics, Institute of Education Sciences, "National Household Education Surveys Program of 2007" (Washington, DC: US Department of Education, 2007), https://nces.ed.gov/nhes/pdf/userman/NHES_2007_Vol_I.pdf.

3. Ruth Spinks et al., "School Achievement Strongly Predicts Midlife IQ," *Intelligence* 35, no. 6 (2007): 563–67.

4. *Encyclopaedia Britannica Online*, s.v. "Alfred Binet," accessed January 28, 2016, http://www.britannica.com/biography/Alfred-Binet.

5. *Encyclopaedia Britannica Online*, s.v. "Lewis Madison Terman," accessed January 28, 2016, http://www.britannica.com/biography/Lewis-Madison-Terman.

6. John Carson, "Army Alpha, Army Brass, and the Search for Army Intelligence," *Isis* 84, no. 2 (March 1993): 278–319.

7. James Coleman et al., *Equality of Educational Opportunity* (Washington, DC: US Office of Education, 1966).

8. Ari Kalechstein and Stephen Nowicki, "A Meta-Analytic Examination of the Relationship between Control Expectancies and Academic Achievement:

An 11-Year Follow-Up to Findley and Cooper," *Genetic, Social, and General Psychology Monographs* 123, no. 1 (January 1997): 27–54.

9. Maureen Findley and Harris Cooper, "Locus of Control and Academic Achievement: A Literature Review," *Journal of Personality and Social Psychology* 44, no. 2 (March 1983): 419–27.

10. Stephen Nowicki and Julia Roundtree, "Correlates of Locus of Control in a Secondary School Population," *Developmental Psychology* 4, no. 3 (March 1971): 477–78.

11. Celeste Pappas, Charlotte Walker, and Stephen Nowicki, "Achievement Correlates of Locus of Control" (paper presented at the Southeastern Psychological Association Meetings, Atlanta, GA, April 1972).

12. Stephen Nowicki, Marshall Duke, and Mary Pat Duncan, "Sex Differences in Locus of Control and Performance under Competitive and Cooperative Conditions," *Journal of Educational Psychology* 70, no. 4 (August 1978): 482–86. Also, for additional study of sex differences, see Duke and Nowicki, "Locus of Control and Achievement: The Confirmation of a Theoretical Expectation," *Journal of Psychology* 87, no. 2 (August 1974): 263–67; Nowicki and Charlotte Walker, "Achievement in Relation to Locus of Control: Identification of a New Source of Variance," *Journal of Genetic Psychology* 123, no. 1 (January 1973): 146–58; Nowicki, "Predicting Academic Achievement of Females from a Locus of Control Orientation: Some Problems and Some Solutions" (paper presented at the American Psychological Association meetings, Montreal, Canada, August 1973).

13. Deborah Stipek, "A Causal Analysis of the Relationship between Locus of Control and Academic Achievement in First Grade," *Contemporary Educational Psychology* 5, no. 1 (January 1980): 90–99.

14. Eirini Flouri, "Parental Interest in Children's Education, Children's Self-Esteem and Locus of Control, and Later Educational Attainment: Twenty-Six-Year Follow-Up of the 1970 British Birth Cohort," *British Journal of Educational Psychology* 76, no. 1 (March 2006): 41–55.

15. Herbert Lefcourt, *Locus of Control: Current Trends in Theory and Research* (Hillside, NJ: Erlbaum, 1976).

16. Donald Gordon, Richard Jones, and Nancy Short, "Task Persistence and Locus of Control in Elementary School Children," *Child Development* 48, no. 4 (December 1977): 1716–19.

17. Ibid., 1718.

18. Mark McLeod, "Locus of Control and Persistence in Structured and

Unstructured Preschool Classrooms," *Journal of Applied Developmental Psychology* 6, no. 4 (October 1985): 299–302.

19. Susan Morris and Stanley Messer, "Effects of Locus of Control and Locus of Reinforcement on Academic Task Persistence," *Journal of Genetic Psychology* 131, no. 1 (September 1978): 3–9.

20. Robert Rosenthal, "Interpersonal Expectancy Effects: A 30-Year Perspective," *Current Directions in Psychological Science* 3, no. 5 (October 1994): 176–79. Also, Herman Spitz, "Beleaguered Pygmalion: A History of the Controversy over Claims That Teacher Expectancy Raises Intelligence," *Intelligence* 27, no. 3 (September 1999): 199–234. The classic study raising the question of teacher expectation was completed by Rosenthal and Lenore Jacobson and then rebutted by Spitz.

21. Prihadi Kususanto, Hairul Ismail, and Hazri Jamil, "Student Self-Esteem and Their Perception of Teachers' Behavior," *Electronic Journal of Research in Educational Psychology* 8, no. 2 (March 2012): 707–24.

22. Morris and Messer, "Effects of Locus of Control."

23. Denise Gifford, Juanita Briceno-Perriott, and Frank Mianzo, "Locus of Control: Academic Achievement and Retention in a Sample of University First Year Students," *Journal of College Admissions* 18, no. 191 (Spring 2006): 19–36.

24. Ibid., 34.

CHAPTER 5: LOCUS OF CONTROL IN ACTION: ACHIEVEMENT IN BUSINESS

1. Ari Kalechstein and Stephen Nowicki, "Social-Learning Theory and the Prediction of Achievement in Telemarketers," *Journal of Social Psychology* 134, no. 4 (September 1994): 547–48.

2. Vance Caesar, "Financial Success and Personality: An Examination of Self-Esteem, Locus of Control and Conative Characteristics in Mid-Life Men in America," *Dissertation Abstracts International, Section A* 56, no. 2-A (1999).

3. Anastasia Semykina and Susan Linz, "Gender Differences in Personality and Earnings: Evidence from Russia," *Journal of Economic Psychology* 28, no. 3 (July 2007): 387–410. Also, Malgorzata Siekanska, "Psychological Determinants of Job Success," *Przeglad Psychologiczny* 47, no. 3 (July 2004): 275–90.

4. June Poon, Raja Ainuddin, and Sa'Odah Junit, "Effects of Self-Concept Traits and Entrepreneurial Orientation on Firm Performance," *International Small Business Journal* 24, no. 1 (February 2006): 61–81.

5. Christophe Boone, Woody van Olfen, and Arjen van Witteloostuijn, "Team Locus-of-Control, Composition, Leadership Structure, Information, Acquisition, and Financial Performance: A Business Simulation Study," *Academy of Management Journal* 48, no. 5 (October 2005): 889–909.

6. Jane Howell and Bruce Avolio, "Transformational Leadership, Transactional Leadership, Locus of Control and Support for Innovation: Key Predictors of Consolidated-Business-Unit Performance," *Journal of Applied Psychology* 78, no. 6 (November 1993): 891–902.

7. Ibid., 893.

8. Christophe Boone, Bert De Brabander, and Johan Hellemans, "Research Note: CEO Locus of Control and Small Firm Performance," *Organizational Studies* 21, no. 3 (May 2000): 641–46. Also, Boone, De Brabander, and Arjen van Witteloostujin, "CEO Locus of Control and Firm Performance: An Integrative Framework and Empirical Test," *Journal of Management Studies* 33, no. 5 (September 1996): 667–99.

9. Martin Kormanik and Tonette Rocco, "Internal versus External Control of Reinforcement: A Review of the Locus of Control Construct," *Human Resource Development Review* 8, no. 4 (2009): 463–83.

10. Qiang Wang, Nathan Bowling, and Kevin Eschleman, "A Meta-Analytic Examination of Work and General Locus of Control," *Journal of Applied Psychology* 95, no. 4 (July 2010): 1–18.

11. Paul Spector, "Locus of Control and Well-Being at Work: How Generalizable Are Western Findings?" *Academy of Management Journal* 45, no. 2 (March 2002): 453–66.

12. Paolo Verme, "Happiness, Freedom and Control," *Journal of Economic Behavior and Organization* 71, no. 2 (August 2009): 146–61.

13. Ibid., 155.

14. Chung-Ming Lau and Richard Woodman, "Understanding Organizational Change: A Schematic Perspective," *Academy of Management Journal* 38, no. 2 (April 1995): 537–55.

15. Justin Sprung and Steve Jex, "Work Locus of Control as a Moderator of the Relationship between Work Stressors and Counterproductive Work Behavior," *International Journal of Stress Management* 19, no. 4 (July 2002): 272–91.

16. Chiewei Hung and Ker-Tah Hsu, "Impact of Locus of Control, Changes in Work Load and Career Prospects on Organizational Commitment of Employees of Life Insurance Companies during Merger and Acquisition," *African Journal of Business Management* 17, no. 5 (March 2011): 7543–56.

17. Sheryl Shivers-Blackwell, "The Influence of Perceptions of Organizational Structure and Culture on Leadership Role Requirements: The Moderating Impact of Locus of Control and Self-Monitoring," *Journal of Leadership and Organizational Studies* 12, no. 4 (July 2006): 28–49.

18. Jingqiu Chen and Lei Wang, "Locus of Control and the Three Components of Commitment to Change," *Personality and Individual Differences* 42, no. 3 (February 2006): 503–12.

19. Thomas Chermack, Susan Lynham, and Wendy Ruona, "Critical Uncertainties Confronting Human Resource Development," *Advances in Developing Human Resources* 5, no. 3 (August 2003): 257–71.

20. Phillip Meilinger, "The Ten Rules of Good Followership," in *Concepts for Air Force Leadership*, 4th ed., ed. Richard Lester and A. Glenn Morton (Maxwell Air Force Base, AL: Air University Press, 2004): 99–101, http://armynursecorps .amedd.army.mil/development/Ten_Rules_of_Good_Followership.pdf. Also, Ronald Riggio, Ira Chaleff, and Jean Lipman, *The Art of Followership* (San Francisco: Jossey-Bass, 2008).

21. Desmond Lam and Dick Mizerski, "The Effects of Locus of Control on Word-of-Mouth Communication," *Journal of Marketing Communications* 11, no. 3 (May 2005): 215–28.

22. Ibid., 217.

CHAPTER 6: LOCUS OF CONTROL IN ACTION:
ACHIEVEMENT IN SPORTS

1. "Vince Lombardi Quotes," BrainyQuote, accessed January 28, 2016, http://www.brainyquote.com/quotes/authors/v/vince_lombardi.html.

2. "Michael Jordan Quotes," BrainyQuote, accessed January 28, 2016, http://www.brainyquote.com/quotes/authors/m/michael_jordan.html.

3. "Spotlight on Statistics: Sports and Exercise," US Department of Labor, May 2008, http://www.bls.gov/spotlight/2008/sports.

4. Physical Activity Council, *2015 Activity Report* (Boston, MA: Physical Activity Council, 2015), http://www.physicalactivitycouncil.com/pdfs/current .pdf.

5. American Council of Sports Medicine, American College of Pediatrics, accessed December 2014, https://www.aap.org/en-us/about-the-aap/ Committees-Councils-Sections/Council-on-sports-medicine-and-fitness.

6. "Facts: Sports Activity and Children," Project Play, Aspen Institute, accessed January 28, 2016, http://www.aspenprojectplay.org/the-facts.

7. "Youth Sports Injuries Statistics," STOP Sports Injuries, accessed January 28, 2016, http://www.stopsportsinjuries.org.

8. Frank Smoll and Ron Smith, "Effects of Enhancing Coach-Athlete Relationships on Youth Sport Attrition," *Sport Psychologist* 6, no. 2 (June 1992): 111–27. Also, Frank Smoll, Ron Smith, and Sean Cumming, "Effects of Coach and Parent Training on Performance Anxiety in Young Athletes: A Systemic Approach," *Journal of Youth Development* 2, no. 1 (Summer 2007): 0701FA002.

9. Robert Rotella, "Locus of Control and Achievement Motivation in the Active Aged," *Perceptual and Motor Skills* 46, no. 3 (May 1978): 1043–46. Also, Alfred Morris, Paul Vaccaro, and David Clark, "Psychological Characteristics of Age Group Swimmers," *Perceptual and Motor Skills* 48, no. 3 (December 1979): 1265–66; Gordon Russell, "Machiavellianism, Locus of Control, Aggression, Performance and Precautionary Behavior in Ice Hockey," *Human Relations* 27, no. 9 (September 1974): 825–37; Richard Celestino, Jack Tapp, and Michael Brumet, "Locus of Control Correlates with Marathon Performance," *Perceptual and Motor Skills* 48, no. 3 (December 1979): 1249–50.

10. Yonaton Porat, Dubi Lufi, and Gershon Tenenbaum, "Psychological Components Contribute to Select Young Female Gymnasts," *International Journal of Sports Psychology* 20, no. 4 (October 1989): 279–86; Suzanne Slenker, "Health Locus of Control of Joggers and Nonexercisers," *Perceptual and Motor Skills* 61, no. 1 (February 1985): 323–28.

11. Margaret Dahlhauser and Michele Thomas, "Visual Disembedding and Locus of Control as Variables Associated with High School Football Injuries," *Perceptual and Motor Skills* 49, no. 1 (February 1979): 254. Also, Elise Labbe' et al., "High School Cross Country Runners: Running Commitment, Health Locus of Control and Performance," *Journal of Sports Behavior* 14, no. 2 (September 1991): 85–91; Francisco Montero et al., "Locus of Control and Vulnerability to Injury in Semi-Professional and Professional Football," *Cuadernos de Psicologia del Deporte* 8, no. 2 (April 2009): 101–12.

12. Corey Nachman, "The 30 Strangest Superstitions in Sports History," *Business Insider*, August 9, 2011, http://www.businessinsider.com/the-strangest-pre-game-rituals-2011-8.

13. Ethan Trex, "The 10 Most Bizarre Athlete Superstitions," *Mental Floss*, March 6, 2008, http://mentalfloss.com/article/18179/10-most-bizarre-athlete-superstitions.

14. Michaela Schippers and Paul van Lange, "The Psychological Benefits of Superstitious Rituals in Top Sport: A Study among Top Sportspersons," *Journal of Applied Social Psychology* 36, no. 10 (October 2006): 2532–53.

15. Melissa Todd and Chris Brown, "Athletes in Action," *Journal of Sport Behavior* 26, no. 2 (June 2003): 168–87.

16. Julien Arnaud and Jerome Palazzolo, "Link between Locus of Control and Competitive Anxiety: Study of 150 High-Level Tennis Players," *Annales Medico-Psychologiques* 170, no. 9 (September 2012): 642–47.

17. Daniel Weigand and Craig Broadhurst, "The Relationship among Perceived Competence, Intrinsic Motivation and Control Perceptions in Youth Soccer," *International Journal of Sport Psychology* 29, no. 4 (July 1998): 324–38.

18. Anne Pensgaard, "The Dynamics of Motivation and Perceptions of Control When Competing in the Olympic Games," *Perceptual and Motor Skills* 89, no. 1 (January 1999): 116–25.

19. David Le Foll, Olivier Rascle, and N. C. Higgins, "Persistence in a Putting Task during Perceived Failure: Influence of State-Attributions and Attributional Style," *Applied Psychology: An International Review* 55, no. 4 (October 2006): 586–605.

20. Je Tsai, Chien-Hsin Wand, and Hung-Jen Lo, "Locus of Control, Moral Disengagement in Sport and Rule Transgression of Athletes," *Social Behavior and Personality* 42, no. 1 (January 2014): 59–68.

21. Jennifer Black and Alan Smith, "An Examination of Coakley's Perspective on Identity, Control and Burnout among Adolescent Athletes," *International Journal of Sport Psychology* 38, no. 4 (October 2007): 417–36.

22. Stephanie Scoffier, Yvan Paquet, and Frans Arripe-Longueville, "Effect of Locus of Control on Disordered Eating in Athletes: The Mediational Role of Self-Regulation of Eating Attitudes," *Eating Behaviors* 11, no. 3 (August 2010):164–69.

23. David Yukelson et al., "Interpersonal Attraction and Leadership within Collegiate Sport Teams," *Journal of Sport Psychology* 6, no. 1 (November 1983): 28–36.

24. Celeste Taylor, J. Schepers, and F. Crous, "Locus of Control in Relation to Flow," *Journal of Industrial Psychology* 32, no. 3 (January 2006): 63–71.

25. M. Csikszentmihalyi, *Living Well: The Psychology of Everyday Life* (London: Weidenfeld and Nicolson, 1997).

26. Bill Russell, *Second Wind: The Memoirs of an Opinionated Man* (San Francisco: Greenwood Biographies, 1980).

27. Taylor, Schepers, and Crous, "Relation to Flow."

CHAPTER 7: COPING WITH RELATING

1. Quotes from Carl Jung, Benjamin Franklin, and Henry Winkler are all from BrainyQuote, accessed May 8, 2015, http://www.brainyquote.com.

2. *Encyclopedia of Psychology*, American Psychological Association, http://www.psychology.org.

3. "RAINN: Rape, Abuse and Incest Network," RAINN, accessed July 8, 2015, https://rainn.org; "Childhelp A Non-Profit Charity Aiding Victims of Child Abuse," Child Help Network: Center for Prevention and Treatment of Child Abuse, accessed January 28, 2016, http://www.childhelp.org; "National Center on Elder Abuse," National Center on Elder Abuse, Administration on Aging, Department of Health and Human Services, accessed January 28, 2016, http://www.ncea.aoa.gov.

4. Ed Diener and Martin Seligman, "Very Happy People," *Psychological Science* 13, no. 1 (2002): 81–84.

5. Stephen Nowicki and Marshall Duke, *Will I Ever Fit In?* (Atlanta, GA: Peachtree, 2003).

6. George Vaillant, *Triumphs of Experience* (Boston: Harvard University Press, 2012).

7. "Strengthen Relationships for Longer, Healthier Life," *Healthbeat*, January 18, 2011, http://www.health.harvard.edu/healthbeat/strengthen -relationships-for-longer-healthier-life.

8. Marshall Duke and Stephen Nowicki, "Personality Correlates of the Nowicki-Strickland Locus of Control Scale for Adults," *Psychological Reports* 33, no. 1 (February 1973): 267–70.

9. Mary Wheeler and Paul White, "The Relationship between the Life-Style Personality Inventory and External Control," *Individual Psychology* 47, no. 3 (September 1991): 372–79.

10. *International Encyclopedia of the Social Sciences*, s.v. "Similarity/ Attraction Theory," accessed January 28, 2016, http://www.encyclopedia.com/ doc/1G2-3045302452.html.

11. Marian Morry, "Perceived Locus of Control and Satisfaction in Same-Sex Friendships," *Personal Relationships* 10, no. 4 (November 2003): 495–509.

12. Ibid.

13. Marian Morry and Cheryl Harasymchuk, "Perceptions of Locus of Control and Satisfaction in Friendships: The Impact of Problem-Solving Strategies," *Journal of Social and Personal Relationships* 22, no. 2 (March 2005): 183–206.

14. Stephen Nowicki and Neil Blumberg, "The Role of Locus of Control of

Reinforcement in Interpersonal Attraction," *Journal of Research in Personality* 9, no. 1 (March 1975): 48–56.

15. Kenneth Dion and Karen Dion, "Correlates of Romantic Love," *Journal of Consulting and Clinical Psychology* 41, no. 1 (January 1973): 51–56.

16. Paul Camp and Lawrence Ganong, "Locus of Control and Marital Satisfaction in Long-Term Marriages," *Families in Society* 78, no. 6 (November 1973): 624–31.

17. Helen Barnet, "Reaction to Divorce," *Journal of Divorce* 13, no. 3 (September 1990): 93–109.

18. Sylvester Miott and Frank Lira, "Dogmatism, Locus of Control, and Life Goals in Stable and Unstable Marriages," *Journal of Clinical Psychology* 33, no. 1 (January 1977): 142–46.

19. Robert Theodore, "The Relationship between Locus of Control and Level of Violence in Married Couples," in *Intimate Violence: Interdisciplinary Perspectives*, ed. Emilio Viano (Washington, DC: Hemisphere, 1992), 37–48.

20. Lilly Dimitrovsky, Ester Schapira-Beck, and Rivka Itskowitz, "Locus of Control of Israeli Women during the Transition to Marriage," *Journal of Psychology* 128, no. 5 (September 1993): 537–45.

21. Stephen Nowicki and Marshall Duke, *Helping the Child Who Doesn't Fit In* (Atlanta, GA: Peachtree, 1992). Also, Duke, Nowicki, and Elizabeth Martin, *Teaching Your Child the Language of Social Success* (Atlanta, GA: Peachtree, 1998); Nowicki and Duke, *Will I Ever Fit In?*; Nowicki, Duke, and Amy van Buren, *Starting Kids Off Right* (Atlanta, GA: Peachtree, 2008).

22. Nowicki and Duke, *Will I Ever Fit In?*

23. Paul Watzlawick, *The Situation Is Hopeless but Not Serious: The Pursuit of Unhappiness* (New York: Norton, 1983).

24. Stephen Nowicki and Marshall Duke, "Dyssemia," in *Encyclopedia of Human Relationships*, vol. 1, ed. Harry Reis and Susan Sprecher (Thousand Oaks, CA: SAGE, 2009): 474–76, https://books.google.com/books?id=E8J1AwAAQB AJ&lpg=PP1&pg=PP1#v=onepage&q&f=false.

25. Stephen Nowicki and Marshall Duke, "Individual Differences in the Nonverbal Communication of Affect: The Diagnostic Analysis of Nonverbal Accuracy Scale," *Journal of Nonverbal Behavior* 18, no. 1 (Spring 1994): 9–36.

26. Stephen Nowicki and Marshall Duke, "The Association of Children's Nonverbal Decoding Abilities with Their Popularity, Locus of Control and Academic Achievement," *Journal of Genetic Psychology* 153, no. 4 (October 1991): 385–93.

27. Howard Friedman et al., "Understanding and Assessing Nonverbal Expressiveness: The Affective Communication Test," *Journal of Personality and Social Psychology* 39, no. 2 (March 1980): 333–51.

28. Stephen Nowicki and Debra Richmond, "The Effect of Standard, Motivation, and Strategy Instructions on the Facial Processing Accuracy of Internal and External Subjects," *Journal of Research in Personality* 19, no. 4 (October 1985): 354–64.

29. Stephen Nowicki and Eileen Cooley, "The Role of Locus of Control Orientation in Speed of Discriminating Facial Affect," *Journal of Research in Personality* 24 (September 1990): 389–97.

CHAPTER 8: COPING WITH PSYCHOLOGICAL DISORDERS

1. Michael Muskal, "In Colorado, 2 Crime Scenes after a Night of Terror," *LA Times*, July 20, 2012, http://articles.latimes.com/2012/jul/20/nation/la-na-nn-colorado-shooting-crime-scenes-20120720.

2. Marshall Duke and Stephen Nowicki, *Abnormal Psychology: A New Look* (New York: Holt, Rinehart and Winston, 1986).

3. Bonnie Strickland, "Internal-External Expectancies and Health Related Behaviors," *Journal of Consulting and Clinical Psychology* 46, no. 6 (November 1978): 1192–211.

4. Ronald Kessler et al., "Prevalence, Severity, and Comorbidity of 12-Month DSM-IV Disorders in National Comorbidity Survey Replication," *Archives of General Psychiatry* 62, no. 6 (June 2005): 617–27.

5. Ibid.

6. E. Jerry Phares, "A Social Learning Approach to Psychopathology," in *Applications of a Social Learning Theory of Personality*, ed. Julian Rotter, June Chance, and Phares (New York: Holt, Rinehart and Winston, 1972).

7. Strickland, "Internal-External Expectancies."

8. Iryna Culpin et al., "Exposure to Socioeconomic Adversity in Early Life and Risk of Depression at 18 Years: The Mediating Role of Locus of Control," *Journal of Affective Disorders* 183, no. 5 (September 2015): 269–78.

9. Ibid.

10. Guro Bjorklofl et al., "Coping and Depression in Old Age: A Literature Review," *Dementia and Geriatric Disorders* 35, no. 1 (August 2013): 121–54.

11. Ibid., 148.

12. Roger Gibson et al., "Locus of Control, Depression and Quality of Life among Persons with Sickle Cell Disease in Jamaica," *Psychology, Health, and Medicine* 18, no. 4 (October 2013): 451–60.

13. Lisa Coyne and Alysha Thompson, "Maternal Depression, Locus of Control, and Emotion Regulatory Strategy as Predictors of Preschoolers Internalizing Problems," *Journal of Child and Family Studies* 20, no. 6 (December 2011): 873–83.

14. Kenneth Kochanek et al., *Deaths: Final Data for 2006* (Hyattsville, MD: National Center for Health Statistics, 1998).

15. Ibid., 1120.

16. Ronald Kessler et al., "Trends in Suicide Ideation, Plans, Gestures, and Attempts in the United States," *Journal of the American Medical Association* 293, no. 20 (May 2005): 2487–95.

17. William Evans, Patsy Owens, and Shawn Marsh, "Environmental Factors, Locus of Control and Adolescent Suicide Risk," *Child and Adolescent Social Work Journal* 22, no. 3 (August 2005): 301–19.

18. James Butcher, Jill Hooley, and Susan Mineka, *Abnormal Psychology*, 16th ed. (Boston: Pearson, 2014).

19. Ronald Rapee et al., "Measurement of Perceived Control over Anxiety-Related Events," *Behavior Therapy* 27, no. 2 (Spring 1996): 279–93.

20. Gerald Nunn, "Concurrent Validity between the Nowicki Strickland Locus of Control Scale and the State-Trait Anxiety Inventory for Children," *Educational and Psychological Measurement* 48, no. 2 (April 1988): 435–38; Harve Rawson, "The Interrelationship of Measures of Manifest Anxiety, Self-Esteem, Locus of Control and Depression in Children with Behavioral Problems," *Journal of Psychoeducational Assessment* 10, no. 4 (December 1992): 319–29.

21. Ho Cheung Li and Oi Kwan Chung, "The Relationship between Children's Locus of Control and Their Anticipatory Anxiety," *Public Health Nursing* 26, no. 2 (February 2009): 153–60.

22. Monica Nanda, Beth Kotchick, and Rachel Grover, "Parental Psychological Control and Childhood Anxiety: The Mediating Role of Perceived Lack of Control," *Journal of Child and Family Studies* 21, no. 4 (August 2012): 637–45.

23. Carl Weems et al., "The Role of Control in Childhood Anxiety Disorders," *Cognitive Therapy and Research* 27, no. 5 (September 2003): 557–68.

24. "Post-Traumatic Stress Disorder," National Institute of Mental Health, National Institutes of Health, accessed January 28, 2016, http://www.nimh.nih.gov/health/topics/post-traumatic-stress-disorder-ptsd/index.shtml.

25. Matt Kushner et al., "Perceived Controllability and the Development of

Posttraumatic Stress Disorder in Crime Victims," *Behavior Research and Therapy* 32, no. 1 (January 1993): 105–10.

26. Karen Karstoft et al., "The Role of Locus of Control and Coping Style in Predicting Longitudinal PTSD Trajectories after Combat Exposure," *Journal of Anxiety Disorders* 32, no. 1 (May 2015): 89–94.

27. Weiqing Zhang et al., "A Longitudinal Study of Posttraumatic Stress Disorder Symptoms and Its Relationship with Coping Skill and Locus of Control in Adolescents after an Earthquake in China," *PLoS One* 9, no. 2 (2014): e88263.

28. Kushner et al., "Perceived Controllability," 109.

29. Georgia Noon, "The Relationship between Locus of Control and Posttraumatic Stress Disorder (PTSD) in Battered Women," *Dissertation Abstracts International* (1996): AAM9611930.

30. Martin Harrow, Barry Hansford, and Ellen Astrachan-Fletcher, "Locus of Control: Relation to Schizophrenia, to Recovery and to Depression and Psychosis: A 15-Year Longitudinal Study," *Psychiatric Research* 168, no. 3 (August 2009): 186–92.

31. Andrew Thompson et al., "Association between Locus of Control in Childhood and Psychotic Symptoms in Early Adolescence: Results from a Large Birth Cohort," *Cognitive Neuropsychiatry* 16, no. 5 (September 2011): 385–402.

32. Brian Rotsztein, "Problem Internet Use and Locus of Control among College Students: Preliminary Findings" (poster presented at the 35th Annual Conference of the New England Educational Research Organization, Portsmouth, NH, September 2003).

CHAPTER 9: COPING WITH PHYSICAL ILLNESS AND INJURY

1. The account of Ben is paraphrased from Rick Reilly, *The Life of Reilly: The Best of* Sports Illustrated*'s Rick Reilly* (New York: Sports Illustrated, 2008).

2. "Facts and Statistics," President's Council on Fitness, Sports and Nutrition, accessed January 28, 2016, www.fitness.gov/resource-center/facts-and-statistics.

3. "Facts about Physical Activity," Centers for Disease Control and Prevention, Division of Nutrition, Physical Activity and Obesity, last modified May 23, 2014, www.cdc.gov/physicalactivity/data/facts.htm.

4. Ibid.

5. Jaqueline Hooper, "Distinguishing Starters from Nonstarters in an Employee Physical Activity Incentive Program," *Health Education and Behavior* 22, no. 1 (January 1995): 49–60.

6. Peter Hassmén and Nathalie Koivula, "Ratings of Perceived Exertion by Women with Internal or External Locus of Control," *Journal of General Psychology* 123, no. 4 (October 1996): 297–304.

7. Deborah Cobb-Clark, Sonja Kassenboehmer, and Stefanie Schurer, "The Connection between Diet, Exercise, and Locus of Control," *Journal of Economic Behavior and Organization* 98, no. 2 (February 2014): 1–28.

8. Ibid., 23.

9. Jane Wardle, Anne Haase, and Andrew Steptoe, "Body Image and Weight Control in Young Adults: International Comparisons in University Students from 22 Countries," *International Journal of Obesity* 30, no. 5 (May 2006): 644–51.

10. Stephen Nowicki et al., "Physical Fitness as Viewed through the Framework of Rotter's Social Learning Theory," *Journal of Social Psychology* 135, no. 5 (September 1997): 549–58.

11. Christine Sheffer et al., "Delay Discounting, Locus of Control, and Cognitive Impulsiveness Independently Predict Tobacco Dependence Treatment Outcomes in a Highly Dependent, Lower Socioeconomic Group of Smokers," *American Journal on Addictions* 21, no. 3 (May–June 2012): 221–32.

12. Ibid., 227.

13. Cobb-Clark, Kassenboehmer, and Schurer, "Connection," 17–24.

14. Andrew Steptoe and Jane Wardle, "Locus of Control and Health Behavior Revisited: A Multivariate Analysis of Young Adults from 18 Countries," *British Journal of Psychology* 92, no. 4 (November 2001): 659–72.

15. Frank Infurna et al., "Long-Term Antecedents and Outcomes of Perceived Control," *Psychology and Aging* 26, no. 3 (September 2011): 559–75.

16. All the measures for Wallston's scale can be obtained by e-mailing him at the address found in his faculty bio, http://www.nursing.vanderbilt.edu/research/bios/wallston3.html.

17. Marilia Zampieri and Elisabete de Souza, "Locus of Control, Depression and Quality of Life in Parkinson's Disease," *Journal of Health Psychology* 16, no. 6 (September 2011): 980–87. Also, Roger Gibson et al., "Locus of Control, Depression and Quality of Life among Persons with Sickle Cell Disease in Jamaica," *Psychology, Health and Medicine* 18, no. 4 (July 2013): 451–60; Laurence Halimi et al., "Severe Asthma and Adherence to Peak Flow Monitoring: Longitudinal Assessment of Psychological Aspects," *Journal of Psychosomatic Research* 69, no. 4 (April 2010): 331–40.

18. National Center for Chronic Disease Prevention and Health Promotion, Division of Diabetes Translation, National Diabetes Statistics Report, 2014

(Washington, DC: Centers for Disease Control and Prevention, 2014), http://www.cdc.gov/diabetes/pubs/statsreport14/national-diabetes-report-web.pdf.

19. "Diabetes Personal Stories," American Heart Association, last modified January 8, 2016, http://www.heart.org/HEARTORG/Conditions/Diabetes/DiabetesToolsResources/Diabetes-Personal-Stories_UCM_313912_Article.jsp#.VqsBP9CleA8.

20. Mohammad Morowatisharifabad et al., "Relationships between Locus of Control and Adherence to Diabetes Regimen in a Sample of Iranians," *International Journal of Diabetes in Developing Countries* 30, no.1 (January 2010): 7–32. Also, Beth Aitzfelder, Charles Engel, and Fred Gilbert, "Substance Abuse in Hawaii: Perspectives on Key Local Human Service Organizations," *Substance Abuse* 19, no. 1 (January 1998): 7–22; Erin O'Shea et al., "Predicting Medical Regimen Adherence: The Interaction of Health Locus of Control Beliefs," *Journal of Health Psychology* 10, no. 5 (September 2005): 705–17.

21. Marzia Raballo et al., "A Study of Patients' Perceptions of Diabetes Care Delivery and Diabetes," *Diabetes Care* 35, no. 2 (February 2012): 242–47.

22. "High Blood Pressure," Centers for Disease Control and Prevention, last modified February 19, 2015, http://www.cdc.gov/bloodpressure.

23. Jens Rollnik, "Cardiovascular Reactions Induced by Unpredictable, Predictable, and Controllable Painful Stimuli during Sphygmomanometry," *International Journal of Psychophysiology* 40, no. 2 (March 2001): 161–65.

24. Tantina Hong et al., "Medication Barriers and Anti-Hypertensive Medication Adherence: The Moderating Role of Locus of Control," *Psychology, Health and Medicine* 11, no. 1 (January 2006): 20–28.

25. Daniel Cukor, Howard Newville, and Rahul Jindal, "Depression and Immunosuppressive Medication Adherence in Kidney Transplant Patients," *General Hospital Psychiatry* 30, no. 4 (July–August 2008): 386–89.

26. Laurence Halimi et al., "Interference of Psychological Factors in Difficult to Control Asthma," 101, no. 1 (January 2007): 154–61.

27. Zampieri and De Souza, "Parkinson's Disease," 980.

28. Svein Bergvik, Tore Sorlie, and Rolf Wynn, "Coronary Patients Who Returned to Work Had Stronger Internal Control Beliefs Than Those Who Did Not Return to Work," *British Journal of Health Psychology* 17, no. 3 (September 2012): 596–608.

29. "Bariatric Surgery: Complete Patient Guide," Bariatric Surgery Source, last modified February 19, 2014, http://www.bariatric-surgery-source.com. Also, Jane Fink, "The Role of the Social Cognitive Variables of Self-Efficacy, Locus

of Control, Weight Loss, and Quality of Life in Post-Bariatric Surgery Patients," *Dissertation Abstracts International, Section A* 68, no. 9-A (2008): 3744.

30. Chris Christie, interview by Matt Lauer, *Today Show*, NBC, April 16, 2015, http://www.today.com/news/chris-christie-2016-my-wife-i-have-not-made -decision-t15546.

31. Fink, "Post-Bariatric Surgery Patients."

32. Andrea Schaller, Stephan Kerth, and Ingo Froboese, "Goal Setting in Activities of Daily Living after Total Joint Arthroplasty: Do Consequences Arise for Patient-Orientation in Exercise Therapy?" *Physickalische Medizin Rehabilitationmedizine Kurortmedizine* 23, no. 3 (2013): 147–53. Also, Christel van Leeuwen et al., "Associations between Psychological Factors and Quality of Life Rating in Persons with Spinal Cord Injury: A Systematic Review," *Spinal Cord* 50, no. 3 (March 2012): 174–87.

33. Pia Thomee, "Determinants of Self-Efficacy in the Rehabilitation of Patients with Anterior Cruciate Ligament Injury," *Journal of Rehabilitation Medicine* 39, no. 6 (November 2007): 486–92.

34. "Knee Injury: Caroline's Story," *TeensHealth*, Nemours Foundation, January 2014, http://kidshealth.org/teen/diseases_conditions/bones/story _caroline.html.

CHAPTER 10: CHANGING LOCUS OF CONTROL
OR MODIFYING THE SITUATION

1. Stephen Nowicki and Jarvis Barnes, "Effects of a Structured Camp Program on the Locus of Control Orientation of Inner City Children," *Journal of Genetic Psychology* 122, no. 1 (January 1973): 247–52.

2. Kristine Daley, "The Effects of a Structured Recreational Activity on the Physical and Psychological Competence of Children with Asthma," *Dissertation Abstracts International, Section B* 55, no. 8-B (1995): 3583.

3. Loretta Autry and Michael Langenbach, "Locus of Control and Self-Responsibility for Behavior," *Journal of Educational Research* 79, no. 2 (November 1985): 76–84.

4. Simona Trip et al., "The Efficacy of a Rational Emotive and Behavioral Education Program in Diminishing Dysfunctional Thinking, Behaviors, and Emotions in Children," *Journal of Cognitive and Behavioral Psychotherapies* 10, no. 2 (April 2010): 173–86.

5. Russ Hill, *How to Teach Internal Locus of Control* (Beach Haven, NJ: Will to Power, 2011).

6. Stephen Nowicki et al., "Reducing the Drop-Out Rates of At-Risk High School Students: The Effective Learning Program (ELP)," *Genetic, Social, and General Psychology Monographs* 130, no. 3 (September 2004): 225–40.

7. John Roueche and Oscar Mink, "Locus of Control and Success Expectancy (A Self-Study Unit)," in *Improving Student Motivation*, ed. John Roueche and Oscar Mink (Manchaca, TX: Sterling Swift, 1976). Also, Roueche and Mink, "Toward Personhood Development in the Community College" (paper presented at the annual meeting of the American Association of Community and Junior Colleges, Seattle, WA, April 1975).

8. Mark McLeod et al., "Evaluating the Study Abroad Experience Using the Framework of Rotter's Social Learning Theory," *Frontiers: The International Journal of Study Abroad* 26 (Fall 2015): 17–28.

9. Frank Knapp Jr. and Lawrence McClure, "Quasi-Experimental Evaluation of a Quality of Life Intervention," *Journal of Community Psychology* 6, no. 3 (July 1978): 280–90.

10. Frederic Wolinsky et al., "Does Cognitive Training Improve Internal Locus of Control among Older Adults?" *Journals of Gerontology Series B: Psychological Sciences and Social Sciences* 65, no. 5 (September 2010): 591–98.

11. Leslie Caplan and Carmi Schooler, "The Roles of Fatalism, Self-Confidence and Intellectual Resources in the Disablement Process in Older Adults," *Psychology and Aging* 18, no. 3 (2003): 551–61.

12. Edward de Bono, *Lateral Thinking: Creativity Step by Step* (New York: Harper and Row, 2015: 1970).

13. James Pennebaker and John Evans, *Expressive Writing: Words That Heal* (Enumclaw, WA: Idyll Arbor, 2014).

14. Krista Fritson, "Impact of Journaling on Students' Self-Efficacy and Locus of Control," *Insight: A Journal of Scholarly Teaching* 3, no. 1 (2008): 75–81.

15. Sean Connolly, "Changing Expectancies: A Counseling Model Based on Locus of Control," *Personnel and Guidance Journal* 59, no. 3 (November 1980): 176–80.

16. Howard Murray and Barbara Staebler, "Teacher's Locus of Control and Student Achievement Gains," *Journal of School Psychology* 12, no. 4 (1974): 305–309.

INDEX